The Crusades
Biographies

The Crusades
Biographies

Written by J. Sydney Jones
Edited by Marcia Merryman Means and Neil Schlager

U·X·L

An imprint of Thomson Gale, a part of The Thomson Corporation

THOMSON
™
GALE

Detroit • New York • San Francisco • San Diego • New Haven, Conn. • Waterville, Maine • London • Munich

THOMSON

™

GALE

The Crusades: Biographies

Written by J. Sydney Jones

Edited by Marcia Merryman Means and Neil Schlager

Project Editor
Julie L. Carnagie

Editorial
Ralph G. Zerbonia

Permissions
Lori Hines, Susan J. Rudolph, William A. Sampson

Imaging and Multimedia
Lezlie Light, Mike Logusz, Kelly A. Quin

Product Design
Pamela Galbreath, Jennifer Wahi

Composition
Evi Seoud

Manufacturing
Rita Wimberley

LIBRARY OF CONGRESS CATALOGING-IN-PUBLICATION DATA

Jones, J. Sydney.

The Crusades: Biographies / written by J. Sydney Jones ; edited by Marcia Merryman Means and Neil Schlager.

p. cm. – (The Crusades reference library)

Includes bibliographical references and index.

ISBN 0-7876-9177-1 (alk. paper)

1. Crusades–Biography–Dictionaries, Juvenile. I. Title: Biographies. II. Means, Marcia Merryman. III. Schlager, Neil, 1966- IV. Title. V. Series.

D156.J66 2004
909.07–dc22

2004018000

Printed in the United States of America
10 9 8 7 6 5 4 3 2 1

Contents

Reader's Guide

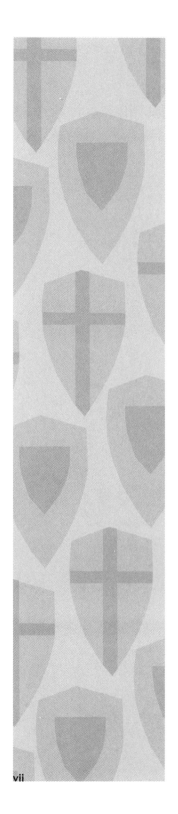

The term "crusade" is commonly used today to refer to a dedicated, enthusiastic effort. It usually means a total, all-out attempt to correct a problem, such as combating drunk driving or saving an endangered species from extinction. When people use the word "crusade," though, they may not recognize its distinctly religious meaning and history, even though they might embark on their crusade with religious enthusiasm.

The "Crusades" (with a capital "C") were a series of military campaigns launched by the Christian countries of western Europe in the late eleventh century. During these battles tens of thousands of people went to war in the Middle East. Their goal was to recapture the Holy Land, or Palestine, from the Muslims and restore it to Christian control. The focus of the Crusaders was the holy city of Jerusalem, now part of the Jewish nation of Israel on the eastern shore of the Mediterranean Sea and still a holy site to three religions: Judaism, Islam, and Christianity. But the impact of the Crusades was felt throughout that region of the world and in Europe.

The First Crusade was launched in late 1095 and ended with the capture of Jerusalem in 1099. The last

Crusade took place in the late 1200s. Historians identify seven separate Crusades, although there were two other highly irregular Crusades that are not generally numbered. The exact number is not important, for the Crusades were a single extended conflict that was fought over the course of two centuries. As the military and diplomatic situation in Jerusalem and the surrounding areas changed, successive waves of European troops flowed into the region to capture a key city or to expel an opposing army that had recaptured the same city. Each of these waves represented one of the Crusades. After each Crusade, particularly the early ones, some of the European invaders remained in the Middle East to rule over Christian kingdoms they had established. Many others returned to their homelands. During the periods between each Crusade, there was relative peace between the warring parties, although tensions simmered beneath the surface.

The Muslim world was slow to respond to the Crusaders. For many decades Muslims were too busy fighting among themselves for power and influence in the Middle East and lands beyond to recognize the threat that the Crusaders posed. Only after they mounted organized resistance were they able to drive the Crusaders out of the Middle East. Hundreds of years later, many Muslims continue to regard westerners as "crusaders" bent on occupying their holy territory.

Historians continue to debate whether, from a European Christian perspective, the Crusades were a success. While the first ended successfully with the capture of Jerusalem, some of the later Crusades were military and political disasters, at least from the point of view of the Europeans. All historians agree, though, that the Crusades would have a profound effect on the development of European civilization. They opened trade routes and promoted commerce, they led to never-before-seen exploration and cultural contact, and they provided inspiration for poets and novelists. They also laid the groundwork for conflict and religious strife that continues in the twenty-first century.

Features and Format

The Crusades: Biographies presents the biographies of twenty-five men and women who lived at the time of the Crusades and experienced the battles or the effects of these wars. Profiled are famous figures, such as King Richard the Lionheart of England; the Muslim warrior Saladin, and Saint Francis of Assisi. Lesser-known people are also featured, among them, the sultana of Egypt Shajarat al-Durr, the Byzantine emperors Alexius I and Alexius IV, and the Arab soldier and writer Usamah ibn Munqidh. There are numerous sidebars that highlight interesting information related to the people who lived at the time of the Crusades. More than forty black-and-white images enliven the text. The volume includes a glossary, a timeline, words to know, sources for further reading, and a subject index.

The Crusades Reference Library

The Crusades: Biographies is only one component of a three-part U•X•L Crusades Reference Library. The set also includes one almanac volume and one volume of primary source documents:

- *The Crusades: Almanac* covers the Crusades in thirteen thematic chapters, each examining an element of the two-hundred-year time period. The volume takes the reader through many aspects of this lengthy conflict. Included are chapters on the origins, history, and aftermath of the Crusades and on the holy city of Jerusalem and the land of Palestine as the focal site of three faiths. There are also profiles of the various groups of Muslims and Christians involved in the fight and descriptions of knights and the conduct of warfare.

- *The Crusades: Primary Sources* offers twenty-four full or excerpted documents, speeches, and literary works from the Crusades era. Included are "political" statements, such as Pope Urban II's speech calling for the First Crusade. There are also accounts of battles and sieges as well as other events, such as the slaughter of Jews in Europe by Crusaders on their way to the Holy Land. Included are samplings from literature, among them, excerpts from the epic poem *The Song of Roland* and a chapter of the Koran. The Arabic view of the times are featured in such writings as a Muslim historian's view of the Mongol invasions. The Byzantine perspective is seen, for example, in portions of *The Alexiad,* a biography of the emperor Alexius I Comnenus by his daughter.

- A cumulative index of all three titles in The Crusades Reference Library is also available.

Acknowledgments

Several people deserve our gratitude for their assistance with this project. We are indebted to everyone at U•X•L and Thomson Gale who assisted with the production, particularly Julie Carnagie, who provided help at all stages; we also thank Carol Nagel for her support.

Marcia Merryman Means

Neil Schlager

About the Author

J. Sydney Jones is the author of eight books of fiction and nonfiction, all with a focus on history and travel. A former journalist, he has also penned more than a thousand articles for newspapers, magazines, and biographical reference works. His works have been translated into French, Russian, Italian, German, and Hebrew.

About the Editors

Marcia Merryman Means and Neil Schlager are managing editor and president, respectively, of Schlager Group Inc., an editorial services company with offices in Florida and Vermont. Schlager Group publications have won numerous honors, including four RUSA awards from the American Library Association, two Reference Books Bulletin/Booklist Editors' Choice awards, two New York Public Library Outstanding Reference awards, and two *CHOICE* awards.

Comments and Suggestions

We welcome your comments on *The Crusades: Biographies* and suggestions for other topics in history to consider. Please write to Editors, *The Crusades: Biographies,* U•X•L, 27500 Drake Road, Farmington Hills, Michigan 48331-3535; call toll-free 800-877-4253; send faxes to 248-699-8097; or send e-mail via http://www.galegroup.com.

Timeline of Events

August 19, 1071 The Seljuk Turk leader **Alp Arslan** defeats the army of the Byzantine Empire at the Battle of Manzikert, establishing Turkish power in Asia Minor and in the Middle East, leading to the First Crusade.

1093 The Byzantine emperor **Alexius I Comnenus** sends a letter to the Catholic pope, asking for assistance against the Muslim Turks, who are threatening to overrun Constantinople and already have attacked the Holy Land in Palestine and sacked Jerusalem.

November 28, 1095 **Pope Urban II** calls for a holy war, or Crusade, against the Muslims in the Holy Land and Constantinople at the Council of Clermont.

Spring 1096 The poor traveling religious man **Peter the Hermit** preaches the Crusade to the people of Europe and mounts the tragic "People's Crusade" to Constantinople.

1096–98 The Byzantine princess **Anna Comnena** depicts the early stages of the First Crusade in her history, *The Alexiad.*

July 15, 1099 The leader of the First Crusade, **Godfrey of Bouillon**, captures Jerusalem. All the Muslims in the city are slaughtered.

1118   The crusader **Hugh de Payens** forms the Knights Templars, which becomes one of the first military orders of the church. Its mission is to battle Muslims, or the infidel (unbeliever), in the Middle East.

1143   At the death of her husband, King Fulk of Anjou, **Melisende** becomes queen of the Kingdom of Jerusalem, serving for nine years, until her son Baldwin III takes over. She is one of the most powerful women during the time of the Crusades and sees the power of the Crusader states diminish as the Muslims begin to organize against them.

March 31, 1146 Preaching at Vézelay, France, **Saint Bernard of Clairvaux** calls for the Second Crusade to battle the rising power of Islam in the Holy Land.

1148–49 The queen of France, **Eleanor of Aquitaine**, and her husband, Louis VII, take part in the unsuccessful Second Crusade.

1159   **Benjamin of Tudela**, a Spanish rabbi, sets out on his travels, documenting Jewish living conditions during the time of the Crusades in *The Itinerary of Benjamin of Tudela.*

1169   The Spanish Arab philosopher and physician **Averroës** begins his commentaries on the works of Greek philosopher Aristotle, forming a bridge between the classical age of the Greeks, the Arab/Islamic world, and the Christian West, as Crusaders bring such scholarship and learning home with them.

1185   The Syrian nobleman **Usamah ibn Munqidh** begins his memoirs, *An Arab-Syrian Gentleman and Warrior in the Period of the Crusades*. This autobiography documents everyday life in the Middle East from the First Crusade until just before the Third Crusade, which began in 1189.

October 2, 1187 The great Muslim military leader **Saladin** rallies all of Islam to the *jihad,* or holy war, against the

Christian Crusaders and captures Jerusalem. This leads to the Third Crusade.

1190 The famous Spanish Jewish scholar **Maimonides** writes *The Guide to the Perplexed,* an attempt to balance the work of Greek philosophy with Jewish religion. Intellectual life in the Middle East continues amid the disruption of the Crusades.

1192 The leader of the radical Shiite Muslim sect the Assassins, **Rashid al-Din Sinan**, dies at his mountain fortress in Syria. His fanatical followers, the *hashashin,* continue to fight both Crusaders and other Muslims for control in the Middle East.

1192 The king of England, **Richard I, the Lionheart**, concludes a truce with the Muslims that ends the unsuccessful Third Crusade.

1198 Pope **Innocent III**, calls for a new Crusade to the Holy Land, resulting several years later in the Fourth Crusade.

1202 The Crusaders of the Fourth Crusade, encouraged by **Alexius IV Angelus**, the next in line to become Byzantine emperor, sack Constantinople.

1219 During the siege of the Egyptian city of Damietta in the Fifth Crusade, **Saint Francis of Assisi** attempts to convert the Egyptian sultan to Christianity.

1221 The Egyptian leader **Sultan al-Malik al-Kamil** defeats the Christian soldiers of the Fifth Crusade at the Battle of Mansurah.

February 18, 1229 Emperor of the Holy Roman Empire, **Frederick II**, reclaims Jerusalem by treaty and diplomacy during the Sixth Crusade.

May–July 1250 **Shajarat al-Durr,** a Mamluk, or slave, who rose from being a member of the Egyptian sultan's harem to becoming his favorite wife, is appointed sultana, or queen, of Egypt, one of only a few medieval Muslim women to attain such power. She also helps command the Muslim armies that defeat the Seventh Crusade.

September 1260 The invading Mongol army is defeated at Ayn Jalut by **al-Zahir Baybars** and his Egyptian Mamluk army. Baybars thereafter becomes sultan of Egypt and pushes the Crusaders into their final strongholds in Palestine.

August 25, 1270 King **Louis IX** of France dies at the outset of what was planned as the Eighth Crusade. His death ends the Crusader movement in Europe.

Words to Know

A

Abbasid: A Muslim religious dynasty that could trace its origins back to the uncle of Muhammad, the prophet and founder of Islam. The Abbasids ruled in Baghdad from 749 to 1258 and were the spiritual heart of Sunni Islam, the orthodox, or mainstream, branch of the faith.

Abbey: A society of monks or nuns governed by an abbot or an abbess, respectively; also refers to the buildings where these monks and nuns resided.

Alhomads: A sect, or subgroup, of Islam from North Africa that conquered Cordova, Spain, in the twelfth century.

Allah: The name of the Muslim god.

Asia Minor: The peninsula between the Mediterranean Sea and the Black Sea that holds most of present-day Turkey; also sometimes referred to as Anatolia.

Assassins: An extremist group of Muslim Shiites organized in the late eleventh century to fight their opponents by any means possible. Known to fortify themselves for their work using *hashishin,* or the drug hashish, they came to be known in French as "assassins," and the name later came to be used to describe those who plotted murder, especially for political reasons.

Atabeg: A Turkish title meaning "prince-father," given to a local leader or governor.

Ayyubid: The ruling dynasty of Egypt, founded by the Muslim military leader Saladin in 1169 and lasting until about 1252.

B

Basileus: The official title of the emperors of the Byzantine Empire.

Bishop: A high rank or office in the medieval church. A person holding this office usually presided over a territory called a diocese, or see.

Booty: The riches and weapons that medieval soldiers had a right to take from defeated enemies.

Byzantine Empire: The Eastern Roman Empire, established in the fourth century in Constantinople and comprising present-day Greece, Turkey, and part of the Balkan countries.

C

Caliph: The English adaptation of the Arab word *khalifa,* which means "successor." This was a title adapted by early Muslim leaders after the death in 632 of Muhammad, the founder of Islam. Rulers in name only by the time of the Crusades, the caliphs were still important religious leaders for the Islamic world. The region a caliph controlled was called a caliphate.

Castle: Defensive residence of a lord or prince.

Cathedral: Major church of a diocese, the religious region of a bishop.

Cavalry: A military body that uses horses in battle.

Chivalry: The principles of courage, courtesy, charity, and skill in arms that marks a true knight.

Constantinople: Capital of the Byzantine Empire, founded by Emperor Constantine in the fourth century; present-day Istanbul, in Turkey.

Crown: The circlet, usually of gold or silver, worn on the head of the king or emperor to show his office. It also means the power of the king or the kingdom.

Crusades: The holy wars fought between Christians and Muslims over occupancy of the shrines of the Holy Land. Begun in 1096, these wars ended with the fall of Acre in 1291 and the final defeat of the Christian armies in the Middle East. Depending on the history consulted, there were seven or eight major Crusades.

D

Diplomacy: The practice of conducting international relations, such as making treaties and alliances.

Dome of the Rock: A shrine in Jerusalem important to both Muslims and those of the Jewish faith.

Duke: Highest level of the nobility, ranking just below prince.

Dynasty: A line of rulers that come from the same family or group.

E

Emir: A Turkish title that indicates a military leader or commander, used widely throughout the Muslim world at the time of the Crusades.

Empire: A political unit consisting of several territories governed by a single supreme authority, usually called the emperor.

Excommunicate: To expel a person from the Catholic Church.

F

Fatimid: The ruling dynasty of Egypt from 969 to 1167. A Shiite dynasty, it based its claim to power on its connection to Fatima, the daughter of the prophet Muhammad.

Feudalism: The political and social organization of Europe during the Middle Ages. In this system, vassals, or loyal subjects, were given land, called a fief, by great lords and kings in return for their military service. The vassals, in turn, would rent their lands to peasants, who would pay annual fees.

Fidai: The loyal followers of Sinan in the Assassin sect of Islam. By extension, the word has become "fedaheen," and describes those willing to sacrifice themselves for their beliefs.

H

Holy Land: For Christians of the West this describes Jerusalem and the sites in Palestine identified with the birth and early life of Jesus Christ.

Holy Roman Empire: A loose collection of German and Italian principalities and territories that lasted from the tenth to the nineteenth century.

I

Imam: The leader of public prayers or the leader of a Muslim community.

Infantry: Foot soldiers.

Islam: The religious faith of the Muslims, which is based on the words and teaching of the prophet Muhammad.

J

Jihad: Holy war of the Muslims against infidels, or unbelievers, in their faith.

K

King: Crowned ruler of a territory or a country called a kingdom. The term comes from the German word *koennen,* meaning "to be able."

Knight: A feudal tenant, usually a member of the nobility, who served his superior, or lord, as a mounted soldier.

Knights Hospitallers: Religious military order established in 1113 to help sick pilgrims in the Holy Land.

Knights Templars: Religious military order established in 1118 to defend Christian pilgrims in the Holy Land.

Koran: See **Qur'an.**

L

Lord: In feudal society, the owner of a manor, or great house, and lands granted directly by the king. The lord, in turn, gave land to the vassals who served him.

M

Mamluk: From the Arab verb for "to own," meaning a slave. In Muslim societies they were usually Turkish slaves trained to be soldiers and commanders. Also refers to the dynasty ruling Egypt from 1252 to 1517.

Middle Ages: The historical period from approximately 500 to 1500 C.E. As an adjective, "medieval" often is used to refer to this era.

Middle East: A term used in the West to indicate the regions that include the present-day countries of Cyprus, the Asian part of Turkey, Syria, Lebanon, Israel, the West Bank and Gaza, Jordan, Iraq, Iran, the countries of the Arabian peninsula (Saudi Arabia, Yemen, Oman, United Arab Emirates, Qatar, Bahrain, and Kuwait), Egypt, and Libya. Also used to describe the lands of the region that have an Islamic culture.

Mongols: A nomadic, warlike tribe from the steppes of Central Asia that, under the leadership of Genghis Khan and his offspring, invaded the Middle East and Europe during the thirteenth century; also called Tatars or Tartars.

Monk: Member of a religious order, or group, that stays out of society and honors hard work, silence, and devotion to God and prayer.

Moors: Muslims from North Africa who settled in Spain in the Middle Ages.

Muslim: Follower of the Islamic faith; also called "Moslem."

N

Nobility: As a group, members of a noble, or aristocratic, family.

O

Outremer (oo-tre-MARE): The name for the Crusader kingdoms and states in the Holy Land. From the Latin, the word means "beyond the sea."

P

Palestine: In the Middle Ages, the region thought of as the Holy Land on the east coast of the Mediterranean Sea. It was made up of present-day Jordan, Israel, and parts of Egypt.

Papacy: The church office of the pope.

Patriarch: Major leaders of the Eastern Orthodox, or Greek Orthodox, Church, similar in power to bishops of the Catholic Church. The four major patriarchs in the East were in Jerusalem, Antioch, Constantinople, and Alexandria.

Pilgrimage: A journey made to a sacred place for religious purposes. A person who takes such a journey is called a pilgrim.

Pope: Leader of the Roman Catholic Church; in the Middle Ages, the religious leader of the Christian West.

Prince: A ruler, from the Latin *princeps,* meaning "first in rank." In general, any ruler came to be known as a prince. A male heir in a royal household, the "crown" prince, was the first in line to the throne, or kingship.

Principality: A subdivision of a kingdom.

Q

Qadi: A judge of religious law in the Islamic faith.

Qur'an: The Muslim holy book, also known as the Koran.

R

Rabbi: A religious leader and scholar in the Jewish faith.

Ransom: The money paid to free a knight or other noble person captured in battle.

Reign: The length of rule of a king, emperor, or other noble.

Relic: A holy object or even a piece of a holy object connected with Jesus Christ or a saint and therefore thought to have mystical powers.

S

Saracen: A member of the nomadic people of the Syrian and Arabian deserts at the time of the Roman Empire; more generally applied by Europeans to all Arabs and Muslims during the Crusades.

Seljuk Turks: A Turkish tribe from Central Asia that converted to Islam and invaded the Middle East in the eleventh century. Religious fanatics, they threatened access to the holy sites of Christianity in Palestine.

Shiite: A follower of the Islamic branch founded by the fourth caliph, Ali, cousin and son-in-law to Muhammad; the first important minority branch of Islam.

Siege: Military blockade of a city or fort to make it surrender.

Sunni: The majority branch of Islam, taking their authority not from direct descendants of Muhammad but from the *sunna,* or practices of Muhammad.

T

Talmud: The body of Jewish laws included in books called the Mishnah and the Gemara.

Teutonic Knights: A religious and military order of knights restricted to German membership, which split off from the Knights Hospitallers.

Torah: The first five books of the Old Testament, which form part of the Jewish tradition of literature and religious laws.

U

Umayyad: An early Muslim dynasty that lost its power in the Middle East and took refuge in Cordova, Spain. There, it established a Spanish Islamic dynasty lasting from 1056 to 1269, noted for an emphasis on scholarship and religious diversity.

V

Vizier: Minister or chief counselor, from the Arabic word *wazir.*

Z

Zangid: Muslim dynasty of Turkish origin founded by the military leader Zengi in 1127. It ruled in Syria and northern Iraq until 1222 and was based in the cities of Mosul, Aleppo, and Damascus.

Alexius I Comnenus

1048
Constantinople

August 15, 1118
Constantinople

Byzantine emperor

Alexius I was the emperor of the Byzantine Empire, the eastern portion of the old Roman Empire based in Greece and Asia Minor, at the time of the First Crusade (1095–99). The first of the Comnenus dynasty, or ruling family, Alexius I inherited a weakened empire at the time of his crowning as emperor in 1081. Byzantium, as the empire was also called, was under attack from all sides, especially from the Seljuk Turks, who had recently converted to Islam. Nevertheless Alexius I managed to restore some of the strength to his land during his thirty-seven-year reign. Alexius I is best known in history as the Byzantine emperor whose call for help against the Turks and Islam was taken up by **Urban II** (see entry), the western pope and spiritual leader of the Catholic Church. This, in turn, played an important part in bringing about the First Crusade and launching the Crusade movement, which resulted in two centuries of conflict between the Christian and Islamic worlds.

"The blood of Christians flows in unheard-of scenes of carnage.... Therefore in the name of God ... we implore you to bring to this city [Constantinople] all the faithful soldiers of Christ."

—*Alexius I, letter to Robert of Flanders, which partly inspired the First Crusade; quoted in* The Story of the First Crusade, *http://www.brighton73.freeserve.co.uk/firstcrusade/People/Eastern_Christians/alexius_comnenus.htm*

Alexius I Comnenus.
Courtesy of the Library of Congress.

An Empire of Many Names

Alexius I ruled an empire that was called many names by different people. Initially these lands were part of the original Roman Empire. But in 284 C.E. this empire was split into an eastern half and a western half for administrative purposes. The part that lay in Asia Minor and Greece was called the eastern Roman Empire. Less than half a century later Constantine, the first Christian emperor, decided to move the capital of the Roman Empire east to Asia Minor, to the city of Byzantium, or Byzantion. Thus the empire gradually began to be called the Byzantine Empire, or simply Byzantium, by Europeans even though Constantine insisted on calling the place "Nova Roma," or New Rome. To confuse matters even more, the city of Byzantium was later called Constantinople after its founder; when the empire ended in 1453, this name was again changed, finally becoming the Istanbul of modern times.

During the time of Alexius I the citizens of the Byzantine Empire nevertheless thought of themselves as the *Rhomaioi,* occupants of New Rome. In medieval times Alexius's empire was often referred to as Romania. In fact, the Byzantine Empire kept many of the aspects of the old Roman Empire for much of its existence. Though Christianity had come to play a more significant public role by the third and fourth centuries, the legal, political, and military structures remained much the same as they had been under the Roman emperors. Even the old imperial Roman title of "Augustus" was used for its emperors. This ultimately changed when the emperor Heraclius (ruled 610–41) declared that from now on the title would be *Basileus,* the Greek word for emperor. Nor was Latin to remain the official language, which was replaced by Greek. Such a change was logical, since the empire was now based both in Greece and Asia Minor. Thus the empire was often referred to as the Greek Empire in the Middle Ages. In turn, the citizens of Byzantium often called their European cousins "Latins." They did not have a very high opinion of these Latins; except for being able to wage war, they were looked upon as dirty and uncivilized barbarians.

Despite all these name changes, the Byzantines continued to think of themselves as Romans. One final name change occurred in 1453, however, which took the "Roman" out of their name. That year Constantinople fell to the Ottoman Turks and the former eastern Roman Empire was no more, replaced first by the Ottoman Empire and then by modern Turkey.

The First of His Line

Born in Constantinople (present-day Istanbul) in 1048, Alexius Comnenus was the third son of John Comnenus and the nephew of the Byzantine emperor Isaac I, who ruled from 1057 to 1059. He thus came from a well-connected and powerful family and was trained from an early age in the arts of war and politics. Both of these skills were necessary for survival in eleventh-century Byzantium. Intrigue and palace plots were the order of the day in this eastern Christian kingdom. Not even emperors were safe from cruel treatment at the hands of their rivals. When the emperor Romanus IV Diogenes lost the Battle of Manzikert in 1071 to the Seljuk Turk **Alp Arslan** (see entry), thus exposing the empire to further attack from these Turkish invaders, Romanus was hunted down by his enemies in Constantinople, blinded, and exiled to a small island prison, where he eventually died. Alexius was thirteen at the time, but the lesson was surely not lost on him: Watch your back!

Alexius was raised mainly by his mother, Anna Dalassena, a woman with a strong sense of purpose for her son, who educated him in matters of politics and diplomacy, or international relations. In the art of war Alexius soon earned a name for himself. This was important, for Byzantium was under attack from enemies on all sides. To the southeast lay the land of the infidel, or nonbelievers: the Islamic world of Mesopotamia (modern Iraq), Syria, and Arabia. Also, following their victory at Manzikert, the Seljuk Turks pressed on into the empire, and by 1081 they had reached Nicaea, an ancient city close to Constantinople. To the west were the Normans, fierce fighters from the French province of Normandy who were of Viking origin. These warriors had carved out a kingdom for themselves in Sicily, in the far south of Italy, where Byzantium also had part of its empire. In 1071, the same year that the Byzantines were defeated by the Seljuk Turks at Manzikert, they were dealt another major defeat by the Normans under the leadership of Robert Guiscard (1016–1085). That year the Normans took the city of Bari, ending Byzantine rule in Italy. Even worse, as far as the Byzantine Empire was concerned, was the fact that Robert and his son Bohemund decided to invade Constantinople itself. Added to these military problems were the Pechenegs, a Turkic nomadic tribe that repeatedly attacked Constantinople from the east.

In 1059 Alexius's father had declined to take the throne after Isaac I stepped down. Thus the Comnendian line was broken, and the role of emperor was taken on by four leaders, including Romanus IV Diogenes, who brought the empire to the edge of ruin. Alexius's daughter, **Anna Comnena** (see entry), wrote a multivolume biography of her father, *The Alexiad,* a book that deals more with military matters than with personal affairs. In it she mentions that her father served under Romanus at the Battle of Manzikert. He served under three other emperors as a military leader and then a general, gaining fame for some of his victories. He was also employed, along with an older brother, Isaac, to put down rebellions against the empire in parts of Greece. Soon, however, he was plotting his own rebellion.

Alexius Becomes Emperor

Alexius's success made others jealous. The emperor Nicephorus III and his ministers thought Alexius was becoming too popular among the people and were about to get rid of him and his dangerously powerful Comnenus family when Alexius struck first, taking the crown away from Nicephorus III and sending him to a monastery (religious community). When Alexius's older brother Isaac refused the crown, Alexius took it, becoming Alexius I on April 4, 1081. He had no time to celebrate, however, for his first job was to deal with the invading Normans, who had already taken the island of Corfu, to the west of Greece.

From the beginning Alexius I combined military might with diplomacy and building alliances to defeat his enemies. While fighting the Normans, he brought in the navy of the powerful state of Venice to help. With this naval force he was finally able to push the Normans back. With the death of Robert Guiscard, duke of Apulia, in 1085, the Norman threat ended for the time being. As a reward for their help, the Venetians gained important trading rights in the Byzantine Empire. Similarly, Alexius made treaties with the Seljuks and other Muslim leaders on his eastern borders, using diplomacy where force would not work. In 1091 he defeated the Pechenegs by hiring a rival Turkish tribe, the Cumans, to help eliminate this threat. He thus managed to secure his northeastern borders.

Such operations were not really victories, however. Each of the negotiations came at a heavy price for Byzantium, especially his deals with the Seljuk Turks, which involved giv-

ing up land in exchange for peaceful relations. Despite his efforts, roving bands of the Seljuks continued to take over and settle various parts of Asia Minor, creating a constant threat of further invasion to the Byzantium empire. Alexius I decided to call for help from a completely different part of the world.

View of the center of Venice, Italy, whose naval fleet Alexius I hired to help in his battle with the Normans in the late eleventh century. © *Archivo Iconografico, S.A./Corbis.*

Alexius Turns to the Pope

It is a sign of how desperate Alexius I was—or how desperate the situation was—that in 1093 he sent a letter to a European noble, Robert of Flanders, to ask for help against the Seljuk Turks. This letter was meant to be passed on to Pope Urban II, but there was no reason Alexius I should have expected any aid from that quarter. The Byzantine Empire saw itself as the legal and moral inheritor of not only the Roman Empire but also the Christian religion. Its Eastern Orthodox Church was a rival to Europe's Catholic Church. For the Byzantines the pope was simply the bishop, or religious leader, of Rome, one among many bishops. The true leader of Christianity was the leader of the faithful in Constantinople—the patriarch, as the office was called. This split between the two parts of Christianity grew even deeper in 1054 when the Eastern Orthodox Church in Constantinople excommunicated, or excluded from the faith, a messenger from the pope in Rome. There had been little communication between the rival branches of Christianity since then.

Alexius's communication, however, caught the attention of Urban II. In his letter Alexius supplied a long list of terrible deeds that the Seljuk Turks supposedly had committed, some of which were true and others of which were not. He also claimed that all of Asia Minor and Byzantium was about to fall to the Turks and that the treasures of his empire, both physical and spiritual, would go to the Turks if that happened. In his letter to Robert of Flanders, Alexius I also provided a motivation for those who might come to his assistance: "Remember that you will find all those treasures and also the most beautiful women of the Orient. The incomparable beauty of the Greek women would seem to be a sufficient reason to attract the armies of the Franks."

What Alexius I was actually looking for was an army of hired soldiers to keep the peace in his empire. He never bargained for the huge forces that landed on his shores in 1096 as a result of the pope's preaching in favor of a holy war to fight Islam and recapture the Holy Land. These Crusaders, as they were called, answered Urban's plea for a variety of reasons: a sense of religious duty, a love of adventure, a desire to occupy new lands, or the need for food and shelter. The armies that arrived in Alexius's city were hardly the manageable group of soldiers he had hoped for. His scheme to get western help clearly backfired.

The first to arrive was the army of common people led by **Peter the Hermit** (see entry), a priest from Amiens in France who inspired thousands of peasants, or poor workers, to follow him to the Holy Land. Once in Asia Minor, his untrained force was slaughtered by the Turks. A second wave of Crusaders arrived shortly thereafter under the leadership of **Godfrey of Bouillon** (see entry), and these soldiers presented even more difficulties for Alexius I. It was clear that these men had not come simply to retake lands in Asia Minor for the Byzantines. Alexius I saw them as mercenaries, or paid soldiers, in his service, but Godfrey and his soldiers had different goals. They intended to move into the Holy Land and conquer Jerusalem for the Catholic Church. From the very beginning the two camps did not get along, but in 1097 they did manage to take the city of Nicaea from the Turks. The Crusaders went south, attacking centers of Muslim power in Syria, such as Antioch. Alexius I ultimately failed to aid the Crusaders in this siege, which completely destroyed relations between the Byzantines and the Crusader armies.

From his viewpoint, Alexius I was right in his less-than-friendly greeting of the Crusaders. After all, they were trying to capture lands in Syria, such as Antioch, that were once held by Byzantium. To Alexius these lands were rightly part of his empire. However, it soon became obvious to him that the Crusaders had no intention of returning such spoils of war to him. Instead, they began setting up Crusader states, or principalities, carving up the Holy Land among themselves. The Crusaders knew only about making war, never thinking of diplomacy or using the skill of playing off one enemy against the other. In fact, their siege of Jerusalem in 1099 and the bloody massacre of Muslims that followed risked uniting the Islamic world against them. The only thing that had allowed Alexius I and his empire to remain partly intact was the fact that Islam was divided politically.

When Alexius's old Norman enemy, Guiscard's son Bohemund, took Antioch for himself, Alexius was suddenly faced with yet another foe at his borders. Between 1104 and 1108 the two fought each other off and on until finally Alexius's forces beat those of Bohemund. The death of Bohemund in 1111 left the question of possession of Antioch unresolved. Alexius I went on to battle the Seljuk Turks in Asia Minor, taking back more lost territory. A battle in 1117 against the Turks marked Alexius's final victory in the field. At home a palace plot—hatched by his wife, Irene, and daughter, Anna, to install his son-in-law on the throne instead of the rightful heir, Alexius's son, John—spoiled his last days. On his deathbed the emperor had to use all his strength to get power transferred to John. He died on August 15, 1118.

Alexius I managed to hold together what was basically a dying empire through his skillful use of diplomacy and his ability to form alliances with even his worst enemies. He played rival tribes against each other and struck with his military might when necessary. But he miscalculated when he invited Latin or European troops into his empire at the beginning of what became known as the First Crusade. For him these troops ultimately became one more power center that he had to battle in the region. They replaced the Byzantine Eastern Orthodox faith with the Catholic Church and created Crusader kingdoms in the Holy Land that rivaled and challenged his own. Alexius's plotting and policies, however, did leave his empire stronger than when he took the throne. By securing his borders through treaty and war alike, he kept the Byzantine Empire alive. He is remembered in history as the man whose call for help to fight Muslims started the Crusades.

For More Information

Books

Comnena, Anna. *The Alexiad of the Princess Anna Comnena: Being the History of the Reign of Her Father, Alexius I, Emperor of the Romans, 1081–1118 A.D.* Translated by Elizabeth A. S. Dawes. New York: AMS Press, 1978.

Hussey, J. M., ed. *The Cambridge Medieval History.* 2nd ed. Vol. 4. New York: Cambridge University Press, 1966.

Norwich, John Julius. *A Short History of Byzantium.* New York: Vintage, 1998.

Ostrogorsky, George. *A History of the Byzantine State.* Translated by Joan Hussey. Piscataway, NJ: Rutgers University Press, 1986.

Treadgold, Warren. *A History of the Byzantine State and Society.* Stanford, CA: Stanford University Press, 1997.

Web Sites

"Alexius I Comnenus, 1048–1118 CE." *The Story of the First Crusade.* http://www.brighton73.freeserve.co.uk/firstcrusade/People/Eastern_Christians/alexius_comnenus.htm (accessed on June 16, 2004).

"Byzantine Empire." *New Advent.* http://www.newadvent.org/cathen/03096a.htm (accessed on June 16, 2004).

"Byzantium: Byzantine Studies on the Internet." *Fordham University.* http://www.fordham.edu/halsall/byzantium (accessed on June 16, 2004).

Comnena, Anna. "Internet Medieval Sourcebook: The Alexiad." *Fordham University.* http://www.fordham.edu/halsall/basis/AnnaComnena-Alexiad.html (accessed on June 16, 2004).

"Emperor Alexius Comnenus." *About's Who's Who in Medieval History and the Renaissance.* http://historymedren.about.com/library/who/blwwalexius.htm (accessed on June 16, 2004).

Alexius IV Angelus

1182
Byzantine Empire

1204
Constantinople

Byzantine emperor

Alexius IV was one of a long line of emperors of the Byzantine Empire, the eastern Roman Empire. Though his reign lasted only six months, his time spent as head of the empire had far-reaching effects. Alexius IV persuaded the Christian soldiers, or Crusaders, who were gathering for the Fourth Crusade (1202–04) against the Muslims in Egypt to set sail first for his home in Constantinople and put him on the throne as emperor of the Byzantine Empire. If they did this, Alexius IV promised, they would receive enough money, weapons, and ships to fight their Crusade in Egypt as originally planned. But such things do not always work out as expected. Alexius's invitation to the Crusaders led to the sacking of Constantinople in 1204 and the end of Byzantine rule in the capital and surrounding lands for more than half a century. Constantinople and the Byzantine Empire never recovered from this incident. Though Constantinople was re-captured in 1261 and survived until the Turks took it in 1453, the Byzantine Empire had been struck a severe blow in 1204. Alexius IV was eventually put to death by yet another Alexius, his successor, Alexius V.

"[The Crusaders] sent two knights to the emperor [Alexius IV] and demanded again that he should pay them. He replied to the messengers that he would pay nothing, he had already paid too much, and that he was not afraid of anyone."

—Robert de Clari, "The Summons to Alexis," in the Internet Medieval Sourcebook, *http://www.fordham.edu/ halsall/source/4cde.html#cp.*

Plots and Stolen Kingdoms

Based on different sources, the Byzantine Empire was between seven hundred and nine hundred years old by the end of the twelfth century. It had gone through numerous family dynasties of emperors, beginning with the Constantinian family and its founder, Constantine I (ruled 306–337), the person who had moved the capital of the Roman Empire from Rome to Asia Minor, setting up headquarters in the city of Byzantion. The empire that grew out of this move was called the Byzantine Empire, after the name of its major city. By the Middle Ages, the city had changed its name to Constantinople (present-day Istanbul) in honor of its founder. When Constantine's reign ended in 337, the empire was run by eight different dynasties over the next 867 years. The Comnenan dynasty ruled from 1081 to 1185; its last emperor, Andronicus I, was so unpopular in Constantinople that his own citizens rebelled and killed him. After that, the Angelan family took over, with Isaac II Angelus becoming *basileus,* or emperor, of a kingdom that included much of present-day Turkey, Greece, and the Balkans.

Ruling Byzantium, as the empire was also called, was always a messy business. The far-flung lands of the empire were constantly rebelling against Constantinople, and there were infighting and court intrigues, or plots, in the capital. This meant that the emperor had to stay alert to enemies all around. Power could change hands by the simple addition of a drop of poison in the emperor's soup. The word "Byzantine" entered the English language as a description not only of the empire and art of the time but also of anything that was very complex and difficult to understand.

That perfectly describes the situation of the Byzantine emperor. Isaac II immediately had his hands full with rebellions in Bulgaria and Serbia and the arrival of the Third Crusade (1189–92)—or at least the German members of that unsuccessful coalition, or partnership, to win back the Holy Land from the Muslims. In fact, the Germans, under King Frederick I, had come to conquer Constantinople, but Frederick I died en route. Crusades had never been an easy business for the Byzantines. Old rivalries between the western and eastern kingdoms, and between the Roman Catholic Church of the European kingdoms and the Eastern Orthodox Church of Byzantium, were stirred up. Though these two branches of Christianity should have been friends and allies, in truth there was a deep and lasting suspicion between the two. Such distrust was felt between the ordinary citizens of the two areas as well. The Latins of Europe and the Greeks of the Byzantine region did not get on well. Emperors of Byzantium looked at Europe as just one of many possible threats.

Isaac II overlooked one threat he should have been aware of—namely his own family. So busy was he dealing with outside threats to the Byzantine Empire that he forgot internal ones and lost control of the political situation in Constantinople. In 1195, with Isaac II away in the Greek region of Thrace, Alexius III, the brother of Isaac II, and Alexius's powerful wife, Euphrosyne, stole the throne with the support of army officers. When Alexius III later captured his brother, he had Isaac II blinded, so that he would be unfit to rule again as emperor, and put him under house arrest. Alexius III and his wife were so busy paying off the bribes that had put him in office that he was an ineffective emperor. His wife was better at governing than he was, but in the end there was much corruption at his court, and Alexius III continued to lose parts of the empire.

Alexius IV Angelus grew up amid all these intrigues. After the overthrow of his father, Isaac II, Alexius IV was also imprisoned by his uncle, Alexius III. He spent six years in confinement before he was finally able to escape in 1201 and make his way to Europe, where his sister was married to a German noble.

The Fourth Crusade

Alexius IV must have known what he was getting into when he asked the nobles of Europe for help, for he had grown up with the complex relations among various nobles in Constantinople. He must also have known about the plans in Europe to conquer Constantinople. The German emperor Henry VI wanted to become master of Constantinople, and it was his brother, Philip of Swabia, to whom Alexius IV's sister, Irene, was married. Philip happily took this young man under his wing, and together they came up with a plan to enable Alexius IV to regain his rightful position.

Alexius IV requesting the help of Enrico Dandolo, the doge of Venice, and his Crusaders in invading Constantinople. *Erich Lessing/Art Resource, NY.*

It so happened that their plan matched the needs of a Crusader army gathering at the Italian port of Venice. The Crusaders, under the leadership of Boniface of Montferrat, had been stuck in Venice for some months because they could not afford to pay the Venetians the fee required to transport them to Egypt, where they planned to fight a new Crusade against the Muslims. The Venetians, led by Enrico Dandolo, their eighty-five-year-old doge (ruler), were pressuring the Crusaders to help them put down a rebellion in one of the cities of their empire in return for part of the fee to transport them. These Christian knights did not feel good about attacking other Christians, for the rebellious city was Zara, on the Yugoslavian coast.

Around this time Philip of Swabia and Alexius IV appeared and presented their plan for liberating Constantinople. According to the plan, Alexius IV would help the Crusaders pay off their debt to the Venetians and finance the rest of their Crusade in Egypt if they agreed to get rid of his uncle, Alexius III. This was too good a bargain to pass up, and on October 1, 1202, with Alexius IV in their company, the Crusaders sailed out of Venice. They made quick work of Zara, capturing it for Venice, and after wintering there they sailed on to Constantinople in April 1203. By this time **Innocent III** (see entry), the pope in Rome, had heard of these battles against Christians and excommunicated, or expelled, the Crusaders from the church. They had nothing more to lose by fighting in Constantinople and arrived in the city by the end of June 1203. Alexius IV rode below the gates of the city, telling his people to throw Alexius III out and to restore their rightful emperor. But the people of Constantinople would not support anyone who, in turn, was supported by the hated Latins. There would have to be a battle for the city.

This battle began on July 5, 1203, when the Venetian army was able to break the huge chain blocking the harbor. Then the Crusaders attacked Constantinople by both sea and land. On July 17 the Venetians, led by their ancient doge, were the first to land, and the battle seemed to be favoring the Crusaders. Alexius III grew nervous. Instead of counterattacking, he fled, taking five tons of gold and one daughter with him. Now it was Alexius IV's turn to take the throne. He was surprised to discover that the Byzantines had already released his father, Isaac II, from prison and, despite his blindness, had made him emperor once again. However, with pressure from the Crusaders, Alexius IV was declared co-emperor.

The Sack of Constantinople

Now it was Alexius IV's turn to keep his bargain. He tried to raise money to pay off the Crusaders by increasing the taxes of the citizens of Constantinople, but this made him unpopular with the people, who also blamed him for bringing the Latins to conquer their city. He attempted to get money from church lands, but this action also angered the people and powerful church officers. The Crusader army, camped near the city, grew restless, and trouble between this army and the citizens of Constantinople was sure to follow. As the winter approached, relations between the Crusaders and Alexius IV broke down. His promises of riches for the Crusaders did not come true, although he managed to raise half the promised funds. He began to withdraw from public life, spending more and more time in his palace. The aged Venetian doge finally confronted Alexius IV, as recorded by Robert de Clari:

> Alexius, what do you think you are going to do? Remember we have raised you from a very humble estate. We have made you lord and ... crowned you emperor. Will you not keep your agreement with us and will you not do more? No, replied the emperor, I will not do anything more. No?, said the doge, "wretched boy, we have raised you from the mire, and we will throw you into the mire again and be sure that I will do you all the injury that I can, from this time on.

In the end, however, it was not the Crusaders who unseated Alexius IV but a rival at court, another Alexius nicknamed "Murzuphlus," or "the Bushy-Eyebrowed." A member of the powerful Ducas family, Alexius Murzuphlus brought anti-Latins together and took power, strangling Alexius IV, throwing his father Isaac II back into prison, and declaring himself Emperor Alexius V. He told the Crusaders that there would be no more payments to them.

This was all the Crusaders needed to set them at the walls of Constantinople once again. On April 9, 1204, they struck the city, agreeing to divide the stolen goods among themselves. Though their initial attack was driven back, the Crusaders struck again on April 13 and broke through the city walls. The Crusaders killed men, women, and children and looted private homes and churches. Much of the city was burned, and its treasures were divided among the Venetians, the German emperor, and the Crusaders, with the Venetians taking the biggest share. Alexius V fled the city but was later captured by Alexius III, who blinded him as he had done his own brother and then turned him over to the Crusaders to finish him off.

The Loot and the Shroud

Ships loaded with loot set sail from Constantinople for Europe after the sack of the city in 1204. Gold and jewels were among this booty, as were works of art and church relics, objects held to be holy because of their association with saints. Even the four horses that now stand so gracefully atop the Basilica of Saint Mark's in Venice originally came from Constantinople. Lands were also part of the stolen goods. Venice won territory on the eastern shore of the Adriatic Sea as well as islands in Greece, including Crete.

The medieval chronicler Nicetas Choniates gives this account of the looting:

> How shall I begin to tell of the deeds wrought by these nefarious [evil] men! Alas, the images, which ought to have been adored, were trodden underfoot! Alas, the relics of the holy martyrs were thrown into unclean places! Then was seen what one shudders to hear, namely, the divine body and blood of Christ was spilled upon the ground or thrown about. They snatched the precious reliquaries [vessels holding holy objects], thrust into their bosoms the ornaments which these contained, and used the broken remnants for pans and drinking cups, precursors of Anti-Christ *[one who opposes Christ]*, authors and heralds of his nefarious deeds which we momentarily expect. Manifestly, indeed, by that race then, just as formerly, Christ was robbed and insulted and His garments were divided by lot; only

one thing was lacking, that His side, pierced by a spear, should pour rivers of divine blood on the ground.

One of the most famous objects to be looted in 1204 was the Shroud of Turin, thought to be the linen cloth placed over the face of Jesus after he was crucified, which is supposed to bear a likeness of his face as a result. The Shroud of Turin had a long history before it ended up in the bag of a Crusader. This cloth first turned up in 544, in Edessa, a city now part of southern Turkey. While repairs were being made to the outer walls of that city, the cloth was discovered and then placed in a church for safekeeping. Called the Edessa Cloth, it became famous throughout the Christian world, for people believed that the shadowy image of Christ that could be seen on the cloth was a miracle and not the work of a human being. By 1204 this cloth had made its way into the treasury of Constantinople. When the city fell to Crusaders, it was among the objects stolen. It was taken to Athens and began to be displayed in Europe, where it has remained ever since. Kept in Italy, it was given the name Shroud of Turin and has been studied widely by scientists and the faithful to discover the secret behind the sacred image many claim to see on it. To this day the mystery of the cloth has not been fully explained.

With the emperors dead, the Crusaders set up a Latin Kingdom in Constantinople and elected the first Latin emperor, Baldwin I. This put an end to the Fourth Crusade, howev-

Mosaic of the fall of Constantinople in 1204 to the forces of the Venetians after the death of Alexius IV. This event ended the Fourth Crusade as well as the Byzantine Empire. *The Art Archive/Dagli Orti.*

er, for the new Latin Kingdom had its hands full fighting enemies on all sides. The idea of moving on to Egypt and from there to Jerusalem was put on hold until the next Crusade. During his very brief reign, Alexius IV had managed to so weaken the Byzantine Empire that it would never recover. By inviting the Crusader army to Constantinople, he signed a virtual death warrant for his empire. The only real winners of the Fourth Crusade were the Venetians, who gained loot and new territories to be added to their own expanding commercial empire.

For More Information

Books

Angold, Michael. *The Fourth Crusade: Event and Context.* New York: Pearson/Longman, 2003.

Bartlett, Wayne B. *An Ungodly War: The Sack of Constantinople and the Fourth Crusade.* Stroud, UK: Sutton, 2000.

Queller, Donald, and Thomas F. Madden. *The Fourth Crusade: The Conquest of Constantinople*. Philadelphia: University of Pennsylvania Press, 1997.

Web Sites

"Constantinople." *New Advent*. http://www.newadvent.org/cathen/04301a.htm (accessed on June 16, 2004).

"Fourth Crusade." *The ORB: On-line Reference Book for Medieval Studies*. http://the-orb.net/textbooks/crusade/fourthcru.html (accessed on June 16, 2004).

"Internet Medieval Sourcebook: The Fourth Crusade 1204: Collected Sources." *Fordham University*. http://www.fordham.edu/halsall/source/4cde.html (accessed on June 16, 2004).

"Internet Medieval Sourcebook: The Sack of Constantinople (1204)." *Fordham University*. http://www.fordham.edu/halsall/source/choniates1.html (accessed on June 16, 2004).

"Internet Medieval Sourcebook: The Summons to Alexius." *Fordham University*. http://www.fordham.edu/halsall/source/4cde.html#cp (accessed on June 16, 2004).

"The Sack of Constantinople." *Illustrated History of the Roman Empire*. http://www.roman-empire.net/constant/1203–1204.html (accessed on June 16, 2004).

"Venetians and Crusaders Take Constantinople." *International History Project*. http://ragz-international.com/Crusades,%20Venetians%20Take%20Constantinople.htm (accessed on June 16, 2004).

Alp Arslan

c. 1026
Khorasan, Persia

November 24, 1072
Turkestan, Central Asia

Military leader and second Seljuk
Turkish sultan of Persia and Iraq

Alp Arslan (ruled 1063–72), second of the powerful Seljuk sultans (Turkish leaders), was indirectly responsible for beginning the Crusades, the two-centuries-long conflict between Christians and the followers of the Muslim religion. A military leader of great fame, he solidified Turkish holdings in Persia and Iraq, pushing their new empire to the doorstep of the Christian Byzantine Empire (395–1493), that portion of the old eastern Roman Empire where religious ceremonies were controlled by the Eastern Orthodox Church, as opposed to the Catholic Church of Europe. This empire was based mostly in Asia Minor, or present-day Turkey. With his victory over the Byzantine emperor Romanus IV Diogenes at Manzikert in 1071, he literally opened the door to the West and Europe for Islam. That same year one of his lieutenants captured Jerusalem. These events caught the attention of the pope, who began calling for a Holy War to take back the lands of Palestine and to return the revenues, or income, of Asia Minor to the Byzantine Empire. A tireless warrior, Alp Arslan, whose name means "Hero" or "Courageous Lion," was killed by a captive commander in 1072.

"Never have I invaded any country or attacked any enemy without seeking God's help in the plan. Yesterday, however, ... I said to myself, 'Now I am master of the world and no-one can stand against me.' Now God has undone me through the least of his creatures."

—*Alp Arslan; quoted in* The Annals of the Saljuq Turks.

Leader of the Seljuk Turks

Under their first sultan, Tughril Beg (990–1063), the Seljuk Turks stormed out of their Central Asian homeland to establish an empire stretching from the Aral Sea to the Euphrates River. Proven warriors and skillful in their use of the horse in cavalry charges and lightning-quick attacks with both their short-bladed scimitar (curved sword) and bow and arrow, they won the favor of the Abbasid caliphate, the reigning Arab Muslim dynasty in Baghdad. The Seljuks became hired soldiers and eventually assumed real political power in Iraq. In 1060 Tughril was proclaimed "King of the East and West" and occupied Baghdad. As such, the Seljuks, recent converts to Islam and its orthodox (traditional) Sunni sect, took on a new task as protectors of Sunni Islam. Sunni is one of the two major religious divisions of Islam. It holds that successors to Muhammad, the founder of Islam, do not necessarily have to come from his descendants. It stresses instead the importance of Sunna, or Muslim law, as a source for leadership in the faith. The Seljuks also inherited two new enemies: the Christian Byzantine Empire to the north in Asia Minor and the Fatimid dynasty, part of the breakaway Shiite Muslim sect based in Egypt, with holdings in Syria.

When Tughril died in 1063, he left behind no male heirs, so his nephew, Muhammad ibn Daud, became the new sultan of the Seljuk Turks. Better known as Alp Arslan, he was born in Persia around 1026 (some chroniclers set the date of his birth as late as 1039), the son of Chagri Beg, chief of the territories of Khorasan in ancient Persia, or today's western Iran. When his father died in 1061, Alp Arslan inherited these Khorasan territories. When he took over from his uncle, his domain increased with the addition of Persian territories around the Caspian Sea and lands in Iraq. This new sultan immediately set to work securing and expanding his empire. Although he was not in the direct line of succession (to inherit the throne), Arslan looked the part of a ruler. As Tamara Talbot Rice noted in *The Seljuks in Asia Minor,* Alp Arslan

> was to prove worthy of his throne. Both his appearance and his character fitted him for the role of sovereign [king]; he was extremely tall, yet he added to the impression created by his great height by wearing an immensely high hat, and he grew his moustache so long that, when out hunting, he was obliged to knot its ends behind his head that they should not interfere with his aim. His strength was as great as his aim was

Nizam al-Mulk

The great Persian statesman Nizam al-Mulk ("order of the kingdom") was an able bureaucrat and administrator and also promoted religious education in Seljuk territories through a series of *madrasahs,* or Islamic colleges and schools. In addition, Nizam wrote a famous book on kingship and statecraft entitled *Siyasat-nameh,* which has been variously translated as *Rules for Kings* or *Book of Government.* Aged forty-two when he became vizier to the Seljuk sultan Alp Arslan, Nizam preferred the art of diplomacy and international relations to the rough-and-ready militarism of his sultan. Persian by birth, Nizam al-Mulk brought with him a rich tradition, not to mention the Persian language, to the Seljuk court. Nizam's book on statecraft outlines how a sultan should rule. In that work he created two important institutions that the Seljuk Turks made their own: the office of the *atabeg,* or military adviser to young sultans, and the right of *iqta,* or the granting of income from land that a minister manages.

Considered one of the most brilliant ministers of the medieval East, Nizam al-Mulk went on to advise Alp Arslan's son and successor, Malik-Shah, in effect becoming the real sultan, for he trained and dominated the young ruler. Nizam became *atabeg* to Malik-Shah, the first time this title was applied after being mentioned in his own book. Nizam attracted many scholars and poets to the Seljuk court in Isfahan, including the Persian mathematician and poet Omar Khayyam (c. 1048–c. 1131), who became famous for his poetry but was far better known in his day for his work in mathematics and reforming the calendar. Under Nizam's leadership, the Seljuks created one of the largest empires in the world, with holdings in the Caucasus, Persia, Anatolia, Syria, Iraq, and parts of Arabia. Unlike Alp Arslan, however, Nizam acquired new lands by means of treaty and negotiation rather than through battle. Such success in the end led to jealousy, and Nizam al-Mulk had many enemies at court. He was murdered in 1092 by an Assassin, a member of the breakaway Islamic religious cult that often committed such political murders for self-defense or for hire. His sultan, Malik-Shah, died less than a month later. Following their deaths, the Seljuk empire was broken up into smaller domains and was never again as strong as it once had been.

true, yet his valor exceeded both. Indeed, he was as noble and brave in his conduct as he was magnificent in appearance.

Alp Arslan was a fighter and a conqueror. Luckily, he had an able administrator to help run his huge empire. Nizam al-Mulk (1018–1092) was a Persian who joined the services of Alp Arslan when he was a governor of Khorasan and soon became his vizier, or chief administrative counselor. Nizam served both Alp Arslan and his son and successor, Malik-Shah (1055–1092). Since Nizam was not only an able administrator but also a statesman, Alp Arslan was free to do what he did best—namely, fight the enemies of Islam and unite the Seljuk Empire. He faced his first challenge in 1064 when his father's cousin, Kutulmish, opposed his succession and took up arms against him. Alp Arslan and his troops fought this renegade at the Battle of Damagan, during which Kutulmish was thrown from his horse and killed. Following this episode, Alp Arslan had to put down revolts from within his own family when his brother, Kawurd, rose up against him in 1064 and again in 1067.

Meanwhile, the sultan also had neighbors to keep in line. He tried to maintain peace with other Turkish rulers to the east. He accomplished this with the Ghaznavid rulers, whose territories stretched from northeastern Iran and Afghanistan into India, but he was forced to engage in military action against the Qarakhanids, who ruled the region known as Transoxania, in Central Asia, with Samarkand as its central city; this area is now known as the regions of Uzbekistan, Tajikistan, Kyrgyzstan, and part of Turkmenistan. With these neighbors to the east finally brought into line, Alp Arslan was able to turn his attention and ambition westward.

Expansionist Policies

In 1064 Alp Arslan first pushed his armies into the valleys of the areas known as Georgia and Armenia, on the borders of Asia Minor, conquering the Georgians, who accepted the Seljuks as their sultans. He also was able to capture the former Armenian capital of Ani as well as the city of Kars. Thus, the Seljuks were in a good position to launch raids into the Anatolian peninsula itself and the Byzantine Empire. Briefly turning south, Alp Arslan and his forces struck the fortified cities of Antioch and Edessa, near the Mediterranean, and then swung north again to invade the Roman Empire in 1068, crossing the Euphrates River, which for centuries had served as the boundary between East and West. He fought Byzantine armies at Keyseri and by 1069 had reached the Aegean Sea, past the fortified town of Konya.

Further action in Asia Minor was put on hold, however, when Alp Arslan took up the request of Baghdad to deal

with the Fatimids in Egypt. He mounted a major expeditionary force, first taking Aleppo in Syria. Now his empire stretched from eastern Persia to the Mediterranean. Meanwhile, however, his troops were resisting renewed efforts by the Byzantine emperor Romanus IV Diogenes to push the Seljuks out of Asia Minor. By 1070 these efforts had succeeded in part, and Alp Arslan's army had been shoved back across the Euphrates again. Word reached Alp Arslan that the Byzantine emperor was planning to mount an even more powerful attack against the Seljuk army left behind in Asia Minor. Romanus assembled an army consisting of two hundred thousand troops, recruiting the faithful and hiring the rest. These mercenaries (paid soldiers) included Norsemen, Slavs, Turks, and even French Normans. Many Sicilians served in his officer corps. Romanus began moving these men east in the summer of 1071, hoping to take the Seljuks by surprise and secure the territory of Armenia as a buffer zone against them.

When word of this Byzantine advance reached Alp Arslan, he cut short his campaign against Egypt and the Fatimids, leaving Atsiz ibn Abaq, his vassal (a person under the protection of a lord) in charge of the campaign, and led his army to rejoin his other men in Armenia. Atsiz used this opportunity and newfound power to attack and greatly damage Jerusalem, thus releasing the city from Fatimid control. Subsequently, however, the Seljuk rulers refused to allow pilgrims of various faiths to gain access to the holy spots of the city, a policy that would have lasting consequences.

Meanwhile, Alp Arslan gathered his forces near Manzikert, north of Lake Van (in the far eastern part of contemporary Turkey, along its borders with Armenia, Iran, and Iraq). Vastly outnumbered by the Byzantine forces, Alp Arslan and his men managed to trap the imperial army thanks to the superior tactics of their cavalry. It also helped that large numbers of mercenary forces deserted Romanus just before the fighting began. The Byzantine soldiers were defeated, and Romanus was taken prisoner—the first time a Byzantine emperor had ever been captured by a Muslim leader. However, instead of taking the captive to Baghdad to show him off, Alp Arslan decided to use the emperor to regain lost land, form an alliance with Byzantium, and attain a long-lasting truce with the Byzantine Empire. Once the ransom for Romanus was paid and he had been returned to Constantinople, the emperor found himself ousted, or removed, from the throne by a new monarch, who imprisoned and blinded him. When Romanus died in prison, the treaty with the Seljuks ended with his death. However, the victory at Manzikert still opened all of Byzantium to Turkish invasions by roving bands, who nibbled away at much of Asia Minor over the next decade.

Alp Arslan Turns East and Faces an Ironic Death

Next, Alp Arslan returned to reconquer his homeland and to battle once again against the Qarakhanids of Transoxania. Before he and his men could cross the Oxus River, south of the Aral Sea, he had to capture a fortress defended by Yussuf Kothual, the governor of the region. When the fortress fell, Yussuf was brought before Arslan, who, forgetting his usual mercy toward prisoners, ordered that the man be killed. Arslan's famous skill at archery came into play in this final act of his life, for when Yussuf began to curse the sultan, Arslan commanded his guards to untie Yussuf's rope bonds. Taking aim with bow and arrow, Arslan had decided to kill the prisoner himself. But his marksmanship failed him at this critical moment, and the arrow missed Yussuf. Taking advantage of the occasion, Yussuf suddenly leaped at Arslan, drawing a hidden dagger, and stabbed the sultan. Arslan died of his wounds a few hours later, but not before making his peace with God for his arrogance. Arslan used his last breath to name his son, Malik-Shah, his successor.

During his short reign Alp Arslan had managed to cut deeply into the Byzantine Empire, delivering a blow at Manzikert from which the empire would never recover. Though the Byzantine Empire stumbled on for almost four more centuries, it would never regain the power it had before the arrival of Arslan and the great Seljuks of Persia. The Battle of Manzikert marked the beginning of Turkish power in the Middle East. Arslan's Seljuks, virtual rulers of Iraq and Syria as well as sultans of Persia and parts of Asia Minor, were now also in control of Jerusalem, the holy city that represented three religions. The coincidence of these events finally led to appeals by the Byzantine emperor to the pope in Rome for help in dealing with the Seljuks. These appeals were at last heard by Pope **Urban II** (see entry), who in 1095 delivered his famous speech at the Council of Clermont, in the south of France, where he pleaded for a holy war against the Muslims. Urban II got his wish, for in 1096 armies set off from Europe bound for the Holy Land, initiating two centuries of periodic war between Christianity and Islam.

For More Information

Books

Barthold, W. *Turkestan down to the Mongol Invasion.* 4th ed. London: E. J. W. Gibb Memorial Trust, 1977.

Bosworth, C. Edmund, ed. *The History of the Seljuq Turks.* Richmond, UK: Curzon, 2001.

Rice, Tamara Talbot. *The Seljuks in Asia Minor.* New York: Praeger, 1961.

Richards, D. S., trans. *The Annals of the Saljuq Turks.* London: Routledge Curzon, 2002.

Web Sites

"The Seljuk Empire." *All Empires.* http://www.allempires.com/empires/seljuk/seljuk1.htm (accessed on June 22, 2004).

"The Seljuk Turks." *Islamic History.* http://islamicweb.com/history/hist_Seljuk.htm (accessed on June 22, 2004).

"The Turks." *Istanbul Life.* http://www.istanbullife.org/turks.htm (accessed on June 22, 2004).

Averroës

1126
Córdoba, Spain

1198
Marrakesh, Morocco

Philosopher, jurist, astronomer, and physician

Known in the West by his Latin name Averroës (pronounced ah-vair-O-ehz), the Spanish Muslim, or Islamic, philosopher known in the East as Ibn Rushd was one of the greatest thinkers of the medieval world. His commentaries on the Greek philosopher Aristotle (384–322 B.C.E.), in which he attempted to balance faith and reason, not only shaped thought in the Islamic world in Spain, North Africa, and the Middle East but also introduced the works of the Greeks to later Latin and Christian philosophers of Europe. Living in Spain and North Africa at the time of the Crusades, he was one of the last in the great line of Muslim scholars of the Middle Ages (c. 500–1500 C.E.). Trained as a philosopher and as a doctor, lawyer, and judge, Averroës created dozens of works in his lifetime, only a fraction of which survive in translation. His major work remains *Tahafut al-tahafut* ("The Incoherence of the Incoherence"), a defense of philosophy or the use of reason.

Descended from a Family of Jurists

Averroës's full Arabic name was Abu al-Walid Muhammad ibn Ahmad ibn Muhammad ibn Rushd. He was born in

"Philosophy is the friend and milk-sister of religion; thus injuries from people related to philosophy are the severest injuries [to religion] apart from the enmity, hatred and quarrels...which are companions by nature and lovers by essence and instinct."

—*Averroës; quoted in* Averroës: On the Harmony of Religion and Philosophy.

Averroës, also known as Ibn Rushd. © *Archivo Iconografico, S.A./Corbis.*

the early twelfth century in Córdoba, Spain, which was then part of the Muslim world and one of the most intellectual and cultured cities in all of Europe. As Philip K. Hitti has noted in his *Makers of Arab History,* the royal library of Córdoba

> is said to have housed 400,000 titles, filling a forty-four-volume catalog. ... The university, housed in the great mosque [religious building], embraced among its departments theology, jurisprudence [law], astronomy, mathematics, and medicine. Its certificate opened the way to the most lucrative [high-paying] posts in the realm.

While the fundamentalist (ultraconservative) Muslim rulers of Spain were outwardly very strict and strictly followed the rules of the holy book, the Koran, the court life they created allowed for intellectual freedom. During Averroës's lifetime two different Moroccan dynasties, the Almoravids and the Almohads, controlled Spain, or *al-Andalus.* Many of the rulers were well educated and curious to gain new knowledge even when it conflicted with the religious teachings in the Koran.

The son of famed jurists and legal minds, Averroës came of age in this rich climate. Both his father and grandfather had been Muslim judges, or *qadi,* in Córdoba, and the grandfather had also been the prayer leader, or *imam,* in the city's great mosque. Destined to follow in their footsteps, as a boy Averroës studied the Islamic sciences, philosophy, and medicine. At the university, located in the great mosque, Averroës studied medicine and law. Study of medicine at that time also implied a further study of philosophy. Averroës was influenced by the work of earlier Arabic philosophers, such as Avicenna (980–1037) and Avempace (c. 1095–c. 1138), who died in Saragossa, Spain, when Averroës was twelve. These scholars and philosophers attempted to create a compromise between religion and philosophy.

At the Court of Marrakesh

Little is known of Averroës's whereabouts from about 1153 to 1169. It seems that he was in Marrakesh, Morocco, by 1153, perhaps helping to develop the colleges that the Almohad caliph, or leader, was founding at the time. He also was involved in research in astronomy, which studied the movement of the planets. While he was in Morocco during this first stay, he observed the star Canope, which was not visible in Spain. This led him to accept Aristotle's theory that the Earth was round, not flat. It is possible that he was employed as a teacher during these years, and he was clearly also working as a physician. His seven-part encyclopedia of medical knowledge, *Kitab al-kulliyat (Generalities),* was written between 1153 and 1169. In this work he covered topics ranging from the anatomy of the organs to therapy and hygiene, or sanitation and cleanliness. He was the first observer to note that patients do not suffer from smallpox twice.

During this time in Morocco he met the court physician and philosopher Ibn Tufayl, who was impressed by some of Averroës's early commentaries on Aristotle. Around 1169 Ibn Tufayl introduced this bright scholar to the new caliph, Abu Ya'qub Yusuf (ruled 1163–84). During this first meeting the caliph asked the Cordoban philosopher how the sky came to be and what it was made of. According to early chroniclers of his life, Averroës, fearing a trap that might lead him to provide a less than traditional answer to this question, hesitated to respond. However, upon hearing the caliph talk with Ibn Tufayl in a learned and even scientific manner, Averroës decided to take a chance and proceeded to give this ruler as much information as possible about the subject from both a scientific and a religious viewpoint.

Taken by Averroës's vast knowledge, the caliph sent him away with gifts that showed his admiration. Soon the caliph had a commission for the Spanish scholar. He complained that the translated works of the famous Greek philosopher Aristotle were too difficult and poorly done to understand. Ibn Tufayl decided not to attempt to explain these works, since such a project might take many years. Averroës agreed to take on the project, and it became his main scholarly occupation for the rest of his life.

Commentaries on Aristotle

In 1169 Averroës was appointed chief judge in Seville, Spain, and thus returned to the region of his birth. Two years later he went back to Córdoba as *qadi*. With access to the great library of the university, he was now able to concentrate more fully on his research. But such work was never made easy, for during the 1170s it seems that he traveled as a roaming judge throughout Spain, and in 1182 he was brought back to Marrakesh to replace Ibn Tufayl as physician to the caliph. When this caliph died in 1184, he was succeeded by his son, nicknamed al-Mansur, "the Victorious" (ruled 1184–99). About this time Averroës was sent back to Córdoba as chief *qadi,* and he remained there until 1195. He died in 1198 in Marrakesh, where his tomb still stands.

Averroës worked on his commentaries of Aristotle and Greek philosophy from 1169 to 1195. They are divided into three types: the *jami,* "epitomes," or short summations, for beginning students; *talkhis,* middle or intermediate commentaries intended for those with some knowledge of the subject; and *tafsir,* extensive commentaries for the advanced student, in which Averroës explains more than just what the original source contains. Over the years Averroës wrote such commentaries on most of Aristotle's works, including the *Organum, De anima, Physica, Metaphysica, Rhetorica, Poetica,* and *De partibus animalium,* as well as other titles by that philosopher, plus works of the earlier Greek philosopher Plato (c. 425–347 B.C.E.), including his *Republic.*

Sometimes Averroës would write all three types of commentaries about the same work. What is amazing about such commentaries is that Averroës did not speak or read Greek. He therefore had to rely on earlier translated texts for his explanations; ironically, it was often these very texts that he was trying to correct. Both in Latin and Arabic scholarship there had been many mistranslations and misunderstandings of the writings of Aristotle. Averroës had to rely on the work of those earlier scholars who had been true to Aristotle but who did not go into great detail in their studies.

The shorter and middle commentaries appeared between 1169 and 1178, with the more extensive studies coming out later. These works as a whole earned Averroës the nickname "Great Commentator" from later Latin and Christian scholars. Between 1174 and 1180 Averroës completed his greatest original works. Of these works, the best known are "The Incoherence of the Incoherence" and *Kitab fasl al-maqal* (*On the Harmony of Religion and Philosophy*). In the first text Averroës defends philosophy and rational thought from attacks made by the Muslim theologian al-Ghazzali, whose *Tahafut al-falasifa* (*The Incoherence of the Philosophers*) had appeared ninety years previously. Averroës takes this earlier argument apart point by point, discussing the creation of the world, the characteristics of God's will and knowledge, and the fate of the soul.

Applying the freethinking reason of Aristotle to such topics, Averroës sometimes came close to being in opposition to pure Islamic thinking. The same is true of his *On the Harmony of Religion and Philosophy,* in which he attempts to bridge faith and reason. In this work he assumes that the two are completely compatible, or similar, or at least are able to coexist. He also notes that people really can believe only what they are able to understand. He wrote that Muslims are in complete agreement "in holding that it is not obligatory [necessary] either to take all the expressions of Scripture in their apparent [seeming] meaning or to extend them all from their apparent meaning to allegorical [symbolic] interpretation."

Because of such statements, Averroës became the enemy of conservative Muslims, for whom the word of the Koran could not be questioned. He also became known in the West as a champion of rational thought and reason over faith. The truth of his thought lies somewhere in the middle. He did apply the philosophy of Aristotle to questions of religion, but according to most commentators he wove this earlier Greek philosophy into Islamic religious thought.

Because his works were not all translated, or were translated gradually into Latin for European readers, two different schools of thought developed from Averroës's philosophy. The early translations, dating from the thirteenth century, seem to present a much more rational picture—one based on reason—of things than his entire body of work does. This more liberal reading influenced Latin scholars and was called Averroism. According to this philosophy, the world has an eternal nature not necessarily created by God. This God, in turn, is distant from human beings, and there is little sense of divine or godly involvement, or taking part, in human affairs. Similarly, there is no indication of an afterlife, or a life after death. Later readings, however, balance these views, showing that Averroës was no believer in a so-called double truth—that is, one truth for philosophy and another one for religion. Instead, being a faithful Muslim, Averroës noted that when the works of philosophy and the Koran disagreed, then the truth about religion came only

Paper and the Spread of Knowledge

Great thinkers such as Averroës would never have had the effect they did without the invention of something all of us take for granted today—namely, paper. The earliest written or sketched information appeared on cave walls tens of thousands of years ago. From there people progressed to stone and clay tablets, but these materials were not very portable and also required great effort to create. Many other materials were tried over the centuries, including bark, silk, metal, and even leaves. The ancient Egyptians developed papyrus from a plant found growing near the Nile River. They created what looked like sheets of paper by peeling and slicing the plant into strips and then layering and pounding them together. Not long after that, parchment was made from animal skins. It had several advantages over papyrus: it was stronger, both sides could be used, and if mistakes were made they could be scraped off.

No further advances in writing surfaces occurred until the Chinese invented paper (the name comes from "papyrus," which it resembles) during the time of Christ. This early paper was made from beaten or pulped plant material and water, which was spread on a bamboo frame to dry. This writing surface was better than earlier ones, because paper could be made much more easily and quickly. The art of papermaking spread throughout Asia to Japan, Korea, and Tibet, and by the seventh century it had reached Central Asia and Persia. From there it passed into Islamic lands, finding a welcome audience in Baghdad in the eighth century. The Arabs made improvements in papermaking, adding linen fibers to the wood to create a finer, smoother surface for writing. Most important, a paper mill was established in Baghdad, permitting the manufacture of paper on a large scale and enabling Arab writers and thinkers to fill libraries with their knowledge, including their translations of Greek texts.

The Christian West, however, resisted paper. The church declared paper was bad because it was a Muslim product. As late as 1221 Holy Roman Emperor Frederick II declared all official documents written on paper to be invalid, or worthless. Only those written on parchment were legal. All this changed with the invention of the printing press in the fifteenth century. Then paper became popular in Europe as well.

from the Koran. Similarly, his idea of an afterlife included a form of resurrection, or rebirth, and if the world were eternal (never-ending) it was only because it depended on God, who is the eternal creator.

In reality, Averroës was walking a tightrope with his philosophy. He understood Greek free will and reason, but as a powerful *qadi,* responsible for maintaining Islamic law as stated in the Koran and the Shar'ia, or Book of Laws, he also needed to blend these two traditions. This position finally landed him in trouble. In 1195 al-Mansur needed to rally his people to fight the Christians in Spain. As a result, he had to please the more conservative elements of Islamic society, who had long criticized the work of Averroës. The philosopher was ordered to appear before a tribunal (court) in Córdoba, where he was blasted by his enemies with both true and false accusations. His books were publicly burned, and he was sent into exile in Lucena, a town south of Córdoba. Not long after this incident al-Mansur won a victory over the Christians at Toledo. Perhaps this made the political climate less difficult for the caliph. In 1198 he summoned the old philosopher out of exile and invited him to come to his court in Marrakesh. Averroës, however, did not have much of a chance to enjoy his changed fortune, for he died later that year.

Averroës was perhaps the most important philosopher of the Middle Ages. Although he lived during a time when two major Crusades were fought, it does not appear that his life was much disturbed by these conflicts. His commentaries on Greek philosophy, especially the works of Aristotle, preserved the thoughts and ideas of that early Greek scholar and introduced him to new generations of Muslim, Christian, and Jewish readers. For those Latin scholars who did not read the full range of his works, Averroës became a symbol of reason and free will. The great Catholic saint and scholar Thomas Aquinas (c. 1225–1274) drew upon the work of Averroës to try to balance faith and reason. Averroës wrote almost eighty books during his lifetime, totaling more than twenty thousand pages. Such works deal not only with philosophy but also with medicine, the law, astronomy, and even grammar. A Renaissance man (a man of many and various skills and interests) before the term was used to describe the rebirth of the arts and sciences in fourteenth-century Europe, Averroës was born into an age of Crusader intolerance but managed to rise above such narrow disputes. As Philip K. Hitti has concluded, Averroës—in his various roles as physician, philosopher, scientist, and commentator—made Aristotle accessible, fathered a long-lasting rationalist movement, and greatly contributed to Europe's Renaissance.

For More Information

Books

Arnaldez, R. "Ibn Rushd." *Encyclopedia of Islam.* 2nd ed. Leiden, Netherlands: E. J. Brill, 1999.

"Averroës." *Encyclopedia of World Biography.* 2nd ed. Detroit, MI: Gale, 1998.

Hitti, Philip K. *Makers of Arab History.* New York: St. Martin's Press, 1968.

Hourani, George F. *Averroës: On the Harmony of Religion and Philosophy.* London: Luzac, 1961.

Leamon, Oliver. *Averroës and His Philosophy.* Richmond, UK: Curzon, 1998.

Web Sites

"Averroës." *Encyclopedia of the Orient.* http://i-cias.com/e.o/index.htm (accessed on June 22, 2004).

"Averroës." *New Advent.* http://www.newadvent.org/cathen/02150c.htm (accessed on June 22, 2004).

"Ibn Rushd (Averroës)." *Islamic Philosophy Online.* http://www.muslim philosophy.com/ir/default.htm (accessed on June 22, 2004).

Al-Zahir Baybars

c. 1223
Southern Russia

July 1, 1277
Damascus, Syria

Mamluk sultan

Called the "Napoleon of medieval Egypt," al-Zahir Baybars, also known as Rukn al-Din Baybars al-Bunduqdari, or simply Baybars, was the savior of Egypt during the critical years of the thirteenth century when that country faced enemies from both Europe and Asia. Baybars, who rose from slave to soldier to sultan (leader), fought the French during the later Crusades, or holy wars, against Islam, and the Mongols, raiders from the plains of Central Asia who tore through the Middle East and destroyed much of Islamic civilization. An intelligent, spirited, and courageous soldier, Baybars was also an able administrator, bringing the centers of Egypt and Syria back to cultural and artistic life during the seventeen years of his rule (1260–77). He was largely responsible for establishing the Mamluk, or slave, dynasty that ruled Egypt, Syria, and Palestine for several centuries and made Egypt the political and religious center of the Muslim world.

A Trained Mamluk

Baybars was born around 1223 near the north shore of the Black Sea, a region in present-day southern Russia. He was a

"Baybars repeatedly demonstrated quickness of action resolution, courage, shrewdness, prescience [foresight], and determination. He seemed to be able to accomplish many things almost at the same time, and to be always on the move directing affairs of state in Egypt and Syria."

—*Mustafa Ziada, "The Mamluk Sultans to 1293," in* History of the Crusades. *Vol. 2,* The Later Crusades, 1189–1311.

member of the nomadic (wandering) Kipchak Turks, who hunted
in this region. As a young boy his people were attacked by the
Mongols, a warrior-like group of nomads who resided in the
steppes, or plains, of Central Asia. These Mongols were originally
led by Genghis Khan (c. 1162–1227) and then later by his sons
and grandsons. By the middle of the 1230s the Mongols had
reached the Black Sea region. During one battle Baybars was taken
prisoner and sold in the slave markets of present-day Turkey.

Purchased by Syrian merchants, the adolescent Baybars was transported farther and farther into the Muslim world, eventually reaching Egypt around 1240, where he was bought by the Egyptian sultan al-Salih Najm al-Din Ayyub. Al-Salih was to be the last of the Ayyubids, a line of rulers of Egypt established by the great Muslim military leader **Saladin** (see entry). This sultan made a point of recruiting Mamluks (from the Arab verb for "to own"), or slaves, and then training them to be soldiers. The sultan placed Baybars in the elite Mamluk training school located on an island in the Nile River. After several years of hard and thorough drills, Baybars was put into the Bahriyya Mamluks, the regiment that served the sultan.

In 1250 Baybars first made a name for himself when he defended Egypt from the Crusader invasion of **Louis IX** (see entry), king of France. This French monarch was a very religious leader and had spent the past several years preparing a Crusader army to free the Holy Land from Islamic control. His Seventh Crusade (1248–54) would be the last major holy war, though many smaller battles would be fought over the next forty years until the Christian Crusaders were finally pushed out of the Holy Land. During the early part of the fighting and eventual standoff between the Egyptians and French, the city of Damietta, located on the Nile delta (mouth) had fallen to the Crusaders. Then the sultan al-Salih died of tuberculosis, a terminal lung disease. His wife, **Shajarat al-Durr** (see entry), a former Mamluk like Baybars, conspired with two advisers of the sultan to keep the death a secret from the troops, both to keep morale up as well as to keep this information from the enemy. Louis IX, however, found out about it through a spy and also discovered a way to cross over the river that separated his men and the sultan's camp. He sent his brother, Robert of Artois, to attack the Egyptians, chasing them as they retreated into the streets of the nearby town of Mansurah. At this point Baybars and his Mamluks struck, cutting down the Crusaders in the narrow streets of the town and saving the day. A large number of the French king's best knights, or noble soldiers, were killed at the Battle of Mansurah in February 1250, thus turning the tide of the war. With the arrival of the sultan's son, Turan Shah, later that month, the French were finally defeated. Louis IX was captured, and Egypt was saved.

The End of the Crusades

The job of chasing the Christians out of the Holy Land once and for all was left to those Mamluk leaders who ruled after Baybars. The final defeat for the Christian Crusaders occurred at the fortified port of Acre in 1291. On April 5 a huge Muslim force consisting of sixty thousand horsemen and one hundred sixty thousand foot soldiers gathered at the gates of Acre. Though this was not the last Crusader city left in the Holy Land, it was the most important. If it fell, those still remaining—such as Tyre, Beirut, and Sidon—would also surely fall. This enormous Muslim force had been assembled by the Mamluk sultan al-Ashraf al-Khalil; it outnumbered by ten to one the Christian defenders inside the walls.

One thing the Crusaders had in their favor was the fact that their defense was largely being directed by the Christian religious and military orders the Knights Templars and the Knights Hospitallers, both of whom had become famous in the Christian and Islamic worlds alike for their courage and honor in battle. The siege lasted almost two months, during which the Templars, Hospitallers, and other Crusaders fought bravely. When it became clear that the city faced defeat, men, women, and children flocked to the docks to try to board ships, for the Muslims were killing every person they captured. Almost thirty thousand people were eventually slaughtered in this final episode of the two-centuries-old Crusades.

During these final tragic moments, Roger de Flor, one of the Templar knights, disgraced the entire Templar order by seizing a ship in the harbor and demanding a high price for any passenger lucky enough to get onboard. Those who did not have the fare, or ticket price—including nuns and children—were left behind to be killed by the Muslim soldiers or taken prisoner and sold as slaves. (He later became known for his harsh treatment of the civilian population.) Roger de Flor's human cargo consisted mainly of noble ladies of Acre who had the necessary funds. Although he created a fortune in this way, he was later stripped of his knighthood by the pope when his cowardly behavior became known. He went on to serve as a soldier of fortune (one who is paid to find and kill specific people) in Sicily and fought the Turks on behalf of the Byzantine emperor. He was planning to set up his own rival kingdom when he was finally murdered on the order of the Byzantine emperor. Roger de Flor's name is usually associated with his ignoble, or dishonorable, actions during the fall of Acre in 1291. His behavior provides an ironic ending to the Crusader movement, which was supposed to have inspired a sense of honor, loyalty, and nobility among fighting men.

when much of the Islamic world was falling apart, threatened by Mongols and Christians alike, this former slave who rose to become sultan made Egypt a strong state at the very center of the Middle East. The Mamluk dynasty he helped create survived the Turkish invasions of 1517 and hung on in Egypt, in one form or another, until the French emperor Napoleon (1769–1821) arrived there in 1798.

For More Information

Books

Glubb, Sir John. *Soldiers of Fortune: The Story of the Mamlukes.* New York: Stein and Day, 1973.

Maalouf, Amin. *The Crusades through Arab Eyes.* Translated by Jon Rothschild. New York: Schocken Books, 1984.

Muir, William. *The Mameluke; or, Slave Dynasty of Egypt: 1260–1517 A.D.* New York: AMS Press, 1973.

Ziada, Mustafa. "The Mamluk Sultans to 1293." In A *History of the Crusades.* Edited by Kenneth M. Sultan. Vol. 2: *The Later Crusades, 1189–1311.* Edited by Robert L. Wolff and Harry W. Hazard. Madison: University of Wisconsin Press, 1969.

Web Sites

"Baybars I." *Encyclopedia of the Orient.* http://i-cias.com/e.o/baybars1.htm (accessed on June 24, 2004).

"Baybars al-Bunduqdari, The First Great Slave Ruler of Egypt." *Tour Egypt.* http://www.touregypt.net/featurestories/baybars.htm (accessed on June 24, 2004).

"The Seventh Crusade." *The ORB: On-line Reference Book for Medieval Studies.* http://the-orb.net/textbooks/crusade/seventhcru.html (accessed on June 24, 2004).

Benjamin of Tudela

c. 1127
Tudela, Spain

1173
Castile, Spain

Rabbi, traveler, and writer

Benjamin of Tudela (pronounced to-DAY-la) is the author of one of the most famous early travel books, *The Itinerary of Benjamin of Tudela.* A rabbi (religious scholar and leader) originally from Spain, Benjamin set out on a world journey around 1159. During the next fourteen years he traveled to more than three hundred cities, including areas in Greece, Syria, Palestine, Mesopotamia, Persia, and Arabia. He is also believed to be the first European to approach the borders of China. The book he wrote to describe these travels, *Massoath Schel Rabbi Benjamin* (first translated in the 1840s), provides scholars with one of the first eyewitness accounts of life in the Middle Ages throughout parts of southern Europe and the Middle East. Benjamin also gave good descriptions of the physical conditions under which Jewish people lived in these regions. Other topics he reported on include politics, commerce (trade), and geography.

"The city of Bagdad [Baghdad] is...situated in a land of palms, gardens and plantations, the like of which is not to be found in Shinar....Wise men live there, philosophers who know all manner of wisdom, and magicians expert in all manner of witchcraft."

—*Benjamin of Tudela*, The Itinerary of Benjamin of Tudela: Travels in the Middle Ages.

A Son of Navarre

Born around 1127 in the city of Tudela, located in the northern Spanish province of Navarre, Benjamin came of age in a time of relative religious tolerance in Spain. Members of the Sephardic community (*Sefarad* is the Hebrew word for Spain), Benjamin's ancestors were part of the diaspora, or migration, of Jews who had come to the Iberian, or Spanish, Peninsula with the Roman legions, though some historians date their arrival to as early as the sixth century B.C.E. In any case, by the twelfth century C.E. the Sephardim (Spanish Jews) made up 90 percent of the world's Jews. In Spain, unlike other regions of Europe, Jews could be found in cities, towns, and villages and were active in all walks of life.

Part of the Spanish mix was also its Moorish history. Since the early eighth century C.E., the Muslims of northwestern Africa of both Arab and native Berber descent had become the rulers of much of the Iberian Peninsula. These Moors, as they were called, formed an Islamic outreach in mainland Europe. The Moorish rulers created a tolerant as well as a multicultural climate, emphasizing science, art, and philosophy. In the Spain, or al-Andalus, in which Benjamin grew up, Muslims, Christians, and Jews all lived in harmony. A golden age of learning and the arts transformed Spanish society. The Jewish philosopher **Maimonides** (see entry) and the Arab philosopher **Averroës** (see entry) were both products of this cosmopolitan, or worldly, atmosphere.

Tudela, a town close to the French border, received its first Jewish families in the eleventh century, when it was still under Moorish control. In 1119—about a decade before the birth of Benjamin—the city and its surrounding kingdom were conquered by Alfonso I, the Christian king of Pamplona and Aragon. As a result of this power shift, the Arab population was forced to relocate to a new quarter beyond the city walls, while the Jewish residents maintained a legal footing almost equal to that of Christians, who were now in control. An atmosphere of tolerance reigned in Tudela, if not in other parts of Spain, where repression and intolerance toward Jew and Muslim alike was becoming the order of the day.

Benjamin studied to be a rabbi, specializing in the *halachah,* or Jewish religious law. Little else is known about his private life until about 1159 (or even later), when he set out on the travels that would take him through much of the known world. Marcus Nathan Adler, translator and editor of

Benjamin's travel journal, *The Itinerary of Benjamin of Tudela,* has suggested possible reasons for the rabbi's journey. Noting that Jews in the Middle Ages were "much given to travel," Adler describes Benjamin as "the wandering Jew, who kept up communications between one country and another. He had a natural aptitude [ability] for trade and travel. His people were scattered to the four corners of the earth." In fact, looking at Benjamin's impressive travel plan, there is hardly a place mentioned that did not have a Jewish population. With fellow Jews so numerous and widespread, it made traveling in these days before organized transportation much easier; at the very least there would be a friendly face awaiting Benjamin at the end of his daily journey.

   Adler also observes that during the Crusades—the two centuries of conflict between the Christian West and the Muslim Middle East over control of Jerusalem and the Holy Land—tolerance for different religions was breaking down. Jews as well as Muslims were discriminated against through-

A map of the Crusades in the Holy Land, a good reference to what Europe and the Middle East would have looked like during the time of Benjamin of Tudela's travels. *Réunion des Musées Nationaux/Art Resource, NY.*

out Europe, especially along the Crusader routes through Europe to Palestine. Adler concludes:

> It is not unlikely, therefore, that Benjamin may have undertaken his journey with the object of finding out where his expatriated [exiled] brethren [brothers] might find an asylum [safe place]. It will be noted that Benjamin seems to use every effort to trace and to afford particulars [give details] of independent communities of Jews, who had chiefs of their own, and owed no allegiance [loyalty] to the foreigner.

Adler also mentions trade and business interests as another possible motive for making this very difficult journey.

On the Road

At the time Benjamin set out on his journey, the Second Crusade (1147–49) was ten years in the past. Benjamin's goal may not have been to give an account of this struggle between Christians and Muslims, but during the course of his travels he did visit flash points, or tense areas, in the ongoing combat between Crusades. Beginning his travels with the Spanish city of Saragossa as his first destination, he took two days to reach the ancient town of Taragona, some of whose buildings dated to the time of ancient Greece. From there he traveled to Barcelona, where, Benjamin wrote (in the Adler edition of the *Itinerary*), "there is a holy congregation, including sages, wise and illustrious men," and listed some of the prominent Jews of the city. Benjamin also described the city in terms of geography and commerce: "This is a small city and beautiful, lying upon the seacoast. Merchants come thither [here] from all quarters with their wares, from Greece, from Pisa, Genoa, Sicily, Alexandria in Egypt, Palestine, Africa and all its coasts."

This is the basic formula Benjamin followed throughout his travels: he noted the presence or absence of a Jewish community in all the places he visited, observing who were the most famous scholars or men of commerce or science. He also commented on the economic conditions in such places and about what sorts of businesses and commercial activities were taking place. Often he included notes of a more "touristy" nature, such as descriptions of famous buildings and, in particular, beautiful scenery.

From Spain Benjamin crossed into France at Montpellier and Marseilles. There he commented on the beginnings of what became known as the Albigensian Crusade, the suppression of a sect, or group, of religious reformers in the south of France who were considered heretics, or persons who hold religious beliefs contrary to traditional church doctrine. From Marseilles he boarded a ship bound for the Italian peninsula, landing in Genoa and also visiting Pisa and Luca on his way to Rome. Benjamin found few Jews in northern Italy. In Rome he estimated that there were about two hundred in all, many of them well known; some even worked for the pope, the leader of the western Christian church. Benjamin also commented on the historical sites of the city, including the ruins of ancient Rome. From there he proceeded south through Naples to the eastern coast of Italy and on to Brindisi and Otranto, where he caught a ship for Corfu, an island near Greece.

Out of Europe

In Thebes, located north of Athens, Benjamin was surprised to find a very healthy Jewish community of two thousand, with rabbis who showed a high degree of learning. Passing through the northern Greek city of Salonika, he traveled on to Constantinople (present-day Istanbul, in Turkey), the capital of the Byzantine Empire, the Orthodox Christian, eastern half of the old Roman Empire. He reached this city in December 1161. Although he was impressed with the magnificent mosque, or Muslim place of worship, of Saint Sophia and was present to document the marriage of Emperor Manuel Comnenus (1143–1180), he was disappointed by the way the Jewish community was being treated in this otherwise great city. The Jews were forced to live in a ghetto, a zone where only Jews resided; were denied such basic rights as riding a horse; and were generally singled out for bad treatment by the rest of the population.

His lengthy stay in Constantinople allowed Benjamin to record some of his most detailed observations. His comments about the military spirit of the city are interesting:

> Wealth like that of Constantinople is not to be found in the whole world. Here also are men learned in all the books of the Greeks, and they eat and drink every man under his vine and his fig tree. They hire from amongst all nations warriors called Loazim (Barbarians) to fight with the Sultan Masud, King of the

Gold hyperperon of Emperor Manuel Comnenus. Benjamin of Tudela was in Constantinople to witness the marriage of Manuel.

Copyright The British Museum. Reproduced by permission.

Togarmim (Seljuks), who are called Turks; for the natives are not warlike, but are as women who have no strength to fight.

From Constantinople, Benjamin sailed past the islands of the Aegean Sea on his way to the island of Cyprus, where he found a Jewish sect that did not observe the holy day of the Sabbath. From there he crossed to the mainland at Antioch, near present-day Syria, entering lands still held by the Crusaders, those Christian soldiers and knights who had first entered the region in 1096 as part of the First Crusade (1095–99) and had maintained their kingdoms in the Holy Land ever since. Traveling south, he recorded observations about the Ismaili religious sect (subgroup of Islam) known as the Assassins, located near Lebanon. The followers of this sect believed in eliminating their opponents by killing them, thus giving rise to the English word "assassin."

Moving farther south, Benjamin praised the harbor of Tyre as being one of the finest in the world. He next passed through Acre and into the Holy Land and Jerusalem, which he described as "a small city, fortified by three walls. It is full of people whom the Muhammadans call Jacobites, Syrians, Greeks, Georgians and Franks, and of people of all tongues," including a Jewish community of about two hundred. He visited many other locations in the Holy Land, such as Hebron and Bethlehem—he was given free access to these places by the Crusaders—before again traveling north to Damascus, a city that, as he noted, was the seat of the powerful sultan Nur al-Din (1118–1174), who was also the patron of the up-and-coming military leader **Saladin** (see entry). There he found a community of three thousand Jews, among whom "are learned and rich men."

From northern Syria he crossed into Mesopotamia (part of present-day Iraq), visiting Baghdad, which was considered the largest city in the world at the time and was the seat of the caliphs, or Muslim leaders, who controlled the entire Islamic region. As Benjamin explained it, Baghdad was

> the great city and the royal residence of the Caliph Emir al Muminin al Abbasi of the family of Muhammad [the founder of the religion of Islam]. He is at the head of the Muhammadan religion, and all the kings of Islam obey him; he occupies a similar position to that held by the Pope over the Christian.

Benjamin noted that he found forty thousand Jews dwelling in "security, prosperity and honour under the great Caliph." Although later observers have questioned this high figure, it is clear that Jews formed a significant part of the population of this city. Some of Benjamin's best descriptions come from his stay in Baghdad. He painted a colorful picture of the court life of the city and also wrote of the schools for the study of Jewish religious and civic law.

From Persia to Egypt

Scholars have noted that Benjamin's descriptions and comments between leaving Baghdad (c. 1164) and arriving in Egypt (c. 1171) seem somewhat far-fetched. It is not known how much of this was the result of his imagination and how much was based on observation. As the writer C. Raymond Beazley noted in *The Dawn of Modern Geography*, Benjamin's *Itinerary* at this point "is no longer, for the most part, a record of personal travel; it is rather an attempt to supplement [add to] the first part 'of things seen,' by a second 'of things heard.'"

An illustration of the Tigris and Euphrates Rivers. Benjamin may have traveled from Basra, at the mouth of the Tigris River, to the island of Kish in the Persian Gulf.

Egyptian National Library, Cairo, Egypt/ Giraudon/Bridgeman Art Library.

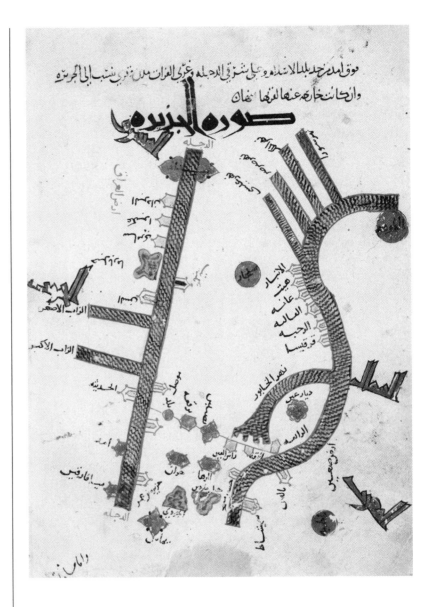

According to his *Itinerary,* for the next seven years Benjamin traveled through Arabia and then north to Persia, visiting Isfahan, and on to Samarkand in Central Asia, Tibet, parts of India, and western China. However, Adler has noted that

> it is unlikely that [Benjamin] went far into Persia, which at that time was in a chaotic [unsettled] state, and where the Jews were much oppressed. From Basra, at the mouth of the Tigris, he probably visited the island of Kish in the Persian Gulf,

which in the Middle Ages was a great emporium [center] of commerce, and thence [from there] proceeded to Egypt by way of Aden and Assuan.

Adler makes no mention of what would have occupied the missing years in Benjamin's travels, but any estimate of the length of his journey is based on a combination of fact and educated guesswork.

It nonetheless is fairly certain that Benjamin reached Egypt in 1171. His descriptions of Alexandria and the Sinai as well as Cairo, the main city of Egypt, are filled with such richness of detail that they appear to be the result of firsthand observation. He makes mention of the Fatimids, a rival dynasty in Cairo belonging to the Shiite group of Islam, who believe that true successors to the prophet Muhammad ended with the death of his son-in-law, as opposed to the caliphs in Baghdad, members of the Sunni sect of Islam, who believe that the Koran, or holy book of the Moslems, provides guidance to the faithful. When Benjamin arrived, these Fatimids were rulers in name only. Saladin, their former military servant, had assumed real power and was in the process of using Egypt to reunite the Islamic forces and fight the Crusaders.

Benjamin sailed back to Europe in 1173, first reaching Sicily. There he provided a good description of Palermo, after which his *Itinerary* enters into the realm of fantasy, with more hearsay about northern Europe, including Germany, France, and Russia. Scholars believe it is far more likely that Benjamin returned to his native Spain from Sicily, there to write up his observations. Down through the centuries Benjamin's *Itinerary* has gained increasing importance due to its eyewitness accounts. After separating those parts of the book that rely on his own observations from those that were clearly invented or borrowed from other sources, readers are left with a detailed and colorful account of the twelfth-century world, particularly the Middle East at the time of the Crusades.

Benjamin traveled in the region during a time of relative peace—between the Second and Third Crusade (1149–1189) —thereby providing inside information on the daily life of the time. More specifically, his travel book is a valuable source of information about the number and status of Jews in the Middle Ages. "Whatever his intentions may have been," Adler concludes, "we owe Benjamin no small debt of gratitude for handing to posterity [future generations] records that form a unique contribution to our knowledge of geography and ethnology [the study of cultural characteristics of different races] in the Middle Ages."

For More Information

Books

Adler, Elkan Nathan, ed. *Jewish Travellers: A Treasury of Travelogues from Nine Centuries.* 2nd ed. New York: Hermon Press, 1966.

Beazley, C. Raymond. *The Dawn of Modern Geography.* 3 vols. New York: Peter Smith, 1949.

Benjamin of Tudela. *The Itinerary of Benjamin of Tudela: Critical Text, Translation, and Commentary.* Translated and edited by Marcus Nathan Adler. New York: Philipp Feldheim, 1907.

Benjamin of Tudela. *The Itinerary of Benjamin of Tudela: Travels in the Middle Ages.* Malibu, CA: Joseph Simon, 1983.

Komroff, Manuel, ed. *Contemporaries of Marco Polo.* New York: Dorset, 1989.

Web Sites

"Benjamin of Tudela." *Jewish Virtual Library.* http://www.us-israel. org/jsource/biography/BenjaminTudelo.html (accessed on July 22, 2004).

"The Itinerary of Benjamin of Tudela: Critical Text, Translation, and Commentary." *Traveling to Jerusalem.* http://chass.colostate-pueblo. edu/history/seminar/benjamin/benjamin1.htm (accessed on July 22, 2004).

Bernard of Clairvaux

1090
Fontaines-les-Dijon, France

August 20, 1153
Clairvaux, France

Catholic religious leader and saint

Bernard of Clairvaux was one of the most powerful figures of the twelfth century. A Catholic priest and abbot (director) of a religious institution at Clairvaux, France, Bernard's influence stretched far beyond the borders of France. A powerful speaker and convincing writer, on one occasion he helped choose the pope, or leader of the Catholic Church, and had significant influence on another pope in religious and civil matters. Bernard could charm kings yet be firm toward fellow Catholics about leading a religious life filled with prayer rather than riches. He preached of love but also spoke forcefully in favor of the Second Crusade (1147–49), a Christian military expedition to the Holy Land to help stop the rising power of Islamic forces there. When that Crusade failed badly, he blamed the sins of the Crusaders. Bernard helped spread the popularity of the Cistercian order, a religious group that believed in a simple and disciplined lifestyle, and wrote widely on church matters. He was canonized (made a saint) in 1174.

"The earth has been shaken; it trembles because the Lord of heaven has begun to lose his land.... What are you doing, you servants of the cross? Will you throw to the dogs that which is most holy?"

—*Bernard of Clairvaux, quoted in* The Crusades.

Bernard of Clairvaux. *The Art Archive/Pinacoteca Virreinel Mexico City/Dagli Orti.*

A Noble Birth

Bernard of Clairvaux was born into a noble family in 1090, in the Burgundy region of France. The males were respected knights, or gentlemen trained in the art of war. His father was killed during the First Crusade (1095–99), when Christian soldiers traveled to Palestine and Jerusalem to free the sacred sites of Christianity from control by the Muslims, or followers of the Islamic religion. The life of a soldier, however, was not for Bernard: Before his birth it was said that there was a prophecy, or prediction, that this child would be a great leader of the church. He was sent to Chatillon-sur-Seine, a famous religious school, where he developed his love for literature and writing. There he memorized religious writings and was recognized by his instructors as a promising church scholar.

Following the death of Bernard's mother in 1107, the youth decided to become a monk, a religious man who withdraws from society and chooses to live a life of prayer and hard work. His noble relatives opposed such a move, wanting him to seek higher church offices, but Bernard had made up his mind. Sometime between 1111 and 1113 Bernard and thirty young noblemen of Burgundy, including several of his brothers and an uncle, joined the Cistercian order at the abbey of Cîteaux (or, in Latin, Cistercium), near Dijon, France. This new religious order took its name from its location. Founded in 1098, the Cistercians were a breakaway branch of the Benedictine order of monks. Bernard was attracted to the reforming philosophy of the Cistercians, who wanted to bring religion back to basics.

The monks at Cîteaux were poor and very religious. They did not interact with society, as did other monastic orders. Their buildings and food were all quite simple, and they led a life close to nature, unlike such wealthier orders as the Cluniacs, named after the abbey church of Cluny in France. In his "Apology," dating from 1125 and quoted in the *Internet Medieval Sourcebook,* Bernard takes these rich and lazy orders of monks to task for their luxurious surroundings:

> In short, so many and so marvelous are the various shapes surrounding us that it is more pleasant to read the marble than the books, and to spend the whole day marveling over these things rather than meditating on the law of God. Good Lord! If

we aren't embarrassed by the silliness of it all, shouldn't we at least be disgusted by the expense?

Bernard and his friends pumped new blood into the Cistercian order and helped it grow. By 1115 Cîteaux had become large enough that additional houses were needed. Bernard and a group of his followers built another monastery at a place called Clairvaux, far from civilization. He was made abbot (director of the house) and planned to devote his life to prayer and hard work. This routine of manual work, little food, and less sleep eventually took its toll. Although Bernard was sick most of his life, he still managed to work long hours. As a preacher he soon became famous locally; people came to pray at his simple monastery. Word of his good deeds and hard work continued to spread, winning new members for the Cistercians. Soon his dream of a simple life had to change, however, for he was drawn into larger matters of the church.

A Battle between Popes

Bernard became so well known in the church that other priests and religious officials came to him for advice. He began writing explanations dealing with church law and sent letters to friends and church leaders alike. He also began to record his sermons in works such as *Eighty-Six Sermons on the Song of Songs*. As his fame grew, however, he had less and less time to attend to the daily affairs at Clairvaux.

For example, in 1128 he played an important role in writing the rules of the Knights Templars, an order of soldier-monks that came into being in the Holy Land under the direction of Bernard's friend **Hugh de Payens** (see entry). These rules were approved at the Council of Troyes that same year. In 1130 bigger matters attracted his interest, involving the election of a new pope, or leader of the Roman Catholic Church and essentially of Christianity in Europe. Innocent II was elected by one group of cardinals, or church officers, but another group elected his rival, Anacletus II. Bernard threw his support behind Innocent II, and as a result the French people accepted Innocent II as the true pope. However, Anacletus II and his friends occupied Rome, the seat of church power, and Innocent II was forced to leave the city. Bernard

Bernard presenting his rules for piety and faith to the faithful. He wrote similar rules for the Knights Templars, and many of his rules were adopted by the Council of Troyes. *The Art Archive/Pinacoteca Nazionale Bologna/Dagli Orti.*

next persuaded Lothair II, the leader of the Holy Roman Empire, a loose collection of mostly German states and kingdoms, to back Innocent II. Lothair ultimately helped restore the pope to his rightful place in Rome.

Bernard also took an interest in church doctrine (beliefs). He fought against what he saw as the misguided policies of the famous medieval philosopher Peter Abelard (1079–

1142). Bernard did not like the way Abelard used reason, or rational and logical thought, to teach about Christianity and the Bible. For Bernard, religion was a matter of faith more than reason. In 1140 Bernard used his influence with Pope Innocent II to have Abelard's theories and writings condemned.

The Second Crusade

Simultaneously, in the Holy Land and the Middle East, events were taking place that directly affected Bernard's life. Since 1099 parts of this region had been held by Crusader knights from the First Crusade, who had carved out kingdoms, or counties, following the defeat of the Muslims at Jerusalem. Edessa was one of these tiny kingdoms to the north of Jerusalem. Throughout the four decades the Crusaders had been in the Holy Land, the Muslims had slowly joined together to fight their own holy war, or *jihad,* to win back land and holy sites that they considered rightfully theirs. For the Muslims these Christian Crusaders—or Franks, as Muslims called them—were foreign invaders and did not belong in the Middle East. Strong leaders rose up and tried to unite the people of Islam, a diverse group that included Turks, Arabs, and North Africans, among others in the region. One such leader was Zengi, the powerful Turkish ruler of Aleppo and Mosul, who managed to capture the Crusader stronghold of Edessa in 1144.

News that the Islamic fighters were on the move again reached Europe and made leaders think of starting another crusade to help their fellow Christians in the Holy Land. Both Louis VII, the king of France, and Eugenius III, the new pope, called for a Second Crusade. This new pope had been a monk at Bernard's abbey for ten years, and it was Bernard who first recommended him to higher church offices that Bernard himself stubbornly refused to accept during his lifetime. Bernard and this pope were thus very close, and Bernard had great influence over Eugenius III. The pope now asked Bernard, who was one of the most prominent of the church's speakers, to begin preaching for a new Crusade to the Holy Land.

At first there was little enthusiasm among the nobles of Europe for such a Crusade, but as Bernard began to write in

Ephraim ben Jacob

Bernard of Clairvaux made a personal appearance in the Rhine Valley of Germany to try to stop the renegade monk Randolph from urging the people to kill Jews at the start of the Second Crusade (1147–49). As had happened during earlier Crusades, the spirit of killing nonbelievers began before the Crusaders reached the Holy Land. Bernard preached that Crusaders who killed in the name of God would have all their sins removed. It also became clear there was a second motivation for these Christian warriors: They were free to plunder (grab the possessions of) those they defeated. The Jews of Europe thus became a prime target for Crusaders even before they set out for the Middle East, not because they were particularly wealthy, but because their outsider status in most European countries made them easy targets.

Such anti-Semitic (anti-Jewish) actions were recorded during the Second Crusade by the German Jewish rabbi and scholar Ephraim ben Jacob (1132–1198). His *Sefer Zechirah* ("Book of Memoirs" or "Book of Remembrance") provides a historical record of these killings and also contains poetic prayers for the dead. It was Ephraim who documented the words of Bernard of Clairvaux when he was attempting to stop the killings in German cities: "Whoever touches a Jew to lay [a] hand on his life does something as sinful as if he had laid a hand on Jesus himself."

Unfortunately, condemning and recording such behavior did not stop it. Anti-Semitic actions occurred again during the Third Crusade (1189–92) in England and parts of continental Europe. Ephraim was still alive and recorded some of the worst atrocities (appalling acts of cruelty), including mass killings. He was also able to record an awful incident that happened in 1171 in France, when thirty-one Jewish men and women were burned after being accused of killing a Christian child as part of a religious ritual. Unfortunately, such tall tales of blood sacrifices by Jews were common in Europe. In this document, part of his *Book of Historical Records,* Ephraim wrote, "O daughters of Israel, weep for the thirty-one souls that were burnt for the sanctification of your Name, and let your brothers, the entire house of Israel, bewail [cry out] the mourning."

favor of a Crusade and to speak at various locations in France and Germany, he soon built up a huge army of supporters. Preaching at a major gathering of nobles and the faithful at Vézelay, in France, on March 31, 1146, he laid out the case for another holy war against the Muslims. He saw this not only as a chance for sinners to win pardons for their previous bad deeds but also as an opportunity for the two halves of the Christian church—the Roman Catholic Church, based in Rome, and the Eastern Orthodox Church, based in Constantinople in the Byzantine or eastern Roman Empire—to come together again. The powerful members of the audience were swept away by the strong words of this "honey-tongued teacher," as Bernard has been called. Among others, the king of France and his wife, the powerful **Eleanor of Aquitaine** (see entry), agreed to go on the Crusade. Bernard ultimately persuaded Conrad III, the Holy Roman Emperor, to lead an army as well. He so excited the common people about the Crusade and fighting non-Christians that commoners began slaughtering Jews in Germany. Bernard himself had to travel to Germany to stop these killings (see box in previous page).

The crusading armies finally assembled and set off for Jerusalem and the Holy Land, but a combination of overconfidence, lack of discipline, and infighting among the various local Christian princes and the leaders of the expedition led to a tragic failure. Thousands of Crusaders died of disease even before reaching the Holy Land. Once there, the rest of them were either killed by the enemy or taken prisoner in battles. They did not capture the city of Damascus in Syria, which was one of their goals. This was a serious setback for the West and made the Islamic fighters even bolder. They now saw that the knights of Europe could be defeated if Muslims united against them. For the people of Europe this defeat put an end to the mass popularity of crusading. The Second Crusade was the last fought by common people; future Crusades would involve professional armies drawn from the West.

Bernard was saddened at this defeat for Christianity, but he felt that he was not personally responsible and blamed the Crusaders themselves for this setback. He defended the role he had played in organizing the Crusade and refused to admit it was a mistake. In his "Apologia for the Second Crusade," quoted in the *Internet Medieval Sourcebook,* he does not apologize at all. Instead, he takes aim at the critics of the Second Crusade:

> The perfect and final apology for any man is the testimony of his own conscience. As for myself, I take it to be a small matter to be judged by those 'who call evil good, and good evil, whose darkness is light, whose light darkness. ...' *I* would rather

that men murmur against us than against God. It would be well for me if He deigns to use me for his shield. ... I shall not refuse to be made ignominious [deserving of shame], so long as God's glory is not attacked.

Although Bernard, feeling ill and near death, tried to retire to Clairvaux, one last public service awaited him. In 1153 he helped work out a peace between two warring German regions. Then, exhausted by a lifetime of service, he returned to Clairvaux, where he died on August 20, 1153, not long after his former student Pope Eugenius III had died. Bernard's influence was many-sided. As the historian Hans Eberhard Mayer has noted in *The Crusades,* Saint Bernard of Clairvaux was "at that time the most distinguished figure in the intellectual and political life of the West." An adviser to popes and kings, he was the power behind the major movements of his day, though he always refused to accept a high church office. His preaching and writings were influential in his day and long afterward. He wrote more than three hundred sermons covering all aspects of Christianity and living a good life, more than five hundred letters, and more than a dozen longer works on themes ranging from love and understanding God to explanations of church doctrine. He also played a very important role in the growth of the Cistercian order. During his lifetime almost seventy additional houses grew out of his abbey at Clairvaux. In 1830, more than six hundred years after he was canonized, Bernard was declared a doctor of the church, a respected explainer of church doctrine. He remains one of the most studied figures in church history.

For More Information

Books

Evans, G. R. *The Mind of Saint Bernard of Clairvaux.* New York: Oxford University Press, 1983.

Hala, James. "Bernard of Clairvaux." In *Dictionary of Literary Biography.* Vol. 208: *Literature of the French and Occitan Middle Ages, Eleventh to Fifteenth Centuries.* Edited by Deborah M. Sinnreich-Levi. Detroit, MI: Gale, 1999.

James, Bruno Scott. *St. Bernard of Clairvaux: An Essay in Biography.* London: Hodder & Stoughton, 1957.

Luddy, Ailbe J. *The Life of St. Bernard.* Dublin: Browne & Nolan, 1963.

Mayer, Hans Eberhard. *The Crusades*. New York: Oxford University Press, 1988.

Web Sites

"Bernard of Clairvaux." *Medieval Church.* http://www.medievalchurch.org.uk/p_bernard.html (accessed on June 24, 2004).

"Bernard of Clairvaux: Apology." *Internet Medieval Sourcebook.* http://www.fordham.edu/halsall/source/bernard1.html (accessed on June 24, 2004).

"Military Orders: In Praise of the New Knighthood." *The ORB: On-line Reference Book for Medieval Studies.* http://the-orb.net/encyclop/religion/monastic/bernard.html (accessed on June 24, 2004).

"Patron Saints Index: Bernard of Clairvaux." *Catholic Forum.* http://www.catholic-forum.com/saints/saintb08.htm (accessed on June 24, 2004).

"St. Bernard: Apologia for the Second Crusade." *Internet Medieval Sourcebook.* http://www.fordham.edu/halsall/source/Bernard-apol.html (accessed on June 24, 2004).

"St. Bernard of Clairvaux." *New Advent.* http://www.newadvent.org/cathen/02498d.htm (accessed on June 24, 2004).

Anna Comnena

December 1, 1083
Constantinople

c. 1148

Byzantine princess, historian, and scholar

nna Comnena was one of the most famous female scholars of the Middle Ages. The daughter of the emperor of the Byzantine Empire (the successor to the Roman Empire) based in Constantinople, she lived in the eleventh and twelfth centuries and was known for her scholarship in medicine, astronomy, mathematics, and music. However, she is best remembered for her fifteen-volume biography of her father, the emperor **Alexius I** (see entry), and for a history of the Byzantine Empire during his reign that she wrote in her old age. This work provides much information about the First Crusade (1095–99), which came about as a result of her father's request for help from the pope, the Catholic leader in Rome, in fighting invading Islamic forces. In this combination of history and biography she paints interesting and detailed portraits of many of the Christian leaders of the First Crusade. She is considered the world's first female historian.

A Princess of Byzantium

Anna Comnena was the oldest child of the emperor Alexius I and his wife, Irene Ducas, who was herself related to

"I swear by the perils the emperor endured for the well-being of the Roman people, by his sorrows and the travails he suffered on behalf of the Christians, that I am not favoring him when I say or write such things....I regard him as dear, but the truth is dearer still."

—*Anna Comnena,* The Alexiad of Anna Comnena, *book 14, chapter 3.*

Anna Comnena. *Courtesy of the Library of Congress.*

67

an earlier line of Byzantine emperors. Thus there was royalty on both sides of Comnena's bloodline, and her early years were spent in training as a future empress. While she was still a young girl she was engaged to Constantine Ducas, a cousin on her mother's side and son of the emperor Michael VII, who ruled from 1067 to 1078, an acceptable engagement for the time period. This strengthened her rights to the crown, but when a baby brother named John came along in 1087 suddenly all rights to the throne went to him. Comnena never got over this loss and refused to forgive her brother. Not long after this Constantine Ducas died, as did Comnena's hopes for a royal career.

Comnena focused much of her attention on scholarship, learning poetry, Greek philosophy, and medicine. It seems that she was familiar with the work of the famous Roman physician Galen (c. 130–200 C.E.), and she may even have taught and practiced medicine at Constantinople's medical school. While she was still young, two further events shaped her life. In 1096, when she was only thirteen, the Crusader armies arrived to fight the Muslims (believers in the religion of Islam). These groups of European Christian soldiers, referred to as the Latins or the Franks by the Byzantines, seemed like barbarians to the inhabitants of the sophisticated city of Constantinople. Worse, they did not come to help the empire regain territory it had lost to such enemies as the Seljuk Turks, a Turkic tribe that practiced the Islamic religion, who were invading the eastern borders of the Byzantine Empire. Instead, these Crusaders came to win their own kingdoms and to free the Holy Land, consisting of Palestine and Jerusalem, from Muslim occupation. The men of the Crusader forces made a very negative impression on Comnena. The second major event of these years was her marriage in 1097 to Nicephorus Bryennius, a scholar and historian, who came from a powerful family and thus had a possible claim to the throne through his grandfather. Comnena was only fourteen at the time of her marriage.

Plots and Exile

Comnena came of age during a time when strong-willed women in the Byzantine Empire were not afraid to get involved in politics. Alexius I was himself the product of such a strong woman: his mother, Anna Desassena. Comnena's mother, Irene, was another strong personality and influenced her husband in making decisions about the empire. Comnena behaved much like these women. If she could not become empress, then she wanted her husband to take power upon the death of her father. She and her mother tried to persuade Alexius I to bypass his own son, John, and make Nicephorus Bryennius next in line to the throne. They continued their efforts even as the emperor lay dying in his bed, but they were unable to make him change his mind.

With the death of Alexius I in 1118, Comnena's brother, John, quickly took power and became Emperor John II. Comnena, however, would not give up. She plotted with others to kill her brother, but her husband would not take part, and the plot failed. She was said to complain later that nature had made a mistake with her husband's gender, for he should have been the woman, so timid was he. John discovered the plot against him and made his sister give up her property and fortune. He exiled her (sent her away) from the court in Constantinople to a place in western Asia Minor where she could not make trouble for him. For nineteen years she remained in exile. When her husband died in 1137, she was allowed to return to Constantinople. Comnena entered a convent (a religious institution for women) that had been founded by her mother.

The Alexiad

It was then that Anna Comnena began the work for which she is best known, *The Alexiad,* a fifteen-volume prose poem (a poem that reads like a story) about the reign of her father. This work had actually been started by her husband. At the time of his death, Nicephorus Bryennius had completed four books covering the nine years just before Alexius I took power, a time when Nicephorus's own grandfather was fighting for the crown against two earlier emperors. As John C. Rouman has noted in the *Hellenic Communication Service,* Nicephorus's "aim in writing was to glorify the reign of Alexius and his Comnenian line." When Comnena took over the project, her goals were no different. Rouman continues: "As

A modern view of Constantinople. In Anna Comnena's *The Alexiad* she describes how knights and common people came through Constantinople to fight the forces of Islam during the First Crusade.
© *Underwood & Underwood/ Corbis.*

one would expect of an educated, dutiful, and devoted daughter, Comnena glorifies the greatness of Alexius." Rouman goes on to compare her history to the work of the Greek historian Thucydides (c. 460–400 B.C.E.), author of the *History of the Peloponnesian War.*

In the volumes of her book Comnena not only presents an outline of Byzantine history from 1081, when her father became emperor, to his death in 1118 but also looks at military technology, weapons, and tactics. In addition, she supplies information on medical theory, writing about her husband's and her father's final illnesses. A large part of the book also deals with Christian or Latin nobles as well as the First Crusade, including descriptions of knights (trained soldiers) and common people who came through Constantinople in the summer and winter of 1096 and 1097 to fight the forces of Islam.

Historians have pointed out that Comnena's account of the First Crusade must be read with caution. First of all, she was only thirteen when these events happened and could hardly have understood all that was going on around her or known of private conversations between her father and the Crusaders. As John France noted in *Reading Medieval Studies Online*, "Anna Comnena cannot be regarded as an eyewitness of the First Crusade. She was writing some forty years after the Crusade had passed through Constantinople, so childhood recollections can only have added an occasional vividness to her use of other sources." France also warned that "*The Alexiad* is a life of her father and is very favorable to him." Despite this slant, the work is still valuable as a piece of history. Comnena had much personal knowledge about events during these years. She also made use of letters and reports from her father's generals and counselors and appears to have had access to the royal archives, or library, where such official documents were kept.

Her view of the Crusades is definitely that of a Byzantine. As such, she does not much care for the Latin soldiers, whom she calls "barbarians." The word in the original Greek simply means someone who does not speak the Greek language. However, even in Comnena's time this word took on the further meaning of an uncivilized person. In fact, these Crusaders were backward by Byzantine standards. Few of them knew how to read or write, and they took little pleasure in arts other than warfare. She presents lively portraits of such Crusade leaders as **Peter the Hermit** (see entry), the French priest who led twenty thousand common people to their deaths at the hands of the Turks; French nobles such as **Godfrey of Bouillon** (see entry), Hugh the Great, and Raymond of Toulouse; and an especially interesting look at Bohemund, son of Robert Guiscard and leader of the Norman forces, who was a longtime enemy of her father's. This last Crusader seemed both to fascinate and anger her. While he was a handsome man, according to Comnena he was also "by nature a liar" and not to be trusted. She also describes him as being greedy and disloyal. In fact, Bohemund was all of these things. He joined the Crusade to enrich himself and the Normans, who had already created a kingdom in southern Italy.

In *The Alexiad* Comnena also writes about battles of the First Crusade, covering the Byzantine and Christian victory at Nicaea, an ancient city close to Constantinople that the Seljuk Turks had once occupied. She gives fewer details of the later siege of Antioch, another former Byzantine possession in

Competing Histories

In *The Alexiad,* Anna Comnena provides a firsthand account of the First Crusade from the Byzantine point of view. Hers is one of several eyewitness accounts that later historians have used to assemble a true picture of events at the end of the eleventh century. Another is *Historia rerum in partibus transmarinis gestarum* (*History of Deeds Done beyond the Sea*), by William of Tyre (1130–c. 1184). Like Comnena's account, William's version of events also comes from someone outside Europe, for he was born and grew up in the Kingdom of Jerusalem, the territory in Palestine that the Crusaders captured after the First Crusade. Unlike Anna Comnena, however, he came from a very humble, simple family. It is uncertain if he was of French or English origin. He showed a talent for scholarship that led him to become a priest, serving as an assistant to the archbishop, or chief religious leader, of Tyre, an ancient city located in present-day Lebanon. He was sent to Europe to complete his education and training and by 1163 was back in Tyre, where he became archdeacon in 1175.

William knew many languages, including French, Latin, Greek, Hebrew, Persian, and Arabic. He soon became the official historian of the Kingdom of Jerusalem. He wrote histories of church councils as well as a history of the Middle East from the time of the prophet Muhammad, but he is best known for his work on the Crusades and the Kingdom of Jerusalem up to 1184. Like Comnena, William was writing long after the fact. Unlike her, however, he was able to use documents in many languages to present a more objective history of the events of the First Crusade. His *History of Deeds Done beyond the Sea,* taking up twenty-three books, became the standard text for centuries. Translated into English by William Caxton, the man who introduced the printing press to England, the book was published in 1481 as *Godeffroy of Boloyne; or, The Siege and Conqueste of Jerusalem.* It is still used today and remains an invaluable resource for scholars and students of the Crusades.

Syria. In his article in *Reading Medieval Studies Online,* France notes that the value of *The Alexiad* "as a source for the First Crusade diminishes as the army gets farther and farther from Constantinople." More errors of fact, especially in the chronology, or timeline, occur in those sections that deal with the Crusaders moving through the Holy Land to lay siege to (attack) Jerusalem and recapture it from the Muslims.

Comnena completed her history in 1148. Little of her life is known after that point. A funeral oration was held in 1156, but this does not appear to have taken place very close to the time of her actual death. Historians think she died around 1148 or, at least, before 1156. *The Alexiad* remains for us a fascinating document from the medieval Byzantine world. As many scholars have pointed out, it is clearly biased—that is, it is not objective. Nevertheless, it provides an inside look at life in the Byzantine Empire during the time of the First Crusade and lets modern readers know how the Byzantines felt about the European Christians of the same period. For James Howard-Johnson, writing in the *English Historical Review,* her biography is "arguably the finest work of history written in the course of Byzantium's ... existence." The fact that the book is less than objective does not take away from its importance: "It ... provides a matchless record of an era of dramatic change in Byzantium and the surrounding world. It is packed with solid data (normally well ordered) and expressed in an elegant but not over-ornate classical style." Also important, according to Howard-Johnson, is the fact that *The Alexiad* "is distinguished by being the first history to come from a woman's pen."

For More Information

Books

Comnena, Anna. *The Alexiad of Anna Comnena.* Translated by E. R. A. Sewter. Baltimore, MD: Penguin, 1969.

Gouma-Gouma-Peterson, Thalia, ed. *Anna Komnene and Her Times.* New York: Garland, 2000.

Hussey, J. M. *The Cambridge Medieval History.* 2nd ed. Vol. 4, *The Byzantine Empire.* New York: Cambridge University Press, 1967.

Norwich, John Julius. *A Short History of Byzantium.* New York: Vintage, 1998.

Ostrogorsky, George. A *History of the Byzantine State.* Translated by Joan Hussey. Piscataway, NJ: Rutgers University Press, 1986.

Treadgold, Warren. A *History of the Byzantine State and Society.* Stanford, CA: Stanford University Press, 1997.

Periodicals

Howard-Johnson, James. "Anna Komnene and Her Times." *English Historical Review* (September 2002).

Web Sites

"The Alexiad." *Internet Medieval Sourcebook.* http://www.fordham.edu/hal sall/ basis/AnnaComnena-Alexiad.html (accessed on April 14, 2004).

"Anna Comnena." *About's Who's Who in Medieval History and the Renaissance.* http://historymedren.about.com/library/who/blwwannacomnena. htm (accessed on June 24, 2004).

"Anna Comnena." *New Advent.* http://www.newadvent.org/cathen/ 01531a.htm (accessed on June 24, 2004).

"Anna Comnena/Komnene (1083–bef. 1186)." *Other Women's Voices.* http:// home.infionline.net/~ddisse/comnena.html (accessed on June 24, 2004).

"Anna Comnena, the *Alexiad* and the First Crusade." *Reading Medieval Studies Online.* 10 (1984). http://www.deremilitari.org/RESOURCES/PDFs/ FRANCE2.PDF (accessed on June 24, 2004).

"Byzantium: Byzantine Studies on the Internet." *Fordham University.* http://www.fordham.edu/halsall/byzantium (accessed on June 24, 2004).

"Nicephorus Bryennius and Anna Comnena: The 'Roman' Xenophon and Thucydides of Eleventh- and Twelfth-Century Constantinople." *Hellenic Communication Service.* http://www.helleniccomserve.com/ comnena.html (accessed on June 24, 2004).

Eleanor of Aquitaine

1122
Bordeaux or Belin, France

1204
Anjou, France

Queen of France and England

Eleanor of Aquitaine was one of the most powerful and interesting people of the Middle Ages. That she accomplished so much at a time when women usually had little standing (power) in society is amazing. The wife of two kings, she gave birth to three more. Called the "grandmother of Europe" for all the royal lines she started or marriages she arranged, Eleanor was more than simply the power behind the throne. A duchess, or ruler, of the wealthy region of Aquitaine in southern France, Eleanor controlled a huge amount of land. She created a royal court at Poitiers, France, that sponsored such arts as music and poetry.

As queen she counseled her husbands and at times went to war against them. She was not the sort of woman to let fate control her. Instead, she gladly bid farewell to her ill-matched first husband, the king of France, and went head to head with her second husband, the fiery king of England. She helped raise armies for the Second Crusade (1147–49) and went along herself, dressed for battle. Eleanor lived a long and active life, traveling throughout Europe when it was more common for noblewomen to be hidden away in their

"Powerful, beautiful, indefatigable [unstoppable], sensuous [appealing to the senses], literary, an eagle soaring above mere mortals, mother of ten royal children she might indeed be. Some regarded her as the Demon mother who had once, in a bath, assumed the shape of a dragon."

—*James Reston Jr.*, Warriors of God: Richard the Lionheart and Saladin in the Third Crusade.

Eleanor of Aquitaine.
© *Bettmann/Corbis.*

castles. Though she lived in the twelfth century, she would also have fit in well in the twenty-first century.

An Aquitaine Heiress

Eleanor was born in 1122 in either Bordeaux or Belin, in southern France. She was the granddaughter of William IX of Aquitaine (1070–1127), a Crusader in the Holy Land during the First Crusade (1095–99), a religious war to free Jerusalem and the holy sites associated with Jesus from Islamic occupation. William brought back romantic tales of fighting and love in the Holy Land, which he set to verse and music. Among the first troubadours, or medieval noble poets of Europe, he ruled one of the most powerful and richest regions of France. During his lifetime, however, William IX paid more attention to the ladies and poetry than he did to keeping his duchy (region) intact. He went through two wives and finally took up with a married woman, whose daughter he married off to his own son, also named William. Upon the death of his father, William X (Eleanor's father) took over Aquitaine. His court was a very sophisticated (learned and cultured) one, where poets were sponsored, or encouraged to compose verse, and the idea of courtly, or polite, love for the ideal woman took hold. Eleanor was five when her father became duke of Aquitaine; she was his oldest child, and after the death of a brother, stood to inherit the duchy.

Eleanor was educated not only in poetry but also in the world of politics, for she would soon become the duchess. She went everywhere with her father, learning at his side. This childhood came to a sudden end in 1137 when William X died of food poisoning while he was making a pilgrimage (visit) to a European religious site. But William had already made plans for Eleanor that would take effect after his death. He knew the powerless status of a woman, and so he had his daughter put in the care of the French king Louis VI, or Louis the Fat. This king, who did not want to see the powerful lands of Aquitaine lost to France, immediately married Eleanor to his son and successor, Louis VII. This future king of France, however, had not been trained for royal duty. Before his older brother, Philip, was killed, Louis VII was planning to adopt a religious life. The strong-willed Eleanor and the stuffy, less active Louis were not a great match. The important thing at the time, however, was that Eleanor brought with her to the marriage the large region of Aquitaine.

Queen of France

In 1137 the couple had barely returned from their honeymoon when Louis the Fat died. Eleanor, who was only fifteen at the time, had in the space of one year become an orphan, the duchess of Aquitaine, a married woman, and the queen of France. Close to him in age yet more worldly than Louis, Eleanor became a powerful queen, advising her husband on political and religious matters. She ran into trouble with the church authorities when she pushed through her younger sister's marriage to an already married man. Eleanor talked Louis into backing her in this effort, and soon she had to deal with the powerful religious writer and preacher **Bernard of Clairvaux** (see entry), who opposed her. It was not until 1145 that Eleanor finally made peace with the church. That year she gave birth to her first child, a daughter she named Marie. Louis, however, had wanted a son to inherit the crown.

About this time, the Middle East forces of Islam were on the march against the Crusader states that had been set up after the First Crusade (1095–99). The powerful Turkish Muslim leader Zengi captured the Crusader city of Edessa in 1144. It was only a matter of time before the Muslims marched on Jerusalem itself. The current pope, Eugenius III, and Bernard of Clairvaux both preached a new Crusade, and Eleanor and Louis, having just patched things up with the church, answered the call. When the leaders of France gathered in the church at Vézelay in 1146 to listen to Bernard call for a new holy war, she knelt with the other nobles and knights and promised that they would fight the Muslims. For Eleanor this was not a matter of staying at home and waiting for her king to return. Instead, she gathered an army of three hundred noblewomen to join the men. Dressed in armor and riding horses, these women planned to take care of the wounded.

The Second Crusade got off to a miserable start. Despite his large army of twenty thousand soldiers, the German king Conrad III was quickly defeated by the Turks and lost most of his men. The French did not do much better, finally

The Missing King

Unlike the First Crusade, a king, a queen, and an emperor actually took part in the Second Crusade. There was one person, however, who failed to show up for the Second Crusade. The legendary King Prester John supposedly tried to come to the aid of the Christians in the Holy Land but was unable to ford, or cross, the Tigris River with his army. Legend has it that he then took his army north because he had heard that the river froze in winter, and he and his troops could thus reach the other side by marching across the ice. He waited for several years, but no ice appeared. The weather was too warm, and his men began to die of fever in this strange climate. Finally, he had to return home to his kingdom, located somewhere in those regions of Asia not yet explored by western-

ers. Such, at any rate, was the tale told by Otto, bishop of Friesing, in 1145. Otto, in turn, had heard this story from others. It was the beginning of the tale of Prester John, who soon took on mythical importance in the West.

John was supposedly a Christian priest who ruled an enormously wealthy empire in Asia or perhaps Africa. His name appears in many forms: Priest John, Priester John, Presbyter John, and other similar-sounding titles. According to the stories that formed around him, he was an offspring of one of the Three Magi, or holy men, who brought gifts to Jesus when he was born. His distant kingdom had so many riches that, according to one version of the tale, he carried a solid-gold scepter (staff). According to another version, this same

reaching the Crusader state of Antioch, where Eleanor's uncle, Raymond, ruled. This uncle, only a few years older than Eleanor, was a handsome, vital man, unlike Eleanor's husband. She openly complained about the king of France, protesting that although she thought she was marrying a man, what she got was a monk. Raymond was no monk. Soon rumors spread that the uncle and niece were romantically involved. When Raymond asked the French king to help him strike at the Muslims in their center of Aleppo, in Syria, and then retake Edessa, Louis refused, instead deciding to head straight for Jerusalem.

When Eleanor learned of this refusal, she sided with her uncle against her husband and even began talking of leaving the king. She told Louis that she was going to stay in Antioch, but in the end the king kidnapped her and had her staff was carved from a large emerald. His was supposed to be the perfect Christian kingdom, and his people or subjects dearly loved Prester John, the perfect king. Unfortunately, he was unable to come to the aid of the Christians in the Second Crusade through no fault of his own. Thus the Crusaders had to go it alone. In the popular imagination the absence of this great Christian king explained the defeat of the Crusader army. Be that as it may, it was a convenient excuse at the time; many scholars have suggested that Prester John was invented to explain the terrible defeat of the Christian armies at the hands of the Muslims during the Second Crusade.

The legend of Prester John took on a life of its own, remaining in the minds of Europeans for several centuries. Letters addressed to the pope, supposedly from Prester John, even arrived in Rome, and the pope is said to have written back. Others claim that Prester John was actually a fictitious, or imaginary, combination of several real kings. Later, when the Mongols began moving out of Asia and attacking Islamic territories in the Middle East, Europeans thought these armies might be Prester John's Christians come to settle a score with the Muslims. By the fourteenth century Prester John's mythical kingdom had moved to Africa. Some maps even located it in present-day Ethiopia. Ironically, these tall tales of Prester John led some Europeans, like the explorer Marco Polo (c. 1254–1324), to develop an interest in Asia and attempt to make contact with the people living there.

taken to Jerusalem. This was the beginning of the end of their marriage. Meanwhile, Crusader armies struck at Damascus, in Syria, where they were defeated. In 1149 Louis stayed in Jerusalem long enough to fight a bit and celebrate Easter, after which he and Eleanor sailed home to France on separate ships. Once again the couple tried to have a son, but when a second girl was born, the marriage was all but over. There was no such thing as divorce in the Middle Ages. Instead, Eleanor claimed that her bloodline and Louis's were too close, and in 1152 she had the marriage annulled, or officially cancelled, by the church. Two months later she remarried.

Queen of England

This time Eleanor married a much younger man known for his fiery and manly character. Henry Plantagenet, duke of

Anjou, was eleven years younger than Eleanor and stood in line to inherit the English throne. To him, Eleanor, with her vast lands in Aquitaine, was a real prize despite their age difference. When Stephen, the current king of England, died in 1154, Henry became Henry II, king of England, and Eleanor was his queen. Thanks to his wife's land, Henry owned more of France than the king of France himself. Together Henry and Eleanor controlled the most powerful kingdom in the Christian West.

At first Eleanor and Henry were inseparable. She traveled with him throughout his lands, living much of the time in less-than-elegant conditions. In thirteen years she gave birth to eight children, five of them boys. But her husband soon showed that he could not be faithful, and his string of lovers and mistresses ruined their marriage. Eleanor left England in 1168 to return to her native Aquitaine, taking her favorite son, **Richard I, the Lionheart** (see entry), with her. There she turned away from politics for a time, enjoying the culture offered at her court. It is said that she was the originator, or founder, of what became known as "courts of love," where noblewomen would gather to judge the love poems recited by knights and other male nobles of the duchy.

Court life, however, was not enough to keep Eleanor's interest. She managed to persuade her absent husband to announce that his eldest son, who was also called Henry, would be the next king. He was crowned Henry III in 1170, though the father still held all the power. After three years, however, this son, his brother Richard I, and a third son named Geoffrey grew restless. Eleanor took their side against their father, and with the help of the French king they rose up against Henry II. The king of England quickly crushed this revolt and imprisoned his rebellious wife in various castles for the next sixteen years. These were hard times for Eleanor, who was used to being out in the world, traveling across Europe and even to the Holy Land. She survived this imprisonment, however, and was let go following the death of her husband in 1189. As Henry III had also died by this time, the crown went to Richard I, who freed his mother from her confinement. It was she, in fact, who arranged the celebrations for his coronation (crowning) in London.

During Richard's reign, Eleanor once again became a close adviser to a king. On his way home after fighting in the

Third Crusade (1189–92) he was thrown in prison by his political rival, the Holy Roman Emperor. Eleanor managed to keep the kingdom together and fight off attempts by her youngest son, John, to steal the crown. She also arranged for the enormous ransom (payment for release of a prisoner) to be paid to the Holy Roman Emperor to free her son and personally delivered the money to Germany. When Richard I died suddenly in 1199, she stood behind her son John in the fight for the crown. He became king, although not a very good or kind one, yet Eleanor remained loyal to him. In her seventies she continued traveling around Europe arranging royal marriages. In her eighties she finally decided that it was time to slow down. She went to live at an abbey (religious institution for women) at Fontevrault, in the French region of Anjou, where she died in the spring of 1204. She was eighty-two, a very old age for a person living during the Middle Ages.

Eleanor of Aquitaine was a woman far ahead of her time. She was not content simply to be the power behind her man. Instead, she took control herself, helping to recruit forces for the Second Crusade and to install her sons as kings of England. Much of the blame for the failure of the Second Crusade was put on her because of the huge supply train she needed for her three hundred female Crusaders. In reality, it was the infighting among the leaders of this Crusade, as well as poor planning, that were responsible for the failure. Eleanor went on to live a life full of adventure and personal sadness, outliving most of her children. A patron, or sponsor, of the arts as well as a powerful and beautiful woman, Eleanor was an early example of what women could accomplish in the world.

For More Information

Books

"Eleanor of Aquitaine." In *Historic World Leaders. Europe: A–K.* Edited by Anne Commire and Deborah Klezmer. Detroit, MI: Gale, 1994.

Gregory, Kristiana *Eleanor: Crown Jewel of Aquitaine.* New York: Scholastic, 2002.

Meade, Marion. *Eleanor of Aquitaine: A Biography.* New York: Hawthorn, 1977.

Owen, D. D. R. *Eleanor of Aquitaine: Queen and Legend.* Cambridge, MA: Blackwell, 1993.

Pernoud, Régine. *Eleanor of Aquitaine.* Translated by Peter Wiles. London: Collins, 1967.

Reston, James Jr. *Warriors of God: Richard the Lionheart and Saladin in the Third Crusade.* New York: Doubleday, 2001.

Seward, Desmond. *Eleanor of Aquitaine.* New York: Times Books, 1979.

Weir, Allison. *Eleanor of Aquitaine: A Life.* New York: Ballantine Books, 2001.

Web Sites

"Eleanor of Aquitaine, 1122–1204." *French-at-a-Touch.com.* http://www. french-at-a-touch.com/French_History/eleanor_of_ aquitaine.htm (accessed on June 24, 2004).

"Eleanor of Aquitaine." *Notable Women Ancestors.* http://www.rootsweb. com/˜wa/aquit.html (accessed on June 24, 2004).

"Eleanor of Aquitaine." *Women in World History.* http://www.womenin worldhistory.com/heroine2.html (accessed on June 24, 2004).

"Eleanor of Aquitaine: The Troubadour's Daughter." *The World of Royalty* http://www.royalty.nu/Europe/England/Angevin/Eleanor.html (accessed on June 24, 2004).

"Queen Eleanor of Aquitaine." *Sherwood Times.* http://www.times1190. freeserve.co.uk/eleanor.htm (accessed on June 24, 2004).

"The Second Crusade." *The ORB: On-line Reference Book for Medieval Studies.* http://the-orb.net/textbooks/crusade/secondcru.html (accessed on April 24, 2004).

Francis of Assisi

1182
Assisi, Italy

October 3, 1226
Portiuncula, Italy

Founder of the Franciscan Order

An Italian of the Middle Ages, Francis of Assisi founded the Franciscans, an important religious order (group) that bears his name. Untrained and not even a priest when he set out on his itinerant (wandering) preaching in the early thirteenth century, Francis wanted to reform the church and bring it more in line with the needs of the common people. Born to a rich family, he gave up his personal wealth and formed a small group of followers who lived a simple lifestyle and preached about nature and the birds and animals of the forest as if they communicated with them. In 1210 Francis and his followers gained the approval and recognition of the pope, **Innocent III** (see entry).

Francis wanted to take his message of love and peace to the Islamic world, preaching to the Moors, or North African Muslims living in Spain. He also attempted to make a truce between battling Christians and Muslims during the Fifth Crusade (1218–21), crossing enemy lines to speak with the leader of the Egyptian forces, **Sultan al-Malik al-Kamil** (see entry). Although he did not convert to Christianity, the sultan was impressed with Francis's honesty and devotion and allowed him to return unharmed to the Crusader camp. Francis was loved by many, but

"Praised be You my Lord with all Your creatures, especially Sir Brother Sun, Who is the day through whom You give us light. And he is beautiful and radiant with great splendor, Of You Most High, he bears the likeness."

—Francis of Assisi, "Canticle of Brother Sun and Sister Moon of St. Francis of Assisi." Catholic Online. http://www.catholic. org/clife/prayers/prayers.php?s ection_id=41&name=Saint%20 Prayers.

Francis of Assisi. *The Art Archive/Bardi Chapel Santa Croce Florence/Dagli Orti (A).*

Five Pillars of Islam

Francis of Assisi tried to convert Sultan al-Kamil to Christianity, but the sultan was also interested in converting the Christian to his religion of Islam. In fact, during the Crusades, one way for prisoners to escape death was to convert to the religion of their captor. The basic tenets, or principles, of Islam—called the Five Pillars of Islam—are organized in five groups.

First, a Muslim must make a *shahadah,* a statement of belief in Allah, the Muslim God, and in Muhammad, as the prophet of Allah. Second are the *salah,* the prayers that a faithful Muslim recites five times a day. Since there are no priests in the Islamic religion, these prayers form a direct link between the believer and Allah. Prayers are said at dawn, midday, late afternoon, sunset, and nightfall, thus setting the rhythm for the entire day. Recited in Arabic, these prayers are chosen from the Muslim holy book, the Qur'an, known in English as the Koran. A typical prayer goes:

> God is Great. God is Great. God is Great. God is Great. I testify that there is none worthy of worship except God. I testify that there is none worthy of

worship except God. I testify that Muhammad is the messenger of God. I testify that Muhammad is the messenger of God. Come to prayer! Come to prayer! Come to success! Come to success! God is Great! God is Great! There is none worthy of worship except God.

The third concept is the *zakah,* which means "purification" or "growth." This is a donation of a part of one's income to charity in order to teach that wealth is not the most important thing in life. The fourth tenet is *sawm,* or fasting, which involves eating nothing between sunset and sunrise during the Muslim holy month of Ramadan. The fifth and final pillar is the *hajj,* a pilgrimage, or spiritual journey, to the Muslim holy city of Mecca for those who are physically able to do so. More than two million Muslims make this pilgrimage each year.

Ironically, many of these same beliefs—praying, fasting, and giving away part of one's wealth—were exactly what Saint Francis was preaching. The Christians and Muslims who fought each other during the Crusades had (and still have) much in common in terms of the basic beliefs of their separate religions.

he also was feared by those who were suspicious of his emphasis on simplicity. In 1126, only two years after his death, Francis of Assisi was canonized, or made a saint of the Catholic Church.

From Riches to Rags

Francis of Assisi's life turned the romantic "rags to riches" tale on its head. Born Giovanni Bernardone, Francis gave up his family fortune to serve what he saw as the will of God. Still, he achieved more than riches in his lifetime; his fame spread far and wide, and he remains one of the best-known and best-loved saints of the Catholic Church, inspiring hundreds of books and several motion pictures. His father, Pietro Bernardone, was among the richest men in the city of Assisi, located in central Italy, where Giovanni was born in 1182. The father, a cloth merchant, was traveling on business in France when his first son was born, and he did not much care for the name his wife had chosen for their son, after the biblical John the Baptist. Pietro wanted a practical child who would follow him into business, not someone who might go into the church. He gave his son the nickname "Francesco" ("Francis" in English), a reminder of Pietro's trip to France at the time of the boy's birth.

Being the first son, Francis was spoiled by his parents. He was more interested in having a good time than in studying. His father taught him French, which was the international language of business at the time, and it is thought that Francis also traveled with his father on business trips to other countries. In addition, the young boy learned Latin, which was the language of the universities and the church. Francis, however, was never a good writer; as an adult he would dictate letters for others to write down and then sign them with a cross. A happy youth, he had many friends and gathered around him a similarly fun-loving crowd—mostly nobles and children of the wealthy—that enjoyed a good party and singing. By day he worked in his father's cloth store and proved to be a good salesman. Francis also had dreams of becoming a knight, or professional soldier, riding a fine horse and being elevated to the ranks of the nobility, for though his family was wealthy, it was not aristocratic. Perhaps in war he could prove himself. He dreamed of becoming "Sir Francis."

He had his chance for military glory in 1202, when Assisi and its rival city, Perugia, went to war. That year Francis fought at the Battle of Ponte San Giovanni and was taken prisoner. He was lucky to survive, since most of the force from Assisi had been wiped out in the battle. He was thrown in prison, not with the common foot soldiers but rather with nobles who had been captured. Still, his imprisonment was not an easy one, for he was chained to a dungeon wall for a year. In 1203 his freedom was finally bought, and he returned to his home in Assisi, where he fell ill for many weeks. When he finally recovered, he had not lost his desire to become a knight.

Next, he took up his sword in the service of Pope Innocent III, who was battling the princes of Germany over the successor to the throne of the German kingdom, or the Holy Roman Empire, as this loose association of German states was called. The leader of that empire thought of himself as the leader of Europe, but the pope also saw himself in that role. This rivalry always caused conflict, and now Francis was going to take part in it too.

A Dream Changes Francis's Life

Francis had been away from Assisi for only one day when he had a dream that changed the direction of his life. While staying at an inn in the town of Spoleto, he dreamed that God told him that the military life was not the way for him to live the good life. Instead of serving a military commander, he should serve the Lord. Francis returned to Assisi in a state of confusion. Unsure what to do, he began visiting the churches of the city and praying. In 1206 he again heard the voice of God telling him to repair a small church in Assisi, which he did, seeing it as his new mission in life. He took money from his father's business to repair the church. His father was angered and took his son before the bishop, or regional church official, demanding that Francis return the money, which he did. Then he also took off all the clothes his father had given him, leaving on only a simple shirt. Francis said he now had only one father—namely, God.

Francis took a vow, or promise, of poverty and began begging for food and shelter. This was at first amusing to the citizens of Assisi and embarrassing for his wealthy father, but Francis was convinced that this was what God had planned for him. While he continued to repair old churches, the meaning of the message he had received suddenly became clear to him during Mass (Catholic church service) one day. God did not mean for him to rebuild churches with stone and mortar but to reform the institution of the church by preaching the truth of Jesus and caring for the sick. Francis followed the exact words of the Bible and went out to spread the word of

God and Jesus Christ in a simple, direct manner. He did not threaten the common people with damnation or a miserable after life in hell, nor did he criticize the wealth of powerful Catholic officials. His was a simple message announcing the joy one could find in Christianity if only one had faith. Soon followers came to Francis, and he formed a small group of the faithful, who called themselves Franciscans.

Francis had never been to a university or studied theology (religious faith and practice). He simply found his calling by preaching to the common people. However, he also wanted official recognition for his group. Tradition has it that in 1210 Francis took matters into his own hands and traveled to Rome to request an audience, or formal visit, with the pope. When Francis came before Innocent III he was almost thrown out because he looked like a tramp. The pope listened to him and then sent him away. That night the pope dreamed of a little man in rags, like Francis, who saved his church from collapsing. The next day Innocent III sent for Francis and gave him official permission to preach. Francis's example encouraged others not only to join his Franciscan order but to begin new ones as well. From Assisi came another child of the wealthy who decided to give up riches in exchange for a life devoted to the church. This religious follower was a young woman named Clare, whom Francis met and inspired. She ultimately went on to form the women's order of the Poor Clares.

Taking the Message to the "Heathens"

As membership in his new order spread throughout Italy—including the towns of Perugia, Pisa, and Florence—Francis decided that he wanted to deliver his message to the larger world, to preach the Bible to the Muslims. In 1212 he set sail for the Holy Land, but when his ship encountered bad weather, he had to return to Italy. In 1214 he set off for Spain to preach to the Muslim Moors who lived there. Again he was unsuccessful, for illness made him cut short his journey and return to Italy. Finally, during the Fifth Crusade, he found an opportunity to spread his message of peace and harmony.

In 1219 the Crusader forces were trying to attack Muslim strongholds in Egypt. It was thought that if they could first destroy the power of Islam in that region, they could move on to the Holy Land in Palestine and liberate Jerusalem, considered a holy city in Christianity. The two armies were fighting over control of the city of Damietta, which was located at the mouth of the Nile River and blocked access to the upriver journey to Cairo, the Crusaders' ultimate target. However, the city of Damietta held off the Crusaders, who were being led by the pope's aide, Pelagius. Al-Kamil, the Egyptian sultan, or leader, and his forces were battling the Crusaders from outside the city walls at their own camp.

For more than a year the two sides fought, with men dying on both sides. In August 1219 Francis arrived in the Crusader camp. As James M. Powell has noted in his *Anatomy of a Crusade, 1213–1221,* Francis "came not to cheer on the discouraged Christian army or to fight the heathen [people who do not acknowledge God and the Bible], but on a mission of peace." Francis had a vision announcing the defeat of the Crusaders at an upcoming battle. In his sermon to the troops he predicted this defeat. On August 29 Francis's vision came true, for the Crusaders were drawn into a trap and suffered heavy losses. Sultan al-Kamil proposed a truce following this defeat, and it was then that Francis saw his opportunity to speak with the Muslims.

Francis was mistaken for a messenger sent from the Crusaders to respond to the proposed truce. He was taken to the sultan and attempted to preach the truth of Christianity to him. The sultan brought into his tent his own religious advisers, who urged him to kill Francis. Al-Kamil, impressed by Francis's honesty and bravery, instead showered him with gifts and sent him safely back to the Crusader camp. Francis had attempted to achieve the final goal of the Crusades—freeing the Holy Land from Muslim control—by converting the Muslims rather than by defeating them in battle. As Powell has noted, this was the beginning "of the long-term commitment of the Franciscan order to missions among the Moslems, and especially to the custody of the Holy Places."

Francis Returns to Italy

Francis's last years were spent in Italy, where his order by that time included thousands of new followers. Ear-

lier, his personality had held the members together, but they now needed rules to live by. Francis insisted that the primary rule of the order be to live in poverty. He did not want to eliminate poverty but instead to make it holy. The houses of the order had to be plain, and friars, as the members were called, were to wear only a robe tied with a cord. If it was really cold, then shoes were permitted. In 1223 he presented the new rule of the order to Honorius III, the pope in Rome;

Francis presenting his rules for the Franciscan Order to Pope Honorius III, emphasizing the simplicity and piety of the order. *© Corbis.*

in fact, some of the emphasis on simplicity was left out of the document the pope approved. The new members of the Franciscan order wanted to adopt a more intellectual approach to their work. In the future the Franciscans would become less known as happy friars wandering the countryside and preaching God's love than as an order associated with learning, whose members became teachers at the great universities of the Middle Ages.

Francis, however, was determined to continue living the simple life and returned to Assisi, where he spent more and more time alone and in prayer. While praying at a mountain chapel north of the city, it is said that he showed signs of the stigmata, the wounds that Christ suffered on the cross. His hands, feet, and side began to bleed in the exact places where nails and a soldier's spear had pierced Christ's body during the Crucifixion, or death on the cross. Francis was marked by these wounds for the rest of his life. Some modern historians say that these wounds may have been signs of leprosy, a disfiguring skin disease, for Francis had worked closely with lepers and other people with diseases throughout his life.

Francis's health was failing. Although he was only in his forties, his life of poverty and serving others had taken its toll. He died in 1226 and was buried in Assisi. Following his death the legend of Francis continued to grow, and he was made a saint in 1228. Assisi still attracts large numbers of tourists who want to see the home of this famous saint, known for his fondness for life and nature and for his devotion to a simple life of peace and love. Francis was the first Christian to carry this message to the Holy Land as a possible alternative to the violence of the Crusades.

For More Information

Books

Bishop, Morris. *Saint Francis of Assisi.* Boston: Little, Brown, 1974.

Green, Julien. *God's Fool: The Life and Times of Francis of Assisi.* San Francisco: Harper and Row, 1987.

House, Adrian. *Francis of Assisi: A Revolutionary Life.* Mahwah, NJ: HiddenSpring, 2001.

Powell, James M. *Anatomy of a Crusade, 1213–1221.* Philadelphia: University of Pennsylvania Press, 1986.

Spoto, Donald. *Reluctant Saint: The Life of Francis of Assisi.* New York: Viking Compass, 2002.

Web Sites

"Canticle of Brother Sun and Sister Moon of St. Francis of Assisi." *Catholic Online.* http://www.catholic.org/clife/prayers/prayers.php?section_id=41&name=Saint%20Prayers (accessed on July 21, 2004).

"Fifth Crusade." *The ORB: On-line Reference Book for Medieval Studies.* http://the-orb.net/textbooks/crusade/fifthcru.html (accessed on July 21, 2004).

"St. Francis of Assisi." *Catholic Online.* http://www.catholic.org/saints/saint.php?saint_id=50 (accessed on July 21, 2004).

"St. Francis of Assisi." *New Advent.* http://www.newadvent.org/cathen/06221a.htm (accessed on July 21, 2004).

"The Testament of St. Francis." *Internet Medieval Sourcebook.* http://www.fordham.edu/halsall/source/stfran-test.html (accessed on July 21, 2004).

Frederick II

December 26, 1194
Jesi, Italy

December 23, 1250
Apulia, Italy

Emperor of the Holy Roman Empire

Given the nickname "Wonder of the World," Frederick II was one of the most powerful emperors who ever ruled what was known as the Holy Roman Empire (962–1806 C.E.), the central kingdom of Europe that included present-day Germany and parts of Italy. Richard Cavendish, writing in *History Today,* called him the "most gifted, vivid and extraordinary of the medieval Holy Roman Emperors." The life of Frederick II can be taken as symbolic of the fight between church and state throughout the Middle Ages; the emperor battled the power of the pope, the Catholic religious leader in Europe, from the beginning of his reign in 1215 until his death in 1250.

Though his attempts at uniting Italy proved unsuccessful, Frederick II did increase the power of the secular (nonreligious) state over that of the church. Frederick II, raised in Sicily, with its large Muslim (believers of the Islamic religion) influence, also formed a bridge between the worlds of Christianity and Islam. He respected Muslim and Arabic learning, and as leader of the Sixth Crusade (1228–29) he recovered Jerusalem and parts of the Holy Land without shooting an arrow. The only bloodless Crusade in the two centuries

"Of faith and God he had none; he was crafty, wily, avaricious [greedy], lustful, malicious [mean], wrathful [angry]; and yet a gallant man at times, when he would show his kindness or courtesy; full of solace [comfort], jocund [cheerful], delightful, fertile in devices [strategies]."

—The Chronicle of Salimbene; *quoted at http://www.fordham.edu/halsall/source/salimbene1.html.*

Frederick II.
© *Bettmann/Corbis.*

of otherwise fierce fighting between Christianity and Islam, the Sixth Crusade showed the power of compromise and bargaining. Unfortunately, it was a lesson ignored by both sides.

More Sicilian than German

Frederick II was the only son of Henry VI, emperor of the Holy Roman Empire, and the Sicilian princess Constance. His father was descended from the German noble family of Hohenstaufen, while his mother was of Norman origin, the daughter of King Roger II of Sicily, who created a culturally rich and intellectual royal court that helped introduce Arabic learning to western Europe. Born in Italy in 1194, Frederick II was an orphan by the time he was four. Though his father had provided for his election as the next German king in 1196, this meant nothing once Henry VI was dead. Even Frederick's uncle, Philip of Swabia, was unable to hold the German electors to their word, for as soon as Henry VI was declared dead they began competing among themselves to take the crown away from the youthful Frederick.

Frederick was kept in Sicily, where he was under the protection of Pope **Innocent III** (see entry), who became his guardian. The boy was raised in the Sicilian kingdom, a region heavily settled by Muslims and deeply influenced by Islamic religion, scholarship, art, and architecture. Having grown up in the Sicilian city of Palermo, he came to understand the traditions of two cultures, the Islamic East and the Christian West, but was a firm believer in neither. He also grew up speaking several languages, and as a future king he learned how to ride and to fight like a knight, or noble soldier.

In 1209 the pope arranged a marriage for the teenage Frederick II with Constance, the sister of Pedro II, the king of Aragon, a region in northeastern Spain. This marriage was planned for political reasons. Though Constance was ten years older than Frederick, the successful match lasted until Constance's death in 1222. Meanwhile, the fighting continued in Germany to see who would become the next emperor. Both Philip and Otto IV were elected as the next king by competing groups of German princes, the first step in becoming emperor of the Holy Roman Empire. This empire was the third most important

Holy Roman Empire

Frederick II was one of a long line of emperors of what was called the Holy Roman Empire. For most of the thousand years of its existence, this empire was more imaginary than real, an empire on paper. Established in 962 C.E., the Holy Roman Empire was thought of as a child of the old Roman Empire. That empire collapsed in the fifth century. In 800 the powerful leader Charlemagne (742–814) once again established control over much of Europe. He was crowned Roman emperor by Leo III, who was the pope at the time. With the last of Charlemagne's dynasty dying out in 899, that empire also fell apart. However, a strong German prince named Otto began to unify the lands of Germany, and in 962 he was crowned the first emperor of the Holy Roman Empire.

This emperor was typically a German king, elected by a group of strong German princes, for much of the existence of the empire. But his imperial crown, or title of emperor, came from the Catholic Church. Becoming king of Germany was the first step in becoming emperor, but it did not always mean that the pope would approve of the choice. Over time, however, the German kingship and the office of emperor were handed down from father to son and from one family to another. It remained in German hands until 1438, when the house of Hapsburg, the rulers of Austria and Spain, took it over.

From the beginning of the Holy Roman Empire there was a battle for power between the emperor, who was the secular leader of the heart of Europe, and the pope, who was the religious leader. This fight continued until 1356, when the Golden Bull, an order from the emperor, allowed the emperor to be chosen without the pope's blessing. Once the rivalry with the pope was settled, the emperor next had to face the rising power of individual princes, kings, and powerful cities. Early on in the history of the empire, the emperor lost control of kingdoms such as France and Italy; his control over others was in name only. Germany and Italy were his center of power, and even this power depended on the emperor: If he was strong enough, he could rule an actual empire; if weak, he was emperor only on paper. Frederick II had such power over his princes, but he was frustrated in his attempts to unite Italy by a still-powerful papacy.

The last emperor, Francis I, a Hapsburg, gave up the title and the empire in 1806. By this time the imperial office was merely a title. Europe was divided into strong kingdoms that no longer needed or wanted one emperor to look after them.

political player in medieval Europe, after France and England. Otto IV won this struggle and persuaded the pope to crown him emperor in 1209.

The pope, however, soon became disappointed in this new emperor when he tried to take over Italy, which was traditionally the pope's territory. Encouraged by the pope, the German electors, or princes, changed their minds about Otto and elected Frederick II the German king, just as his father had earlier arranged. In 1212 Frederick traveled to Germany to take up his duties, but first he had to defeat his rival, Otto IV. With some help from Philip Augustus, the king of France, Frederick II was able to accomplish this, and in 1215 he was officially crowned king of Germany.

Frederick II was never as interested in his German kingdom as he was in his Italian one in Sicily and southern Italy. However, he remained in Germany for five years, securing his office and making sure he had the princes of Germany on his side by giving them new rights and powers. He also eased tensions with the pope by promising to lead a Crusade to free the Holy Land from the Muslims and by pledging to separate the kingdom of Sicily from the Holy Roman Empire. The papacy, or office of the pope, had long feared having Rome caught between the German regions and the south of Italy. They were against any attempt to unite Italy as part of the Holy Roman Empire, for the papacy regarded Italy as its own region. With such promises to Honorius III, the new pope, Frederick II won the favor of the papacy and in 1220 was crowned Holy Roman Emperor.

Frederick II Returns to Sicily

Leaving his young son, Henry, behind as the new king of Germany, Frederick II returned to the warmer climate of Italy. He went back on his promise to the papacy about giving up his lands in Sicily and in southern Italy, claiming that he needed them in order to support his Crusade. He set about getting Sicily in shape, creating a strong central government under his rule and putting down any rebellions. As a result of all this reorganization, he kept putting off the time of his Crusade and was able to send only a small force on the unsuccessful Fifth Crusade (1218–21). With the founding of the University of Naples in 1224, he established the first state university of the Middle Ages. The following year he married Yolande, a teenage girl who was next in line to the Kingdom of Jerusalem, a Crusader state established in the Holy Land after the First Crusade (1095–99). This marriage, which brought with it the title of King of Jerusalem for Frederick II, ultimately led him to go on a Crusade himself.

The Sixth Crusade

Frederick's marriage to the fourteen-year-old Yolande (he was thirty-one) did not work out well. He liked women too much to remain faithful. He soon sent Yolande to live in Palermo, where she died at seventeen after giving birth to a son, Conrad. The two sons he had with his first two wives were the only ones that were legitimate—that is, born in marriage. But Frederick also fathered numerous illegitimate sons to whom he often awarded important positions. Frederick learned of his wife's death on his way to the Holy Land. It was not the only bad news he received during his trip. When malaria (a disease with symptoms of chills and fever, spread by mosquitoes) struck him and his Crusader army, Frederick II delayed the Crusade once again, and the pope excommunicated, or expelled, him from the church. Once he recovered, he set out again for the Holy Land. When the pope learned of this, as if to emphasize his displeasure, he excommunicated Frederick a second time for daring to set off on the Crusade after being excommunicated.

However, Frederick really did not care about such things. He had his own plans. While he was still in Sicily, he had been communicating with **Sultan al-Malik al-Kamil** (see entry), the powerful ruler of Egypt and Palestine, who let Frederick understand that he might be willing to negotiate a peaceful deal concerning Jerusalem, one of the sultan's holdings. Thus, when Frederick reached the Holy Land with a very small army and with little local support from the religious fighting orders (such as the Knights Templars and Knights Hospitallers) because of his excommunication, he was not really concerned. He knew al-Kamil needed to strike a deal over Jerusalem because the sultan was busy with his own internal fights, trying to take Damascus, Syria, from his nephew.

Frederick II also badly needed a victory in this Crusade in order to reestablish his power base in the empire. Both men were willing to compromise. Frederick made it look as if he were ready to fight, but in the end no battles were fought. On February 18, 1229, the sultan and the emperor simply signed the following agreement: The Christians would get Jerusalem, Nazareth, and Bethlehem back, as well as a small strip of land along the coast. These lands, long in the hands of the Muslims, had been won by the Christian Crusaders in the First Crusade (1095–99) under **Godfrey of Bouillon** (see entry) and then lost to the Muslims in 1187 under the Islamic leader **Saladin** (see entry). For the past forty years Christians and Muslims had been fighting over this city and region, for it was important to both religions. However, Frederick and al-Kamil were politicians first and believers second. The Muslims got something out of the deal, too. Al-Kamil was promised a truce for ten years, during which time he could fight rival Muslims to secure his own empire. Also, the Crusaders were forbidden to rebuild the destroyed walls of Jerusalem in order to defend it. The city was thus open to attack at any time. In addition, Muslims retained possession of al-Aqsa, their mosque, or place of worship, and were allowed free access to the city.

This agreement pleased both Frederick II and al-Kamil, though both were sharply criticized for it. The Christians, who had settled the area since the First Crusade, felt that Frederick had never really intended to fight. His was a public-relations trick. If al-Kamil had agreed simply to hand over Jerusalem without a fight, these critics argued, just think what could have been achieved with a real battle. The Muslim world also cried out against the handover of Jerusalem. Yet both leaders survived, and their agreement brought a period of peace to the region and temporarily ended the battle over who controlled Jerusalem. Though a Seventh Crusade was fought in the mid-thirteenth century, Frederick's agreement took the wind out of the arguments for a Crusade.

Battles for a United Italy

Frederick II stayed on in the Holy Land for a short time, declaring himself king of Jerusalem, but there was little enthusiasm locally for his leadership. Besides, a new pope, Gregory IX, was in power in Rome and was using the emperor's absence as an opportunity to attack his lands in Sicily. Returning to Italy, Frederick II defeated the pope's army and then forced Gregory IX to nullify, or end, his excommunication. Frederick II spent the next twenty years trying to unify Italy. In 1231 he issued a group of laws, called the Constitutions of Melfi, that provided for a strong central government, a system of taxes, an army, a standard currency (type of money), and a court system, all of which turned Sicily into a wealthy kingdom.

Once Sicily was under his control, Frederick II attempted to dominate northern Italy, but the pope would not stand for this. Gregory IX again excommunicated Frederick II and managed to get cities in the north, which were members of the Lombard League, to resist the emperor. Although he was almost constantly at war with one group or another, Frederick found the time to marry Isabella, the sister of the king of England. In 1235 he also passed what are known as the Laws of the Empire, establishing an imperial court of justice. This was an extremely important move, for it later served as the basis for national law.

The emperor also had to put down a rebellion by his son Henry in Germany. Frederick II sent forces to Germany, defeated the rebels, and threw his young son in prison, where he died in 1242. He replaced Henry as German king with his second son, Conrad. Now Frederick could once again turn his attention to Italy. After the death in 1241 of his enemy Pope Gregory IX, he kept the papacy from electing a new pope for two years. Finally, Innocent IV became pope and was at first controlled by Frederick. But he fled Rome for France, where he held a church council in 1245 that condemned Frederick II as the Antichrist (the biblical enemy of Christ).

Relations were never repaired between Frederick II and the papacy. He suffered a defeat in 1248 by the pope's army and the cities of the Lombard League. Two years later he was beginning to get the upper hand again when he died of dysentery, an infection of the intestines.

Although Frederick II was unable to achieve his goal of uniting Italy, he was still one of the most powerful medieval Holy Roman Emperors. His advances in centralized government—one governing body and set of laws that ruled over large portions of land such as entire countries—paved the way for modern governments. He was in many ways a man before his time. Religion did not dominate his life, as it did for many other rulers of the Middle Ages. His interest in the arts and learning created a multicultural environment at his court in Sicily. He corresponded with Christians, Jews, and Muslims about philosophical and scientific questions. A rationalist (one who believes in reason over blind faith), Frederick II was an amateur scientist, creating his own experiments on digestion by examining the contents of the stomachs of executed prisoners or seeking an answer to the riddle of language by raising children in silence to see which language they would choose. Such experiments show both Frederick's curiosity and his lack of sensitivity for basic human rights. As king and emperor he made the laws, but he did not always abide by them. That next step in the development of government would have to wait many centuries.

For More Information

Books

Abulafia, D. *Frederick II: A Medieval Emperor.* London: Pimlico, 2002.

Barraclough, G. *The Origins of Modern Germany.* New York: Norton, 1984.

"Frederick, II." In *Historic World Leaders. Europe: A–K.* Edited by Anne Commire and Deborah Klezmer. Detroit, MI: Gale, 1994.

Maalouf, Amin. *The Crusades through Arab Eyes.* New York: Schocken Books, 1984.

Mayer, Hans Eberhard. *The Crusades.* 2nd ed. Translated by John Gillingham. New York: Oxford University Press, 1988.

Van Cleve, T. C. *The Emperor Frederick II of Hohenstaufen.* Oxford: Clarendon Press, 1972.

Web Sites

"Death of the Emperor Frederick II." *History Today* (December 2000). http://articles.findarticles.com/p/articles/mi_m1373/is_12_50/ai_68147618 (accessed on June 26, 2004).

"Emperor Frederick II." *Best of Sicily Magazine.* (July 2002). http://www.bestofsicily.com/mag/art57.htm (accessed on June 26, 2004).

"Frederick II." *New Advent.* http://www.newadvent.org/cathen/06255a.htm (accessed on June 26, 2004).

"Frederick II, Holy Roman Emperor." *RoyaList Online.* http://www.royalist.info/execute/biog?person=1068 (accessed on June 26, 2004).

"The Frederick–Al-Kamil Compromise of 1229." *Aljazeerah Online.* http://aljazeerah.info/Opinion%20editorials/2003%20Opin

ion%20Editorials/August/13%20o/The%20Frederick-Al-
Kamil%20compromise%20of%201229,%20David%20Abulafia.htm
(accessed on June 26, 2004).

"Salimbene: On Frederick II." *Internet Medieval Sourcebook.* http://www.
fordham.edu/halsall/source/salimbene1.html (accessed on June 26,
2004).

"The Sixth Crusade." *The ORB: On-line Reference Book for Medieval Studies.*
http://the-orb.net/textbooks/crusade/sixcru.html (accessed on June
26, 2004).

Godfrey of Bouillon

c. 1060
Boulogne, France, or Baisy, Belgium

July 18, 1100
Jerusalem

Knight and duke of Lower Lorraine, leader of the First Crusade and first ruler of the Kingdom of Jerusalem

G odfrey of Bouillon (pronounced boo-YOHN) was a medieval knight, or trained soldier, as well as a duke of the region of Lower Lorraine (in present-day northwestern Germany). He played a major part in directing military operations in the latter part of the First Crusade (1095–99), the European Christian mission to retake the Holy Land in Palestine from the Islamic and Turkish forces that held it. One of several powerful families of landed nobility who raised and commanded armies against the Muslims, or faithful followers of Islam, he was chosen, after Jerusalem fell to the Christians in 1099, as the first ruler of what was called the Kingdom of Jerusalem.

From Minor Knight to Major Crusader

Godfrey of Bouillon was born around 1060 in either Boulogne in France or Baisy, a city in the region of Brabant (part of present-day Belgium). During Godfrey's lifetime this region was part of the German or Holy Roman Empire, a loose collection of principalities, or small royal states. Godfrey was the second son of Count Eustace II of Boulogne and Ida of

> "He was a religious man, mild mannered, virtuous, Godfearing. He was just, he avoided evil, he was trustworthy and dependable in his undertakings.... He was considered by everyone to be most outstanding in the use of weapons and in military operations."
>
> —William of Tyre, "History of Deeds Done beyond the Sea," in The Crusades: A Documentary History.

Godfrey of Bouillon.
© Hulton Archive.

Lower Lorraine. That he was the second son was very important to Godfrey's future. In the Middle Ages it was the first son who inherited the lands of the parents. As the second-born son, Godfrey had fewer opportunities. Were it not for a bit of family luck, he would have become just one more minor knight in service to a rich landed nobleman. It happened that Godfrey the Hunchback, his uncle on his mother's side, died childless, naming his nephew, Godfrey of Bouillon, as his heir and next in line to his duchy (region) of Lower Lorraine. This duchy was an important one at the time, serving as a buffer (safety zone) between the kingdom of France and the German lands.

In fact, Lower Lorraine was so important to the German kingdom and the Holy Roman Empire that Henry IV, the German king and future emperor (ruled 1084–1105), decided that he would place it in the hands of his own son and give Godfrey less important lands in exchange, as a test of Godfrey's abilities and loyalty. Godfrey served Henry IV loyally, supporting him even when Pope Gregory VII (the leader of the Catholic Church) was battling the German king over who should have more power in Europe, the church or the secular (nonreligious) powers of the kings and princes. Godfrey fought with Henry IV and his forces against the rival forces of Rudolf of Swabia and also took part in battles in Italy when Henry IV actually took Rome away from the pope.

At the same time, Godfrey was struggling to maintain control over the lands that Henry IV had not taken away from him, for the widow of his uncle said that these lands should have come to her. Another enemy outside the family also tried to take away other bits of his land, and Godfrey's brothers, Eustace and Baldwin, both came to his aid. Following long struggles, and after proving that he was a loyal subject to Henry IV, Godfrey finally won back his duchy of Lower Lorraine in 1087, becoming Godfrey IV, duke of Lower Lorraine. Still, Godfrey would never have had much power in the German kingdom or in Europe if it had not been for the coming of the Crusades.

Godfrey Takes Command of Crusader Forces

In 1095 **Urban II** (see entry), the new pope, called for a Crusade (holy war) against the Islamic forces that held

Jerusalem and other religious locations in Palestine. Crusader fever caught on throughout Europe, partly because of the power of the pope but also because there were many knights and second and third sons, such as Godfrey, who were looking for opportunities outside Europe. The pope promised that all sins would be forgiven for anyone who served in the Crusades, but there was also talk of lands to be won there, of new duchies that could be carved out of Muslim lands.

Godfrey took out loans on most of his lands or sold them to the bishops, or regional church leaders, of Liège and Verdun. With this money he gathered thousands of knights to fight in the Holy Land. In this he was joined by his older brother, Eustace, and his younger brother, Baldwin, who had no lands in Europe. He was not the only major nobleman to gather such an army. Raymond of Saint-Gilles, also known as Raymond of Toulouse, created the largest army. At age fifty-five he was also the oldest and perhaps the best known of the Crusader nobles. Because of his age and fame, Raymond expected to be the leader of the entire First Crusade. Adhemar, the assistant to the pope and bishop of Le Puy, traveled with him. There was also the fiery Bohemund, a Norman knight who had formed a small kingdom in southern Italy. He had Viking blood in his veins and fought like a warrior of old, going into battle himself and fiercely combating the enemy until they perished. For Bohemund this Crusade was simply another chance to add lands to his kingdom. There was also a fourth group under Robert of Flanders. No kings participated in this First Crusade.

Each of these armies traveled separately, some going southeast across Europe through Hungary and others sailing by water across the Adriatic Sea from southern Italy. Their first destination was Constantinople, capital of the Byzantine Empire, or eastern Roman Empire. The pope had, in fact, called the Crusade in order to help **Alexius I** (see entry), the emperor of this eastern Christian kingdom, fight the Islamic Turks who were invading his lands from Central Asia and Persia.

Godfrey and his troops were the first to arrive in Constantinople, just before Christmas 1096. During the next several months the other Crusader armies arrived; suddenly, the

The conquest of Antioch by the Crusaders, one of the first battles of the First Crusade that Godfrey of Boullion took a role in.
© *Archivo Iconografico, S.A./Corbis.*

Byzantine emperor had an army of about four thousand mounted knights and twenty-five thousand infantry (foot soldiers) camped on his doorstep. The Crusader leaders Godfrey and Alexius I had different goals. The Byzantine emperor wanted the help of these professional soldiers to recapture lands that the Seljuk Turks, his enemies to the east, had taken. The Crusaders, however, had the main aim of taking the Holy Land in Palestine from the Muslims and setting up a Christian occupying force there. For them, Alexius I and his Turks were only a sideshow. Worse, the Byzantine emperor expected the Crusaders to take an oath, or promise, of loyalty to him. Godfrey and the other knights agreed to a modified version of this oath, promising to help return some lands to Alexius I. By the spring of 1097 the Crusaders were ready to march into battle.

Their first major victory, with Byzantine soldiers at their side, was at the city of Nicaea, close to Constantinople, which the Seljuk Turks had taken some years earlier. Godfrey

Godfrey of Bouillon and the Crusaders break through into Jerusalem and overtake the city in 1099, ending the First Crusade. © *Corbis.*

and his knights of Lorraine played a minor role in this action, with Bohemund successfully commanding much of the action. Just as the Crusaders were about to storm the city, they suddenly noticed the Byzantine flag flying from atop the city walls. Alexius I had made a separate peace with the Turks and now claimed the city for the Byzantine Empire. These secret dealings were a sign of things to come in terms of relations between Crusaders and Byzantines.

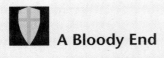

A Bloody End

When the Crusaders took Jerusalem on July 15, 1099, they seemed to forget the tenets, or ideals, of Christian behavior. Only the Arab Muslim commander of the city and his guards were allowed to leave unharmed. The rest of the inhabitants of Jerusalem—Muslims and Jews alike—were murdered by the Crusaders. Since they were the only ones left alive in the city, the Crusaders assembled at the Holy Sepulchre, or tomb of Jesus Christ, to pray.

Raymond d'Aguilers, one of the Crusaders who took part in this bloody massacre, left a written description of the scene, as found in "The Siege and Capture of Jerusalem: Collected Accounts":

> Now that our men had possession of the walls and towers, wonderful [extraordinary] sights were to be seen. Some of our men (and this was more merciful) cut off the heads of their enemies; others shot them with arrows, so that they fell from the towers; others tortured them longer by casting them into the flames. Piles of heads, hands, and feet were to be seen in the streets of the city. It was necessary to pick one's way over the bodies of men and horses. But these were small matters compared to what happened at the Temple of Solomon, a place where religious services are ordinarily chanted. What happened there? If I tell the truth,

On to Jerusalem

Godfrey continued to play a minor role in the battles against the Muslims until the Crusaders finally reached Jerusalem in 1099. Before that time, he took part in the attack on the fortified city of Antioch in 1098, which fell in June of that year after long and bitter fighting. During the siege some of the Crusaders felt that the battle was hopeless and left the Crusade to return to Europe. Alexius I, hearing of the desperate situation, thought that all was lost at Antioch and did not come to help the Crusaders as promised. When the Crusaders finally took the city, they decided that their oaths to Alexius I were no longer in effect. Bohemund, the first to enter the city gates, claimed the prize for himself. A Muslim force under Karbugah, from the city of Mosul, arrived and battled the Crusaders, but the Christians finally defeated these Turkish Islamic troops.

After this victory, the Crusader army headed south. The bishop of Le Puy, the pope's assistant, had died at Antioch. Bohemund remained behind to secure his new kingdom, it will exceed [strain] your powers of belief. So let it suffice to say this much, at least, that in the Temple and porch of Solomon, men rode in blood up to their knees and bridle reins. Indeed, it was a just and splendid judgment of God that this place should be filled with the blood of the unbelievers, since it had suffered so long from their blasphemies [lack of respect for sacred things]. The city was filled with corpses and blood. Some of the enemy took refuge in the Tower of David, and, petitioning Count Raymond for protection, surrendered the Tower into his hands.

At this point another Crusader, named Fulk of Chartres, takes up the awful tale:

Some Saracens, Arabs, and Ethiopians took refuge in the Tower of David, others fled to the temples of the Lord and of Solomon. A great fight took place in the court and porch of the temples, where they were unable to escape from our gladiators [professional soldiers]. Many fled to the roof of the Temple of Solomon, and were shot with arrows, so that they fell to the ground dead. In this Temple almost ten thousand were killed. Indeed, if you had been there you would have seen our feet colored to our ankles with the blood of the slain. But what more shall I relate? None of them were left alive; neither women nor children were spared.

and Godfrey's younger brother, Baldwin, also stayed in the north at the Crusader state he had established at Edessa. As they traveled south into Palestine, the Crusaders faced a new enemy. No longer were the Seljuk Turks the rulers of these lands. Now the Christian army had to deal with armies of North African Muslims called Fatimids, who had adopted the name of the ruling family in Cairo, Egypt. These Fatimids had taken Jerusalem in August 1098. The Crusaders would be battling them for the final prize of the First Crusade.

It was in Jerusalem that the legend of Godfrey of Bouillon was born. The army reached the city in June 1099 and built wooden ladders to climb over the walls. The major attack took place on July 14 and 15, 1099. Godfrey and some of his knights were the first to get over the walls and enter the city. Once inside, the Crusaders went wild, ultimately killing every Muslim man, woman, and child. Jews were also slaughtered. It was a shameful end to three years of fighting by the Crusaders, but they had finally done what they had set out to do in 1096—namely, to recapture the Holy Land and, in particular, the city of Jerusalem and its holy sites, such as the Holy Sepulchre, the tomb of Jesus Christ.

Once the city was captured, some form of government had to be set up. So popular was Godfrey that the other knights chose him to rule what became known as the Kingdom of Jerusalem. The knights wanted to crown Godfrey king, but he refused such a title, saying that he would not wear a golden crown in a place where Christ had worn a crown of thorns. Instead, he took the title of Defender of the Holy Sepulchre. He had his work cut out for him, for soon his army shrank as a result of the loss of knights, some of whom returned to Europe and others of whom competed with one another to create their own kingdoms, or states, in the Holy Land. Godfrey successfully repulsed, or fought back, an attack by Egyptian Muslim forces and also began rebuilding the port of Jerusalem at Jaffa. In June 1100 he led a force to help the Christian soldiers at Damascus, Syria, but on the way he fell ill and was taken back to Jerusalem, where he died on July 18.

Because Godfrey never married, there was no son to take over from him. Instead, his brother Baldwin took the title of king, ruling in Jerusalem until his death. This set the tone for other states formed in the Holy Land. Rather than becoming church lands run by the pope, they ended up in the hands of the Crusader noblemen, who created their own little kingdoms much as they had done in Europe. Godfrey's remaining lands in Europe were soon divided up into smaller holdings.

With the fall of Jerusalem the First Crusade came to a close. Crusader states such as the Kingdom of Jerusalem, the Counties of Edessa and Tripoli, and the Principality of Antioch were created in these former Muslim lands along the coast of the eastern Mediterranean Sea. Jerusalem was regarded as the unofficial capital of these lands. Godfrey's fame spread as a result of his position as the first Christian ruler of the city following the Crusades. Thanks to his good looks and his fighting ability, he became a symbol of the perfect knight, finding his way into medieval histories of the Crusades as well as romances, or early stories, of the Crusades sung by troubadours, or wandering entertainers. The reality was somewhat different. Bohemund was the real military leader and Raymond of Toulouse the best-known nobleman at the time. Godfrey's own brother Baldwin was the first king of Jerusalem. Godfrey really did not lead the Crusader armies until the siege of Jerusalem. It seems he was chosen because he was respected by the other knights and had no obvious negative qualities. Every special event needs a romantic hero, and Godfrey ended up being the hero of the First Crusade.

For More Information

Books

Andressohn, John C. *The Ancestry and Life of Godfrey of Bouillon.* Freeport, NY: Books for Libraries Press, 1972.

Brundage, James A. *The Crusades: A Documentary Survey.* Milwaukee, WI: Marquette University Press, 1962.

"Godfrey of Bouillon." In *Historic World Leaders, Europe: A–K.* Edited by Anne Commire and Deborah Klezmer. Detroit, MI: Gale, 1994.

Riley-Smith, Jonathan. *The First Crusade and the Idea of Crusading.* Philadelphia: University of Pennsylvania Press, 1986.

Runciman, Steven. *A History of the Crusades.* Volume 1: *The First Crusade.* Cambridge, UK: Cambridge University Press, 1951.

Web Sites

"Crusaders at Constantinople: Collected Accounts." *Internet Medieval Sourcebook.* http://www.fordham.edu/halsall/source/cde-atcp.html (accessed on June 26, 2004).

"The First Crusade." *The ORB: On-line Reference Book for Medieval Studies.* http://www.the-orb.net/encyclop/religion/crusades/first_crusade.html (accessed on June 26, 2004).

"Godfrey of Bouillon." *New Advent.* http://www.newadvent.org/cathen/06624b.htm (accessed on June 26, 2004).

"The Siege and Capture of Jerusalem: Collected Accounts." *Internet Medieval Sourcebook.* http://www.fordham.edu/halsall/source/cde-jlem.html#raymond1 (accessed on June 26, 2004).

Hugh de Payens

c. 1070
Champagne or Burgundy, France

1136
Jerusalem

Crusader; founder of Knights Templars

Hugh (also called Hugues) de Payens was a French noble-man who fought in the Holy Land during the First Cru-sade (1095–99), the initial stage of what became a two-hundred-year conflict between the Christian West and the Islamic Middle East over control of Jerusalem and Palestine. Staying on after the fall of Jerusalem to the Crusader forces, Hugh and a small group of other knights, or trained soldiers of noble birth, founded a protective service that would escort pilgrims, or religious visitors, from the port city of Jaffa to Jerusalem. Given quarters in what was formerly the Temple of Solomon, built by the Jews in Jerusalem, this group of knights adopted the name of Knights Templars in 1118. Ten years later this unofficial group was made a Catholic order of mili-tary monks (religious believers) who promised to live a sim-ple life without family and away from society. By the time of Hugh's death in 1136, the Knights Templars had become one of the strongest fighting forces in the Holy Land. The order lasted for almost two hundred years, until in 1314 it was fi-nally disbanded, or broken up, by the French king Philip IV.

"In [1118] certain noble men of knightly rank, religious men,...promised to live...without possessions, under vows of chastity [purity] and obedience. Their foremost leaders were the venerable Hugh of Payens and Geoffrey of Saint Omer."

—William of Tyre, "The Foundation of the Order of Knights Templars," in the Internet Medieval Sourcebook, http://www.fordham.edu/halsall/source/tyre-templars.html.

Hugh de Payens. *Réunion des Musées Nationaux/Art Resource, NY.*

Gerard de Martigues and the Hospitallers

Hugh de Payens' Knights Templars was not the only military order fighting in the Holy Land. Another important order, both then and now, is the Hospitallers of Saint John of Jerusalem, otherwise known as the Order of Saint John. Like Hugh's Templars, the Hospitallers began with a specific function—namely, to provide assistance to the growing number of Christian pilgrims coming to the Holy Land. As early as the eleventh century there was a hospital set up in Jerusalem specifically for these western visitors, attached to the small church of Saint John. When the Crusaders took Jerusalem in 1099, the master of the hospital was Gerard de Martigues (1040–1120), a former soldier or merchant from Provence, a region in France. At this time the institution was part hospital and part hospice (hotel) for pilgrims. Wounded Crusader knights were treated in this hospital after the Christians took Jerusalem. Gerard, however, saw a larger, military role for members of the religious order that ran the hospital and helped to create an order of knights whose job also included protection of Christians in the Holy Land.

In 1113 his order, the Friars of the Hospital of Saint John of Jerusalem, was recognized by Pope Paschal II, with Gerard becoming the first grand master of the order.

In addition to their medical duties, the monks of this order also fought the infidels, or nonbelievers, in the Holy Land. While the Templars wore a white tunic (a knee-length slip-on top) with a red cross, the Hospitallers' uniform was a black tunic with a white cross. With the death of Gerard in 1120, rule passed to Raymond de Puy. These Knights Hospitallers—or Knights of Saint John, as they were also called—took on an increasingly military role. When Jerusalem fell to the Muslim (followers of the Islamic religion) leader **Saladin** (see entry) in 1187, the Hospitallers moved their base to Acre. They also developed a rivalry with the Templars that ultimately led to civil war between the two Christian orders. Their hospital work nevertheless managed to continue.

When Acre fell in 1291, these knights first moved to the island of Rhodes and later to Malta, where they became known as the Knights of Malta and, still later, as the Order of Saint John of Jerusalem, the name they bear today. Their primary function in the modern world is medical; members of the order are involved in hospital and ambulance work. In their nine-hundred-year history the Hospitallers have thus come full circle back to their origins.

From France to Jerusalem

Not much is known of the early career of Hugh of Payens. It appears he was born to the lower nobility in the

French region of Champagne or Burgundy. The date of his birth is not recorded. However, John J. Robinson, who has written about the Templar order in *Dungeon, Fire and Sword: The Knights Templar in the Crusades,* notes that Hugh was forty-eight when he became grand master of the order (1118) and that by that time he had already served in the Holy Land for twenty-two years. This would seem to set his birth in 1070 or perhaps a little later. He was known to be a very religious man. While in France, it seems that Hugh was in the service of the count of Champagne, a distant cousin. Later, this count donated lands to a young French priest to build a religious institution. This young priest was, in fact, Saint **Bernard of Clairvaux** (see entry), a powerful speaker and writer who preached in favor of the Second Crusade (1147–49). Bernard and Hugh would later be linked as a result of the process of making the Knights Templars an official Catholic order.

Hugh was one of thousands of knights inspired by the words of Pope **Urban II** (see entry) during his speech to the Council of Clermont in 1095, when he called for a holy war against the Islamic forces that had taken over the holy sites in Jerusalem and Palestine. It is not known which Crusader army he fought alongside, but according to Charles G. Addison, in his online essay "Foundation of the Order of Knights Templars," Hugh "fought with great credit and renown at the siege of Jerusalem." After Jerusalem fell to the Crusaders in 1099, various principalities, or states, were carved out of the Holy Land and were ruled by the local nobility according to the European fashion. Jerusalem became known as the Kingdom of Jerusalem, with its first ruler, **Godfrey of Bouillon** (see entry), refusing to accept the title of king. Instead, he was called Defender of the Holy Sepulchre, or the tomb of Christ. Upon his death in 1100, his younger brother, Baldwin I, took the title of king and ruled the Kingdom of Jerusalem until 1118. He, in turn, was followed by Baldwin II.

Hugh Forms a Guide and Escort Service for Pilgrims

During these early years of Christian or Latin occupation of Jerusalem and the Holy Land, the situation for these new settlers was not always safe and secure. Beyond those cities protected by towers and walls—Jerusalem, Acre, Antioch, and Edessa, among other Crusader holdings—the countryside was dangerous. Armed bands of Egyptians and Arabs made life difficult for those Europeans living in the region. It was also risky for pilgrims who had come to Jerusalem in order to visit the Holy Sepulchre; to Bethlehem to see where Christ was born; or to be baptized in the Jordan River and visit Nazareth, where Christ had lived. Such pilgrims were in constant danger of being attacked by these roving bands of Arabs and Egyptians.

Hugh de Payens had stayed on in Jerusalem following the end of the First Crusade. Like many knights of lesser rank, he had nothing to return to in Europe; as firstborn son, his older brother, Edmund, had taken over the lands of the Payens family. Instead, Hugh dedicated his life to serving the kings of Jerusalem. He married Catherine Saint Clair, but it is not clear if this was before or after he arrived in the Holy Land. He had three sons, one of whom entered church service in France. After his wife died, Hugh decided to live a life devoted to God. In 1118 he and several other knights decided to form an organization to help pilgrims in their visits to the Holy Land. The men included Geoffrey de Saint Omer (or Saint Aldemar), Payen de Montdidier, Archambaud de Saint Agnan, André de Montbard, Geoffrey Bisol, and two other knights known only by their first names of Rossal and Gondamer. These men all promised the patriarch, or head of the church in Jerusalem, that they would live a life of poverty, obedience, and chastity (no sexual relations). At first they were only too true to their word: the knights were so poor that Hugh and Geoffrey had just one horse between them and had to ride together. In fact, the seal, or stamp, of the order showed two knights riding a single horse.

Hugh and his men acted as unofficial escorts to pilgrims landing at the nearby port of Jaffa. They would ride with these people on their journey to Jerusalem, chasing off any attackers. So helpful did these knights prove to be that the king of Jerusalem gave them a home in al-Aqsa Mosque, near the Dome of the Rock, in Jerusalem, which was the original site of the Temple of Solomon of biblical fame. They took their name from these lodgings and were called the Poor Fellow Soldiers of Jesus Christ and the Temple of Solomon, or the Knights Templars for short. They chose Hugh as their first grand master, or leader. For nine years these men carried on their protective work. As the historian Robert Payne has noted in his book *The Dream and the Tomb: A History of the Crusades,* Hugh inspired his fellow "brothers" in the Templars

> with the energy of chastity and obedience. No women might enter the Temple; they were not permitted to embrace any woman, not even their sisters or their mothers. A lamp burned in their dormitories all night; their breeches [pants] were tightly laced, they were never permitted to see each other naked. They were permitted no privacy, and letters addressed to individual Templars had to be read aloud in the presence of the Grand Master or chaplain. They never shaved their beards. Their Spartan [simple and strict] lives were directed toward the single end of protecting the pilgrims and the Kingdom of Jerusalem by killing the enemy.

They were easily recognized wherever they went: they wore a white knee-length top, called a tunic, with a red cross on it.

Hugh and his followers went about their work with single-minded determination. They even learned Arabic and studied the Islamic faith so that they could better understand their enemy. Because of these skills, they also made good diplomats, or middlemen, to talk with the various Muslim leaders at the request of the kings of Jerusalem. So successful were they in protecting pilgrims that soon they were given the task of defending the Kingdom of Jerusalem. However, this was only after their numbers had grown. They began to attract notable, or famous, members not long after organizing. In 1120 Fulk V, the count of the French region of Anjou, became a member of the order even though he was married. He was followed in 1124 by Hugues, the count of Champagne, the cousin of Hugh de Payens. It appears that such memberships were more honorary than actual, however. These men donated money to the cause rather than lifting their swords.

The Templars Gain Recognition by the Pope

Up to this point Hugh de Payens and his men were an unofficial troop. But Hugh wanted to make his Knights Templars an official order of monks, a special order permitted to use violence against its enemies. Through the count of Champagne, Hugh was put in touch with another distant relative, Bernard of Clairvaux. It seems that the Knights Templars had strong connections in France. André de Montbard, another original member of the Knights Templars who would later become a grand master, was also related to Bernard. This powerful French priest began to push for making the Templars an officially recognized religious order. Hugh himself, accompanied by several members of the Knights Templars, left Jerusalem for Rome to meet with Pope Honorius II, who was impressed with their organization. Meanwhile, Bernard had been busy behind the scenes. He arranged a meeting, called the Council of Troyes, that was attended by important officers of the church. Here the rules of the order were established, written up by Bernard from basic suggestions provided by Hugh. These rules are contained in seventy-two chapters and deal with a variety of matters, from dress to religious practices. Most important, Bernard permitted the use of deadly force by these military monks. In the case of fighting the infidel, such killings were not considered "homicide" (killing a human) but "malicide" (killing evil).

After this meeting, Hugh and his men traveled throughout Europe to raise money to help support the Templars in their work. Hugh went to England and Scotland, where he was warmly greeted and given gold and land grants, creating Knights Templars orders in these countries. He also won new recruits to the order in Jerusalem, but only after the knight proved himself willing to take a vow of poverty and obedience. As a result of this visit to Europe, Templar houses were created in many areas, from Spain to Scotland. Adding to this newfound fame was a work by Bernard of Clairvaux, *In Praise of the New Knighthood,* which honored the life of these warriors for Christ.

In 1130 Hugh returned to the Kingdom of Jerusalem with his new recruits from France and England, where he was welcomed by King Baldwin II. When Baldwin died the following year, he was succeeded by Fulk of Anjou, who was a member of the Knights Templars and who increased their role as protectors of the Kingdom of Jerusalem. Funds and land continued to come into their possession in Europe, making the order very wealthy. By the time Hugh de Payens died in 1136, the Knights Templars order was well established. The order gained more independence in the following years, becoming answerable only to the pope. During the Second Crusade (1147–49) the Templars entered a new field of activity when the French king was forced to accept a loan from the wealthy order. They soon became international bankers, launching a scheme similar to modern traveler's checks, whereby pilgrims could deposit their money in a Templar house in Europe and a coded letter would be handed over to the order upon their arrival in Jerusalem, allowing them to receive the amount they had left behind in Europe. This banking role expanded over time and eventually led to jealousy on the part of secular (nonreligious) rulers; ultimately, it led to the destruction of the Knights Templars in the early fourteenth century.

Formed as a private army and police force, the Knights Templars had many legends created about them and their time spent in the Temple of Solomon. They were supposed to have discovered secret and powerful knowledge while digging in the temple. Various legends claim that they recovered the Ark of the Covenant, the box where the Ten Commandments had been stored, or the Holy Grail, the cup that Jesus used at the Last Supper and into which his blood was supposedly gathered at the Crucifixion. These legends were spread, in part, because of the secret signals and codes the Templars developed for their banking practices. In reality, however, these military monks were both feared and respected by their enemies, the Muslims of the Middle East, until the order was finally defeated in 1291 and was forced to leave the region.

For More Information

Books

Addison, Charles G. *History of the Knights Templars: The Temple Church and the Temple*. Kempton, IL: Adventures Unlimited Press, 1997.

Payne, Robert. *The Dream and the Tomb: A History of the Crusades*. New York: Cooper Square Press, 2000.

Read, Piers Paul. *The Templars: The Dramatic History of the Knights of Templar, the Most Powerful Military Order of the Crusades*. New York: St. Martin's Press, 2000.

Robinson, John J. *Dungeon, Fire and Sword: The Knights Templar in the Crusades*. New York: M. Evans, 1992.

Seward, Desmond. *The Monks of War: The Military Religious Orders*. New York: Penguin, 1996.

Web Sites

"Foundation of the Order of Knights Templars." *International History Project.* http://ragz-international.com/templar.htm (accessed on June 26, 2004).

"Hugues de Payens." *Templar History.* http://www.templarhistory.com/hugues.html (accessed on June 26, 2004).

"The Knights Templars." *New Advent.* http://www.newadvent.org/cathen/14493a.htm (accessed on June 26, 2004).

"Military Orders: The Primitive Rule of the Templars." *The ORB: On-line Reference Book for Medieval Studies.* http://the-orb.net/encyclop/religion/monastic/t_rule.html (accessed on June 26, 2004).

"The Templars." *The Military Orders of the Crusades.* http://www.adambennington.com/military_orders/templars.html (accessed on April 21, 2004).

"William of Tyre: The Foundation of the Order of Knights Templars." *Internet Medieval Sourcebook.* http://www.fordham.edu/halsall/source/tyre-templars.html (accessed June 26, 2004).

Innocent III

c. 1160
Anagni, Italy

June 16, 1216
Perugia, Italy

Pope

The most powerful of the medieval popes (leaders of the Catholic Church), Innocent III was a strong and talented administrator who brought the church to the zenith, or highest point, of its political power. Using the threat of excommunication (expulsion from the church) for princes, kings, and even entire countries, Innocent III put his papacy, or office, above that of political rulers of the time, including the kings of England and France as well as the German emperor. He called for the Fourth Crusade (1202–04), and though the Crusader armies eventually were beyond his control once they left Europe, Innocent III kept a grip on the religious and political affairs inside Europe for the eighteen years of his papacy, which stretched from 1198 to his death in 1216. The year before his death he called the Fourth Lateran Council, the most important church meeting of the Middle Ages, in which he demanded church reform and a new Crusade, or holy war, against the Muslims (believers in the Islamic religion) in the Holy Land of Jerusalem and Palestine. He did not live to see that fifth installment of the long-standing war between Christianity and Islam.

"I have decided...to convoke a general council, by means of which evils may be uprooted...morals reformed, heresies wiped out, the Faith strengthened princes and people won to the cause of aiding the Holy Land..."

—*Pope Innocent III, calling for the Fifth Crusade at the Lateran Council in 1215; quoted at http://www.catholicism.org/OGP/pope_chapter7.htm.*

Pope Innocent III. © *Archivo Iconografico, S.A./Corbis.*

A Noble Background

Like many popes, Innocent III came from an old aristocratic (noble) family. Born Lothario de Segni, he was descended from the Trasimunds, one of the four oldest noble families in Italy, and was educated at the best universities of the day in Paris and in the Italian city of Bologna. There he studied civil (for ordinary citizens) and canon (religious) law. As a youth he was deeply impressed by the martyrdom (death for a cause, usually religious in nature), of the English religious leader Thomas Becket (1118–1170), who was murdered by agents of the king of England. Lothario de Segni had not only aristocratic roots but also excellent connections within the church. His uncle was Clement III, who served as pope from 1187 to 1191. Thanks to his uncle's influence, Lothario rose quickly through the church ranks, becoming a deacon, a rank just below a priest, when he was twenty-seven, and a cardinal, a leading official of the Catholic Church, at the age of thirty.

This rapid rise stopped with his uncle's death in 1191. The new pope, Celestine III, was a rival, and Lothario made no progress in the church for the next seven years. He continued to study law and began to be known for his legal writings. When Celestine III died in 1198, it was Lothario's turn. At the young age of thirty-seven he was selected by the cardinals in Rome to be the next pope, taking the name Innocent III. This election came as a complete surprise to Lothario, since his confirmation as a priest in the church had not yet been completed.

Innocent III Sees the Papacy as a Powerful Office

From the beginning of his rule, it was clear that Innocent III felt that the pope should play the most important part not only in church-related matters, or religious life, but also in temporal, or nonreligious, matters. He followed up the reforms that an earlier pope, Gregory VII (1020–1085), had started. These reforms were intended to affect not only the church itself but also its relations with kings and princes. For Innocent III all power came from God. The pope was God's messenger on earth. Therefore, the pope's power was stronger than that of any king or emperor. Innocent III called himself the "Vicar [religious representative] of Christ." The medieval papacy did not have much of an army, so Innocent could not hope to use force to keep the nobles of Europe in line. Instead, he used three powerful weapons: excommunication—the removal of the rights and advantages of the church—for an individual; interdict, or the stopping of all religious activities in a country; and the placing of canon law above civil law, thus limiting a king's power in his own kingdom.

Innocent III used these tools to help establish the church's dominance over the major political rivals of the day. He threw his weight behind one of the contenders (competitors) for the crown of the Holy Roman Empire, which basically included the German lands of Europe, and finally had his favorite, **Frederick II** (see entry), placed on the throne. When King John of England (1167–1216) tried to name the next archbishop of Canterbury, the highest church office in his land, Innocent III told him that this was the pope's job, not his. When John went ahead anyway, the pope declared an interdict on the country of England and excommunicated John. After several years of closed churches, the religious citizens of England demanded that their king give in to the pope so that they could go to church again and save their souls. Innocent III handled the king of France, Philip Augustus (1165–1223), in much the same way. When the king wanted to give up his legal wife and take a mistress (lover), the pope placed an interdict on all of France, forcing Philip to submit to the rule of the church.

Innocent III, ruling from his pontifical seat after assuming the title of pope in 1198. © *Courtesy of the Library of Congress.*

Innocent III Calls for a Crusade

One of the new pope's first acts following his election was to call for a Crusade, a holy war to rid the lands of Palestine and Jerusalem of Muslims. There had already been three such Crusades by this time; the First Crusade (1095–99) was the only successful one. At that time the knights, or Christian soldiers, had taken Jerusalem back from the mostly Turkish Islamic forces then occupying the city and had set up Crusader states in the region under the control of the Kingdom of Jerusalem. However, Muslim forces regrouped during the next century—guided by such powerful leaders as Kengi, who died in 1146; Nur al-Din, who died in 1174; and **Saladin** (see entry), who lived from 1137 to 1193—and ultimately took Jerusalem back in 1187. Two more Crusades failed to stop the Muslim advance. Now the Crusader states were pushed into a narrow strip along the eastern Mediterranean coast in the present-day lands of Israel, Lebanon, and Syria.

Innocent III wanted to retake Jerusalem and thereby demonstrate the power of the church. He began by calling for a new Crusade as early as 1198. In this call to arms the pope made himself the leader of the new holy war, promising to forgive the sins and debts of all those who took part in the military adventure. To get the kings of England and France to stop fighting each other was a difficult job. In 1199 a truce (peace agreement) was called between those two warring kingdoms; this was the same year Innocent III said that the Crusaders should leave for the Holy Land, but nobody went. Innocent III got help from many preachers, who reached out to the faithful and preached a new Crusade; by the end of 1199 men began to volunteer. It was Innocent III's plan that the Crusaders would gather in the Italian port of Venice and then sail to the Holy Land. However, once the Venetians were involved, Innocent III lost control of the Crusade.

The French made a deal with the Venetians to transport more than thirty thousand Crusaders, but only a third of them showed up. The Venetians said a deal was a deal, however, and asked for the full price to carry the Crusaders. Finally, a new bargain was struck. Now Venice would share in the profits of this holy war. They talked the Crusaders into helping them defeat the residents of the city of Zara, on the Dalmatian (Yugoslavian) coast. This city, which had a large trading empire in the Mediterranean Sea, was causing Venice problems. Against the wishes of the pope, in late 1202 the Crusaders attacked and defeated the Christian city of Zara in order to help pay off their debt to the Venetians.

The Crusaders also decided that they should take over the capital of the eastern Roman Empire, or Byzantium, as it was then called. Centered at Constantinople, this eastern empire consisted of present-day Greece, the Balkans, and Turkey and was led by the Eastern Orthodox Church, a Christian rival to the Catholic Church of Europe. Other Crusades had set off from Constantinople, which was considered a friend and ally in the fight against the "infidels," or nonbelievers. However, this alliance had weakened over the years. The Latins, as the Byzantines called the European Christians, were not to be trusted. The Europeans felt the same way about the Greeks, as the Crusaders called the people of Byzantium. A plan developed in which the Fourth Crusade would actually take over the city of Constantinople and, using Byzantium's riches to finance the war effort, go on to the Holy Land and conquer Jerusalem.

When the pope heard of this plan, he again wrote to the Crusaders, ordering them not to attack a Christian empire. Once again the Crusaders ignored him. In April 1204 they stormed the city, stealing the wealth collected by the empire over nearly a thousand years and destroying many of the buildings. It was the worst defeat Constantinople had ever suffered, and the city never recovered from it. The sacking (destruction) of the city made the Venetians rich, for they claimed almost half of the loot. However, this "victory" did little to advance the Fourth Crusade. The Crusaders were stuck in Constantinople for decades, trying to maintain their power and fighting for their very survival. The forces of the Fourth Crusade got no farther than Constantinople, and the Crusade ended in failure.

This, however, did not kill the Crusader spirit in Europe. Innocent III next declared a Crusade against heretics, or Christians who practiced religion in ways not permitted by the church. The heretics in question were a French sect (religious group) called the Albigensians. Their belief in an active Satan got them into trouble with Rome, and Innocent III sent two large armies to the region to defeat their strongholds. This action against heretics was the beginning of Innocent III's formation of the Inquisition, or tribunals and courts that would investigate and determine the guilt or innocence of accused heretics. During his rule Innocent III also approved two new groups of friars, or roving priests, the Franciscans and

Two Churches

The writer Mark Twain once jokingly described England and the United States as two countries separated by the same language. A similar statement can be made for the two early branches of Christianity. The western, or Roman Catholic Church, based in Rome, and its eastern partner, the Eastern Orthodox Church, which had its base in Constantinople, are two faiths separated by the same religion. The differences that divided these two branches of the Christian religion were partly political and partly religious. When Emperor Constantine moved the capital of the Roman Empire to Byzantion—or Constantinople (present-day Istanbul), as it came to be called in the fourth century—he was one step ahead of the defeat of that empire in Europe by warring tribes from the north. He took with him the practices of the Roman Catholic Church and set up a new home for it in Constantinople.

While Christianity merely survived during the Middle Ages in Europe, the faith blossomed in Byzantium, with differences growing between the two branches. The first of these differences was language. In the West, Latin was the language of the church. But in the East, most of the faithful spoke Greek, which became the primary language. In the East the priests (ministers of the faith) were allowed to marry, but in the Catholic Church marriage was (and still is) forbidden for priests. In Europe the leader of the church was called the pope, but the leader of the Eastern Orthodox Church was called a patriarch—and there were several rather than just one. Many other differences, both large and small, separated the two religions.

In 1054 this schism (division) between the two religions became even greater when the patriarch of Constantinople was excommunicated over an argument about control of Latin, or European, churches in Constantinople. Then came the Crusades. The next two centuries witnessed a series of wars between Christianity and Islam over control of the Holy Land. The First Crusade was called in 1095 in order to protect the Byzantine Empire from the Muslim forces of the invading Seljuk Turks—or so claimed **Urban II** (see entry), the pope at the time. Actually, this pope hoped to repair the damage between the two faiths and perhaps also to gain more influence over Constantinople. Relations were never perfect between the Christian Crusaders and their Byzantine allies, but it was not until the Fourth Crusade that the schism was made permanent. When the Crusaders, drunk and disorderly, sacked Constantinople in 1204, it was the final blow to relations between the two main branches of Christianity. Where earlier the competition between the two religions had been among church leaders, now the hatred trickled down to the masses, the ordinary people. The schism between the Roman Catholic Church and the Eastern Orthodox Church remains today.

Dominicans, who would work toward ridding the church of heretics. In later centuries these policies led to the awful extremes of the Inquisition in Spain, where supposed heretics were tortured in order to gain a confession.

One of Innocent III's last achievements was the Fourth Lateran Council, a huge meeting consisting of church officials from both East and West, as well as kings and emperors. Here Innocent III called for still another Crusade and also discussed reforms in the church. These reforms included the abolition (outlawing) of simony, which is the practice of charging a price for religious services such as baptism and the mass, as well as selling religious positions or offices to the highest bidder. Simony is now considered a serious sin and can result in excommunication. Innocent III also proposed a change in the frequency of confession, in which believers admit their sins to a priest and ask for forgiveness. Although Innocent III decided that the faithful should do this every year, later centuries made this a weekly practice.

Numerous other reforms were agreed to at this conference, but the unexpected death of Innocent III in 1216 cut his rule short. Following his death, many of these reforms were not put into effect. If they had been, the later history of the church might have been quite different, and corrupt (dishonest) practices that hurt the church might have been prevented. One thing is certain: never again would the Catholic Church enjoy the power it had during Innocent III's rule. Symbolic of that lost influence is the fact that while waiting for burial, the pope's corpse, which was not well guarded, is said to have been stripped of its fancy clothes and jewels and left half naked. More respected than loved, Innocent III took his power with him to the grave.

For More Information

Books

Bokenkotter, Thomas. *A Concise History of the Catholic Church*. New York: Doubleday, 2004.

Elliott-Binns, L. *Innocent III*. London: Methuen, 1979.

"Innocent, III." In *Historic World Leaders. Europe: A–K*. Edited by Anne Commire and Deborah Klezmer. Detroit, MI: Gale, 1994.

Martin, Malachi. *The Decline and Fall of the Roman Church.* New York: Putnam, 1981.

Powell, James, ed. *Innocent III: Vicar of Christ or Lord of the World?* Washington, DC: Catholic University of America Press, 1994.

Queller, Donald, and Thomas Madden. *The Fourth Crusade: The Conquest of Constantinople.* Philadelphia: University of Pennsylvania Press, 1977.

Smith, Charles Edward. *Innocent III, Church Defender.* Westport, CT: Greenwood Press, 1971.

Web Sites

"The Fourth Crusade." *The ORB: On-line Reference Book for Medieval Studies.* http://www.the-orb.net/textbooks/crusade/fourthcru.html (accessed on June 26, 2004).

"Innocent III." *Medieval Church.* http://www.medievalchurch.org.uk/p_innocentiii.html (accessed on June 26, 2004).

"Innocent III: Summons to a Crusade, 1215." *Internet Medieval Sourcebook.* http://www.fordham.edu/halsall/source/inn3-cdesummons.html (accessed on June 26, 2004).

"Pope Innocent III." *New Advent.* http://www.newadvent.org/cathen/08013a.htm (accessed on June 26, 2004).

"Pope Innocent III (1198–1216)." *Our Glorious Popes.* http://www.catholicism.org/OGP/pope_chapter7.htm (accessed on June 26, 2004).

Sultan al-Malik al-Kamil

1180
Cairo, Egypt

1238
Damascus, Syria

Sultan of Egypt, Palestine, and Syria

Al-Malik al-Kamil was sultan, or leader, of Egypt and later of Syria during both the Fifth (1218–21) and the Sixth (1228–29) Crusades. After successfully defending Cairo, the capital of his caliphate (kingdom) in Egypt from the Crusaders in 1221, he once again needed to deal with a Crusader army in 1228, under the leadership of the German emperor **Frederick II** (see entry). This time, however, he used diplomacy, or bargaining, rather than force. The result was that Jerusalem passed to the Christian West and al-Kamil was criticized by most of the Islamic world. However, the sultan had reasons for his choices. The city of Jerusalem was no longer as defensible as it once had been, nor were the Crusaders the only enemy al-Kamil was facing in the region. He also had to battle his own family for ultimate control of Egypt and Syria. His diplomatic tactics during the Sixth Crusade created the only bloodless Crusade. Al-Kamil was the last powerful ruler of what is known as the Ayyubid dynasty (1171–1252), founded by the great Muslim leader **Saladin** (see entry).

"In [1229] al-Kamil gave Jerusalem to the emperor [Frederick II].... The news of the handing over of Jerusalem to the Franks arrived and all hell broke loose in all the lands of Islam."

—Medieval Muslim chronicler Sibt bin al-Jawzi; quoted in The Crusades: Islamic Perspectives.

The End of the Ayyubids

Born in 1180, al-Malik al-Kamil Nasir al-Din Muhammad ibn al-Malik al-Adil ibn Bakr—or simply al-Kamil, as he is known in history—was the son of the sultan al-Adil, who was called Safadin in the West. Al-Adil, in turn, was the brother of the famous Saladin, a Muslim of Kurdish origin who rose from the rank of military leader to become the ruler of Egypt and Syria. Saladin recaptured Jerusalem for Islam in 1187, thus bringing about the Third Crusade (1189–92), in which the Christian West tried unsuccessfully to recapture the Holy Land from the Muslims. At his death in 1193, Saladin's Ayyubid Empire, named after his father, Ayyub, stretched from Cairo in Egypt to Damascus in Syria. His seventeen sons and several brothers began fighting among themselves for power.

In 1201 al-Adil finally managed to gain control of the empire and ruled from Cairo. Once his son, al-Kamil, was old enough, he served his father as vizier, or chief adviser, and was second in command. Another son, al-Kamil's brother al-Muzzam, was sent to Damascus to manage the Syrian part of the empire. During the lifetimes of both al-Adil and al-Kamil, they not only were faced with Christian enemies, who launched several Crusades, or holy wars, against Islam, but also had to deal with numerous relatives who still wanted a chunk of the Ayyubid Empire. They both tried to reduce the number of these enemies by means of diplomacy and negotiation. Thus, both father and son attempted a risky policy of trying to avoid direct conflict with the Franks, or Crusaders, in Palestine. They did not want to give the Christians living there a reason for uniting with the invading Crusader armies against them. This policy defined much of what al-Kamil did when he became sultan.

For example, when the Europeans were beginning preparations for the Fourth Crusade (1202–04), al-Adil had his vizier son al-Kamil make a deal with the Republic of Venice, which was responsible for transporting the Crusaders. Al-Kamil and his father knew that the Christian Crusaders were planning to attack Egypt and then use it as a base to move on to Jerusalem and the Holy Land. Al-Kamil offered the trading-minded Venetians full access to Egyptian ports at Alexandria and Damietta on the Nile delta, or mouth of the river. In return, Venice agreed not to support any expedition into Egypt. The bargain was made and kept. The Fourth Crusade never got past Constantinople, the capital of the Byzantine Empire, an eastern Christian kingdom in Asia Minor that includes present-day Turkey and Greece. Egypt and the Ayyubids won a long period of peace, during which they could secure their power against threats from other Muslims.

The Fifth Crusade

During these years of peace al-Kamil continued to fortify Cairo, a process that had been begun by his uncle, Saladin. He added several towers to the Citadel, the main fortification of the city, and also finished building the walls, which were thirty feet high and ten feet deep. By the late fall of 1217 Crusaders began arriving as part of the Fifth Crusade, led by King John of Jerusalem and the armies of the Christian West, under the command of Cardinal Pelagius, the pope's representative. By the summer of 1218 these forces had arrived in Egypt and begun attacking the Egyptian port of Damietta, which lay between the Crusaders and the Ayyubid capital of Cairo, up the Nile River.

The Crusaders had the first victory in this lengthy war, capturing a small fortress that guarded Damietta. However, al-Kamil was able to raise an opposing force and stop their advance. Neither side was strong enough for a direct attack. The Crusaders were waiting for reinforcements from Italy, and al-Kamil was waiting for more men from his brother, al-Muzzam. When al-Adil suddenly died on August 31, 1218, al-Kamil became sultan. The Christians were encouraged both by this news and by the arrival of more men. They advanced to the fortified walls of Damietta. Al-Kamil, fighting outside, tried to break through the Christian lines but managed only to block the Crusaders' progress upriver. All winter long the two sides fought until, in February 1219, al-Kamil had to leave the battlefield to put down a rebellion within his own court in Cairo. With al-Kamil gone, the Christians advanced, but the Egyptians were finally able to hold them off.

Al-Kamil put down the rebellion in Cairo and made a peace offer to the Crusaders: he agreed to return the Holy

Manuscript illustration of the battle between the Egyptian forces of al-Kamil and the Crusaders at Damietta during the Fifth Crusade. © *Archivo Iconografico, S.A./Corbis.*

Lands (except for a couple of fortresses) in return for a truce lasting thirty years. Jerusalem itself could not be defended, since his brother had destroyed the city walls. Many of the professional soldiers in the Crusader forces wanted to accept this offer, but Cardinal Pelagius was against it. He wanted total victory. When his offer was refused, al-Kamil got many additional men and was able once again to take the offensive.

The Fifth Crusade dragged on through the summer, with attack and counterattack. Meanwhile, the citizens inside the walls of Damietta were running low on food and water. In late August of 1219 the sultan received an amazing visitor. Saint **Francis of Assisi** (see entry), the founder of the Franciscan order—a Christian brotherhood that traveled to spread ideas of Christianity, poverty, and charity—came to Egypt to try to find a peaceful solution to the Crusades. He decided to convert the sultan. Crossing the Muslim lines, Saint Francis and his companion were nearly killed. They were finally captured and delivered to al-Kamil, who offered to spare their lives if they would convert to Islam. He was amazed to hear Saint Francis make the same offer to him—if he would convert to Christianity. So impressed was al-Kamil with the honesty and sincerity of this Italian religious man that al-Kamil did not kill him, as his religious advisers urged him to do. Instead, he presented Francis of Assisi with gifts and a safe-conduct back to the Crusader lines and promised to protect him during his visits to Jerusalem. Some historians mention a month-long visit, during which al-Kamil was in daily contact with Saint Francis, while others claim that the visit lasted only a matter of hours or days.

By August 29 the battle was on again. Al-Kamil drew the Crusaders into a trap, killing large numbers of them. After this victory, al-Kamil once more offered the same peace deal. Again Cardinal Pelagius refused, thinking more men were being sent from Europe to aid him. That November the Christians captured Damietta, which was now nearly a ghost city; almost all of its eighty thousand inhabitants had been killed during the fighting or had starved to death during the siege. When the Crusaders could not agree on their next move, it gave al-Kamil a chance to regroup. The two armies continued their standoff, with frequent small battles through 1220 and into 1221.

When more Crusaders arrived in the summer of 1221, that force once again set out on the offensive but were drawn into another trap by the Muslims: They were cornered between the waters of the Nile and a canal whose waters were slowly rising. As the Christians attempted to retreat, the sultan struck, handing the Crusaders a final defeat at the Battle of Mansurah. By September 1221 the Crusaders had sailed back to Europe, and al-Kamil was once again in control of Damietta.

The Sixth Crusade

Al-Kamil had no sooner strengthened his kingdom than he received word of another Crusade on the horizon. The Sixth Crusade was led by the German emperor Frederick II, a man who was said to admire Islamic culture and civilization. In fact, al-Kamil had earlier sent a representative to the German emperor, and a correspondence had started between Frederick II and al-Kamil, who discussed topics ranging from Greek philosophy to history. Thus, when the German emperor arrived in Acre in September 1228, al-Kamil was prepared to make a deal rather than start fighting immediately. Working in al-Kamil's favor was the fact that the sultan and his brother in Damascus, al-Muzzam, had not been on good terms since the Fifth Crusade and were battling for control of the two parts of the Ayyubid empire, Egypt and Syria. When al-Muzzam died in 1227, he passed on his power to his son, al-Nasir, who was also responsible for Jerusalem. Al-Kamil quickly laid siege to Damascus and was involved in this military operation when Frederick II arrived.

Both al-Kamil and Frederick II were realists rather than being driven by religion. For the sultan, Jerusalem was merely a bargaining chip. It could no longer be defended, and he had no real concern for the holy aspect of the city in terms of Islamic tradition, with its mosques (religious buildings) and shrines. It was similar for Frederick II. He was not motivated by a religious desire to recapture the Holy Land from the Muslims but by the fact that such a victory would strengthen his position as emperor against the religious power of the pope in Europe. The emperor led his small army toward Jerusalem as if to attack. For a time nothing happened, but by early 1229 al-Kamil had signed a treaty to avoid bloodshed. In reality, however, all arrangements for transferring Jerusalem had been made before the emperor's arrival. The Crusaders got Jerusalem, Bethlehem, Nazareth, and a few castles leading to the port of Jaffa. The Muslims kept control of some locations inside Jerusalem, including al-Aqsa Mosque and the Dome of the Rock. Most important, al-Kamil won a ten-year truce from the Crusaders. Now he could concentrate on taking back Syria from his nephew.

Al-Kamil, however, was not prepared for the storm of protest his action caused. In Islamic eyes the sultan was supposed to be the defender of the faith, and for most Muslims he had not taken this role in the case of Jerusalem. Nevertheless, he pressed on in Damascus, finally driving al-Nasir out of that city in the summer of 1229. After having survived criticism for not defending Jerusalem, he spent the rest of his life protecting his empire against repeated invasions from Khwarismian Turks in the north and the Mongols of Central Asia, both of whom were the newest enemies of Islam. In addition, there was again a rebellion, led by another of his brothers, resulting in a civil war that finally ended in 1237.

Al-Kamil died in 1238, exhausted by fighting enemies within and without his empire. The following year his nephew al-Nasir took Jerusalem back from the Christians. However, nothing could hold the Ayyubid Empire together now. Al-Kamil's sons in Damascus and Cairo fought another bloody civil war over control of the empire that lasted until 1240. Fifteen years after al-Kamil's death, the dynasty had been eliminated and was replaced by the Mongols and Turks in Syria and by the Mamluks, or soldier-slaves, in Egypt, who finally turned against their Ayyubid masters and seized power

Ibn al-Baitar

Like many Muslim leaders, al-Kamil hired numerous experts to study and teach at his courts in both Cairo and Damascus. One of the prominent scientists he managed to attract was Ibn al-Baitar, who was born in Malaga, Spain, at the end of the twelfth century. He studied botany and began collecting plants. This knowledge led him to become one of the most famous pharmacists of the Middle Ages, for at that time all medicines were made from herbs. In 1219 he journeyed along Africa's northern coast and into Asia Minor, where he visited Constantinople.

Sometime after 1224 Ibn al-Baitar joined the service of Sultan al-Kamil as chief herbalist, or pharmacist. Once settled in Egypt, he expanded his knowledge of plants to include varieties growing along the southern coast of the Mediterranean Sea. His botanical knowledge grew following al-Kamil's conquest of Syria in 1229. He collected plants and herbs in Syria as well as in Arabia and Palestine, using Damascus as his new base.

His most famous works include *Kitab al-Jami fi al-Adwiya al-Mufrada,* an encyclopedia of medicinal plants, and *Kitab al-Mlughni fi al-Adwiya al-Mufrada,* an encyclopedia of medicine. The first book lists more than a thousand different medicinal plants and quotes both Arab and Greek scientists. When he died in Damascus in 1248, Ibn al-Baitar was already recognized as the greatest authority on medicinal plants in the Islamic world. When his *Jami* was translated into Latin in 1758, he was hailed as the greatest botanist and pharmacist of the Middle Ages.

for themselves. Al-Kamil was the last powerful leader of the Ayyubids. With his passing it became clear that the empire was in decline.

For More Information

Books

Hillenbrand, Carole. *The Crusades: Islamic Perspectives.* New York: Routledge, 2000.

Maalouf, Amin. *The Crusades through Arab Eyes.* Translated by Jon Rothschild. New York: Schocken Books, 1984.

Mayer, Hans Eberhard. *The Crusades.* 2nd ed. Translated by John Gillingham. New York: Oxford University Press, 1988.

Powell, James M. *Anatomy of a Crusade, 1213–1221.* Philadelphia: University of Pennsylvania Press, 1986.

Web Sites

"The Citadel of Cairo." *Tour Egypt.* http://www.touregypt.net/citadel.htm (accessed on June 21, 2004).

"Egypt." *Islamic World to 1600.* http://www.ucalgary.ca/applied_history/tutor/islam/fractured/ (accessed on June 21, 2004).

"The Fifth Crusade." *The ORB: On-line Reference Book for Medieval Studies.* http://the-orb.net/textbooks/crusade/fifthcru.html (accessed on June 21, 2004).

"The Frederick–Al-Kamil Compromise of 1229." *Aljazeerah Online.* http://aljazeerah.info/Opinion%20editorials/2003%20Opinion%20Editorials/August/13%20o/The%20Frederick-Al-Kamil%20compromise%20of%201229,%20David%20Abulafia.htm (accessed on June 21, 2004).

"The Sixth Crusade." *The ORB: On-line Reference Book for Medieval Studies.* http://the-orb.net/textbooks/crusade/sixcru.html (accessed on June 21, 2004).

Louis IX

April 25, 1214
Poissy, France

August 25, 1270
Tunis, North Africa

King of France

Louis IX, who ruled as king of France throughout much of the thirteenth century, was a deeply religious and moral man, a legendary figure in French history who was so much admired by other leaders that he was asked to settle international disputes. As a youth he ruled jointly with his mother, Blanche of Castile (1188–1252). He came to the throne in 1236, governing one of the richest kingdoms in the Christian West. He used much of that wealth to fight two holy wars against the Muslims in Egypt and the Holy Land: the Seventh Crusade (1248–54) and another, shorter Crusade in North Africa in 1270, during which he died of fever. Beloved by the people of France, he was called a saint even before being formally canonized, or officially made a saint, by the Catholic Church in 1297. His Crusades marked the end of large-scale holy wars against Islam by the Christian West. Known for his sense of justice, his diplomacy (tact in political matters), and his deeply held religious beliefs, Louis IX became, during the Middle Ages, a positive symbol of how a king should govern.

"The crusades of Louis IX mark both the culmination and the beginning of the end of the crusading movement. None of the earlier expeditions was as well organized or financed, none had a more inspiring leader, none had a better chance of success."

—Joseph R. Strayer, "The Crusades of Louis IX," in History of the Crusades. Vol. 2, The Later Crusades, 1189–1311.

King Louis IX. *Courtesy of the Library of Congress.*

A Youthful King

Louis IX was the fourth child of King Louis VIII of France and Blanche of Castile, who was the granddaughter of **Eleanor of Aquitaine** (see entry), queen of England. Married to Louis while she was still a child of eleven, Blanche proved to be a wonderful choice as a mate for a future king, being both intelligent and strong-willed, like her grandmother. Louis VIII became king in 1223, ruling a realm that had been enlarged by his own father, Philip II. The France that Louis VIII ruled was the largest ever, and when he died just three years later he passed this enlarged kingdom on to his son, Louis IX (his other three children having died). In 1226 Louis VIII died of an illness while returning from southern France after battling the Albigensians, a heretical, or nonconforming, religious group. As he lay dying, Louis VIII made his son the next king, with the heir's mother jointly ruling with him. Louis IX was crowned king of France on November 29, 1226, in the magnificent cathedral of Rheims, France. Blanche was to act as co-regent, or coruler, until the boy reached twenty-one years of age. The most influential person in the young boy's life was his mother, who transmitted her strength of character to her son. She taught him to be religious and to have a strong sense of right and wrong as well as a sense of duty toward his country and people. As a youth, Louis was also trained in the arts of warfare, learning to ride, fight, and lead men. Although he was not a true scholar, he was well educated in religious matters.

At this time France was still a feudal state—that is, one in which powerful noblemen pledged their loyalty to a king in return for large tracts of land. In return, the barons, or noblemen, supplied the king with knights and other fighting forces to protect the kingdom. They accumulated their wealth from the labor of peasants, the poor who rented their farmland for a share of the crops. Now that the kingship was held by a young boy and a woman, these barons thought that they could rebel and gain more power or even total independence from the crown. Blanche, however, was intelligent about using alliances to protect her realm. She first won the influential count of the region of Champagne to her and her son's side. The count helped Blanche protect the kingdom from powerful princes and barons in the north of France as well as from England's King Henry III, who wanted to win back lost territory from France.

Blanche was able to keep the monarchy and its lands together through these difficult years. In 1234 Louis IX married Margaret of Provence, helping to create further alliances among the nobles, and two years later he became the sole ruler, thus ending the stated reason for the rebellion of the barons. Now that there was a male king of mature age on the throne, the kingship was again secure. However, for the rest of her life, Louis IX continued to seek the counsel and advice of his mother.

Louis IX as Christian Monarch

Louis IX continued many of the policies of his father and grandfather in extending the power of the monarchy, or throne, and placing his close relatives in important administrative positions involving control of the provinces. For example, he named his brother Robert count, or chief noble, of Artois and his brother Alfonso count of Poitiers; a third brother, Charles, became count of Anjou. Louis IX also proved to be skilled in international affairs, staying out of the feud between the pope, the religious leader of the West, and his main rival, the emperor of the Holy Roman Empire, also known as the German kingdom. Louis IX also showed that he was a true Christian by buying back relics (objects held in reverence because of their association with saints) from the time of Christ, including the crown of thorns that Jesus supposedly wore during his crucifixion. For this relic Louis IX constructed a beautiful chapel in Paris called Sainte-Chapelle.

One international situation Louis IX refused to stay out of, however, was the Crusades. These holy wars against the Muslims, whom the Christians called infidels, or unbelievers, in the Holy Land and Middle East were already 150 years old. Jerusalem and its Christian holy sites had been won and lost, bargained over and lost again. Six major Crusades had already been launched against Islam, the most recent ending in the peaceful handing over of Jerusalem to the Christians during the Sixth Crusade (1228–29), which was led by Holy Roman Emperor **Frederick II** (see entry). Since then, however, the Muslims had won the city back. As early as 1244 Louis IX answered the pope's call for a new Crusade, promising to raise an army and reconquer the Holy Land for Christianity.

Stained-glass window of Crusader knights from Sainte-Chapelle, the chapel Louis IX built in Paris to house religious relics such as Jesus' crown of thorns.
© Royalty-Free/Corbis.

Louis IX was a careful planner. During the next four years he raised money and a mostly French army. In 1248 he and his army were finally ready to set sail. Louis had decided he would first capture the Muslim strongholds in Egypt, now the center of power of the Islamic world, and then move on from there to Jerusalem. His was the first Crusade to be solely sponsored by a single king. Although Louis IX took his wife and two brothers along, he left his mother, Blanche, in France to run the government and keep the nobles in line.

The Crusaders spent the winter months of 1248 to 1249 on the island of Cyprus and then traveled on to Egypt that spring. Arriving off the coast of Egypt on June 4, he and his men quickly took the city of Damietta, at the head of the Nile River, defeating Fakhr al-Din, who was leading the Mamluk (slave) army of the Egyptian leader Sultan al-Salih Najm al-Din Ayyub; the latter was the last member of the Ayyubid dynasty, which had begun when the powerful Muslim leader **Saladin** (see entry) conquered Egypt in 1169. The sultan was deathly ill from tuberculosis (a disease of the lungs) and was in Cairo during this battle, but soon he left the capital to set up a defensive position near the small town of Mansurah, site of an earlier battle between Crusaders and Egyptians during the Fifth Crusade (1218–22). The sultan was accompanied by his favorite wife, **Shajarat al-Durr** (see entry), who took over command of his forces when her husband died in November 1249.

Although the news of the death of the sultan was kept from the Egyptians, Louis IX learned of it through his spies. In February 1250 he decided to launch a surprise attack, aided by another spy who showed the French where to cross a river separating them from the Muslim and Mamluk forces. Louis IX sent his brother, Robert of Artois, to lead this attack, carefully instructing him not to get too far ahead of his reinforcements. In the heat of battle Robert forgot these orders and chased the retreating Egyptians into the narrow streets of Mansurah, where the Crusaders were cut down by the Mamluk leader **al-Zahir Baybars** (see entry). Many of the Crusader's most important knights, including Robert of Artois, were killed, forcing the French to retreat.

Not long after this defeat, Turan Shah, the son of Sultan al-Salih, arrived in Egypt with a large force of fighters and finally captured Louis IX and his men even as his wife, Queen Margaret, was giving birth to a son in Damietta. Margaret, learning of her husband's capture, named the son John-Tristan (meaning "sadness" or "sorrow") and made sure to hold Damietta so that the French would have some bargaining power in negotiating the return of the king. The French situation was aided somewhat by the confusion resulting from a palace revolt in Cairo, in which the Mamluk general Baybars killed Turan Shah, the new sultan, and placed Shajarat al-Durr on the throne as sultana. Following payment for the release of Louis IX, he and his wife and newborn son sailed to the Crusader stronghold of Acre in the Holy Land, leaving behind many wounded Crusaders, who were slaughtered by the Mamluks once the French had left.

Louis IX remained in Acre from 1250 to 1254, becoming the leader of the Crusader states that had been left in the region since the time of the First Crusade (1095–99) and helping to unify and fortify (make strong) the states against a possible attack from both the Muslims and the Mongols, a new

The Pen and the Sword

While organizing and fighting in the Crusades, Louis IX also found the time to improve domestic life and to sponsor the arts in France. He built hospitals and institutions for the poor, as well as the glorious chapel at Sainte-Chapelle in Paris to house the crown of thorns worn by Christ.

Such sponsorship of scholarship and the arts was also a typical feature of Islamic courts, from Baghdad to Cairo. Although we generally do not associate the arts with the Mongols—those warring tribes from Central Asia who swept into Europe and the Middle East in the mid-thirteenth century—even they honored the skills of famous scholars. One such man of learning was Nasir al-Din (1201–1274), who served as a minister for the powerful Mongol leader Hulagu.

Fresh from his sacking (destruction) of Baghdad in 1258, in which it is estimated that at least one hundred thousand Muslims were slaughtered, Hulagu attacked the strongholds of the Assassins, an Islamic religious sect, or group, who used politically arranged murder to maintain their position in the Middle East. These Assassins had earlier kidnapped the famous scientist and philosopher Nasir al-Din. After freeing him, Hulagu became impressed with the man's learning and brought him to his court as an adviser.

Nasir al-Din was famous in his time as a philosopher, scientist, physician, mathematician, and writer. He made major advances in the mathematical field of trigonometry, and in science his work in astronomy helped move forward the study of the heavens. He built an observatory that contained many instruments the Mongols stole from Muslim cities they conquered. He was able to produce astronomical (of the solar system) tables, the *Al-Zij-Ilkhani* ("The Ilkhanic Tables"), that revealed the motion of the planets. Nasir al-Din thought this work would take thirty years to finish, but on orders from Hulagu he completed the monumental task in only twelve. In philosophy his *Akhlaq-i-Nasri* ("Nasirean Ethics") became one of the most famous writings on ethics, or moral living. He also wrote widely on religion and produced other scientific studies—all while in the service of the so-called barbarian Mongols.

menace in the region. This warlike tribe came from the plains of Central Asia and, under Genghis Khan and his sons and grandsons, were pushing into Europe and the Middle East, battling Christians and Muslims alike. In the Middle East, Hulagu, a grandson of Genghis Khan, was fighting his way to the Mediterranean Sea. Although they were pagans—nonbelievers in the major religions who worshiped several gods—the Mongols considered Muslims even worse enemies than

Christians and planned to destroy Islam first. However, Louis IX could not help but see the ultimate threat to the Crusader states in these wild warriors from the steppes.

Louis IX Returns to France and Launches a Final Crusade

Louis IX was finally forced to return to France. His mother had died in late 1252, and the kingdom needed its king at home. He immediately set about enacting domestic reforms, sending royal commissioners, or representatives, to check on the running of the local administrations to make sure there was no abuse of power. He also established a fair tax system in France. Internationally, by signing the Treaty of Paris in 1259, he reached a settlement with England's Henry III over the regions of Normandy, Anjou, and Poitou, also making a similar agreement with the regions of northern Spain.

Louis IX, however, was restless. He never gave up the idea of a new Crusade to the Holy Land, where the situation had grown more desperate for the Crusader kingdoms. Under Baybars's leadership, the Mamluks had defeated the Mongols, but they now turned their attention to the Christians. In 1267 Louis IX decided to mount another Crusade. Preparations again took several years, and in 1270 he was ready to depart. For some reason he decided to set out first for Tunis, in North Africa, to establish a base for the Crusade, instead of heading directly for the Holy Land. Landing in Tunis in the height of summer, many of the Crusaders fell ill, including the king and his son. John died of fever on August 3, and his father followed him to the grave three weeks later, his death officially ending this Crusade.

Not long after the king's death, miracles were reported in connection with his burial and remains. As a result of these miracles and his devotion to the Crusades, in 1297 Louis IX was officially canonized (made a saint) by the Roman Catholic Church. As king, he strengthened the French monarchy, introduced administrative reforms, and generally made the position of king of France a respected one. However, his energetic support of both Crusades cost the kingdom dearly in terms of wealth and men; his losses forever changed the nature of the Crusader movement. As has been noted in "The Crusades of Louis IX,"

> the very magnitude of [his Crusades] brought disillusion [disappointment] when [they] failed. If Louis, the richest and most powerful ruler in western Europe, could not conquer the Moslems and recover the holy places, who could? The failure of Louis contributed to the loss of confidence, the hesitations, and even the cynicism which weakened all later crusades.

For More Information

Books

Labarge, Margaret Wade. *Saint Louis: Louis IX, Most Christian King of France*. Boston: Little, Brown, 1968.

Maalouf, Amin. *The Crusades through Arab Eyes*. Translated by Jon Rothschild. New York: Schocken Books, 1984.

Mayer, Hans Eberhard. *The Crusades*. 2nd ed. Translated by John Gillingham New York: Oxford University Press, 1988.

Strayer, Joseph R. "The Crusades of Louis IX." In *History of the Crusades*. Vol. 2, *The Later Crusades, 1189–1311*. Edited by Robert L. Wolff and Harry W. Hazard. Madison: University of Wisconsin Press, 1969.

Periodicals

Lloyd, Simon. "The Crusades of St. Louis (King Louis IX of France)." *History Today* 47, no. 5 (May 1997): 37–43.

Web Sites

"Louis IX: Advice to His Son." *Internet Medieval Sourcebook*. http://www.fordham.edu/halsall/source/stlouis1.html (accessed on July 21, 2004).

"The Seventh Crusade." *The ORB: On-line Reference Book for Medieval Studies*. http://the-orb.net/textbooks/crusade/seventhcru.html (accessed on July 21, 2004).

"St. Louis IX." *New Advent*. http://www.newadvent.org/cathen/09368a.htm (accessed on July 21, 2004).

Maimonides

April 6, 1135
Córdoba, Spain

December 13, 1204
Cairo, Egypt

Spanish-Hebrew philosopher, theologian, and author

One of the foremost scholars of the medieval world at the time of the Crusades, Rabbi Moses Maimonides (pronounced my-MON-uh-deez)—who was also known as Ramba'm (from the first letters of his name)—was as influential outside the world of Jewish thinkers as he was within it. In his *Mishneh Torah,* Maimonides organized Jewish law and tradition in a way that could be understood by the average faithful person without an interpretation provided by a rabbi, or Jewish religious leader and scholar. In *The Guide of the Perplexed,* Maimonides attempted to balance the ideas of rational thought—that is, thinking based on reason, explanation, and faith. He concluded that philosophy (a branch of learning that focuses on values and concepts rather than practical, everyday knowledge) supports faith rather than working against it. Beloved in his own age and widely respected into the twenty-first century, Maimonides was the subject of a popular Jewish expression of the Middle Ages (c. 500–1500 C.E.): "From Moses [of the Old Testament] to Moses [Maimonides] there was none like Moses."

"...May neither avarice nor miserliness, nor thirst for glory or for a great reputation engage my mind; for the enemies of truth and philanthropy could easily deceive me and make me forgetful of my lofty aim of doing good to Thy children."

—*Maimonides, "Oath of Maimonides," in the* Internet Medieval Sourcebook, *http://www.fordham.edu/halsall/source/rambam-oath.html.*

Maimonides. © *Corbis.*

Spanish Origins

Moses ben Maimon was born in Córdoba, Spain, in 1135, the son of a rabbi. From his father the young Maimonides (Greek for "son of Maimon") studied mathematics; astronomy; the literature of the Torah, which consists of the first five books of the Old Testament; and the Talmud, the body of Jewish laws not covered in the Torah. In the multicultural atmosphere of southern Spain, Maimonides also came into contact with Greek and Arabic thought and learned to read and write in several languages.

When the strict North African Islamic sect (subgroup) called Alhomads, or "followers of the prophet Muhammad," conquered Córdoba in 1148, Maimonides and his family were forced to leave their home. The Alhomads demanded that non-Muslims convert to Islam. If they refused, there were only two choices: exile or death. Maimonides' family chose exile, and for a dozen years they moved from place to place throughout southern Spain. It was during these years of wandering that Maimonides began his first important work, the *Commentary on the Mishnah,* the ancient oral code of Jewish law, which was finally written down in the third century C.E.

The Mishnah and the Gemara, representing centuries of scholarly interpretation (explanation) of Jewish scripture, are the two books that form the Talmud. However, by the twelfth century such scholarly writings could not be understood by average believers, making it hard to grasp the basics of Judaism. In his article "Maimonides," Elliot Wachman noted that Maimonides' task in his *Commentary on the Mishnah* was an important one: "He brought brief, lucid [clear] explanations to each passage in the Mishnah whose meaning was not otherwise evident [clear]." The *Commentary* was written in Arabic and then translated into Hebrew and was read by Jews everywhere. Even in the twenty-first century, it was considered one of the best explanations of the Talmud.

Already in this first work Maimonides was attempting to blend Greek philosophy—especially the belief of the famous thinker Aristotle (384–322 B.C.E.) that nothing is real that cannot be understood by means of reason—with traditional Jewish faith. As part of these commentaries, Maimonides also developed the thirteen articles, or statements, of faith—dealing with such topics as the origins of the Torah, the

Rashi

Maimonides, or Ramba'm, as he was also called, was one in a long line of famous commentators, or writers, on the Torah and Talmud, the Jewish holy books. Rabbi Shlomo Itzchaki was another medieval scholar who, like Maimonides, was also popularly known by the initials of his name, Rashi (from RAbbi SHlomo Itzchaki). Born in the French city of Troyes in 1040, as a youth Rashi wanted to spend his life studying at Talmudic, or religious, schools in Germany. The early death of his father forced him to take over his father's vineyards instead. He spent the rest of his life balancing two occupations: managing the family wine business and writing long, detailed, and very clear explanations of the Old Testament and the Talmud.

Ironically, Rashi's fame spread as a result of tragedy. With the beginning of the First Crusade (1095–99), Jewish persecution in Europe increased. Crusader armies on their way to the Holy Land to battle Islam first began killing non-Christians in Europe. They attacked Jewish communities along the Rhine River, killing thousands, including major Jewish scholars. Students of these scholars eventually came to study with Rashi, who opened his own school, which became one of the most famous centers of Jewish religious study in Europe. There Rashi's scholars helped him write down much of the Jewish oral tradition of laws and rituals, thus saving them for future generations. His students and sons-in-law spread his work throughout Europe. Rashi, who died in 1105, was one of the best-known Jewish scholars of his day.

afterlife [life after death], and the oneness of God—that ultimately became a primary set of beliefs of Judaism. (Unlike Christians, who believe that the godhead, or divinity, is made up of three, or a Trinity—God, Christ, and the Holy Spirit—Jews believe that God is one.) They were later adapted to serve as the popular "Yigdal" prayer found in most Jewish prayer books, among other prayers that many Jews recite daily.

Exile

At length, Maimonides and his family had to flee Spain to avoid death at the hands of the Alhomads. In 1160 they settled in Fez, Morocco, where he continued to work on his *Commentary,* often from memory, clarifying complex Talmudic passages without a text. Five years later he and his family were again forced to move after angering the Islamic rulers of Morocco by working with Jews who had been required to convert to Islam. In 1165 the family moved to Palestine, in the Holy Land, where much of the territory was in the hands of the Christian Crusaders who had taken Jerusalem in 1099—an event that marked the beginning of two centuries of hostilities between Christians and Muslims over who should control this place considered sacred by several religions. Maimonides and his family traveled throughout the Holy Land for a little more than a year, finally deciding that the Jewish community residing there was oppressed and living in poverty. They decided to move on once again, this time to the relatively settled regions of Egypt.

In 1166 Maimonides and his family arrived in Fostat (Old Cairo), Egypt. His father died shortly thereafter. Maimonides' younger brother, David, a rabbi who also traded in jewels, supported the family for the next five years, allowing Maimonides to continue his studies and writing. In 1168 he published his *Commentary on the Mishnah,* which first brought attention to him in the Jewish world. This settled existence came to an end in 1171, when David was drowned in a shipwreck, taking the family's fortune down with him. So saddened was Maimonides that he fell ill for a year. After recovering, he realized that he now needed to support his family. He took up the study of medicine and eventually became the physician to the vizier (chief counselor) of the Muslim Egyptian ruler **Saladin** (see entry) and then to Saladin himself. It is reported that during the Third Crusade, King **Richard I, the Lionheart** (see entry), asked Maimonides to become his personal physician, but he refused and stayed in Egypt for the rest of his life.

A Busy Life

Maimonides led a very busy and productive life. Between 1170 and 1180 he wrote his monumental work, *Mishneh Torah,* a complete code of Jewish law. At the same time, his duties to the sultan (a Muslim ruler) were "very heavy," as Maimonides wrote in a letter quoted by Wachman:

> I am obliged to visit him every day, early in the morning; and when he or any of his children, or any of the inmates of his harem [female relatives living in private, isolated housing],

מה אהבתי תורתך כל היום
היא שיחתי

והוא ספר | ספר שני

הלכות ק"ש

הלמותי שש וזהו סדורן | הלכות קריתשמע
הלכות תפלה וברכתכהנים הלכות תפלין ומזוזה
וספר תודה | הלכות ציצית הלכות כרבות
הלכות מילה | הלכות ק"ש | מצות
עשה אחה וזהאו למרות ל"ש ט"ומים ביום | הלכות

Page from the *Mishneh Torah*, the systematic code of Jewish law written by Maimonides in 1180 that applied Jewish law to everyday problems.
© *National Library, Jerusalem, Israel, Lauros/Giraudon/ Bridgeman Art Library.*

are indisposed [ill], I dare not quit Cairo, but must stay during the greater part of the day in the palace. It also frequently happens that one or two of the royal officers falls sick, and I must attend to their healing. Hence, as a rule, I repair [go] to Cairo very early in the day, and even if nothing unusual happens, I do not return to Fostat until the afternoon.

Once home, Maimonides ate a quick meal (the only one of the day) and then faced another heavy load of patients, both Jews and Gentiles (non-Jews). As he described it, "When night falls I am so exhausted that I can scarcely speak." In 1177 Maimonides was made *nagid,* the head of all the Jewish communities in Egypt, a position of great honor that brought no income but many more duties. Despite these commitments, Maimonides was still able to continue his scholarly activities.

His *Mishneh Torah* (the title means "Second Torah") expanded the work begun in the *Commentary.* According to Wachman, it provided "a clear, practical source to which people could turn to answer day-to-day questions of law." Maimonides arranged the code by topic in order to give the average person "reliable, definitive [final] rulings of Jewish law," as Wachman further explains. Maimonides divided his huge work into fourteen books, dealing with Jewish laws by subject, so that readers could quickly and easily find what they were looking for. This collection was intended to function as the only book on Jewish law a person would need to consult.

Upon publication, the *Mishneh Torah* became one of the most important books in Judaism and was studied and consulted by Jews around the world. As Wachman noted, Maimonides' book "was soon acclaimed as the greatest work of Jewish scholarship since the Talmud." However, the book also had its critics among conservative, more traditional rabbis, who felt that the work undermined, or lessened, their authority. One French rabbi even wanted the book banned by the Inquisition, the Roman Catholic Church's tribunal (court), which punished heretics, or those who went against the faith. As a result, there were public burnings of *Mishneh Torah* in France.

Balancing Faith and Reason

Maimonides continued with his busy schedule. In 1190 he wrote the third of his greatest works, the *Moreh Nevuchim,* known in English as *The Guide of the Perplexed,* or confused. With this work the name of Maimonides became well known outside the Jewish world of the Middle East and Spain, for he balanced the work of Greek philosophy with Jewish religion. Written in the form of a very long letter, divided into three parts, to one of his students, the *Guide* mainly attempts to settle differences between the "scientific," or rational, tradition of Aristotle and the biblical approach to the concept and existence of God. Maimonides concludes that reason and faith can both be useful, for there is much that science and reason cannot explain. According to the *Guide,* where reason and philosophical explanations fail to find answers to deep questions, such as the creation and the eternal nature of the world, it is left to faith and revelation, or divine inspiration, to supply meaning. Maimonides also analyzes questions concerning good and evil, the purpose of the world and of life, and the meaning of the Ten Commandments.

Scholars have noted that Maimonides' *Guide* must be read with care, for the language is difficult and can easily be misunderstood. Maimonides himself warned against such misunderstandings in the introduction to the work:

> What I have written in this work was not the suggestion of the moment; it is the result of deep study and great application [hard work]. ... Do not read superficially [lightly], lest you do me an injury and derive [receive] no benefit yourself. You must study thoroughly and read continually.

Despite such difficulties, the influence of the *Guide* "was great in both Jewish and non-Jewish circles," according to Wachman. Translated into all the major European languages, this final work of Maimonides influenced thinkers from the Catholic philosopher and saint Thomas Aquinas (c. 1225–1274) to the English scientist and philosopher Roger Bacon (1214–1292), serving as a basic text for medieval philosophy.

Maimonides lived until 1204, dying in Fostat, where he was mourned for three days. His passing was also noted throughout the Jewish world. He was buried in Palestine, at Tiberias. As a doctor he was known as a compassionate healer. His lasting contribution to that profession was his emphasis on preventive medicine, or early treatment before the onset of illness. His gift to the world of religion and learning remains huge. Wachman has called his last two works "landmarks in the history of Jewish thought." To mark the anniversary of his birth, in 1985 an international conference was held in Paris to celebrate his achievements, concluding that Maimonides was the most influential thinker of the Middle Ages.

For More Information

Books

Arbel, Ilil. *Maimonides: A Spiritual Biography.* New York: Crossroad Publishing, 2001.

Maimonides, Moses. *The Guide of the Perplexed.* Translated by Shlomo Pines. Chicago: University of Chicago Press, 1963.

Muenz, J. *Maimonides (the Ramba'm): The Story of His Life and Genius.* Translated by H. T. Schnittkind. Boston: Winchell-Thomas, 1935.

Web Sites

"Maimonides." *Encyclopedia of the Orient.* http://i-cias.com/cgi-bin/eo-direct.pl?maimonid.htm (accessed on July 21, 2004).

"Maimonides." *Wellsprings Online.* http://www.e-wellsprings.org/Article. asp?Category=8&Article=22 (accessed on July 21, 2004).

"Maimonides: The Greatest Medieval Jewish Thinker, Talmudist and Codifier." *My Jewish Learning.* http://www.myjewishlearning. com/history_community/Medieval/MedThoughtTO/Maimonides.ht m (accessed on July 21, 2004).

"Maimonides/Ramba'm (1135–1204)." *Jewish Virtual Library.* http:// www.us-israel.org/jsource/biography/Maimonides.html (accessed on July 21, 2004).

"The *Mishneh Torah.*" *University of Calgary.* http://www.ucalgary.ca/~elsegal/ TalmudMap/Maimonides.html (accessed on July 21, 2004).

"Oath of Maimonides." *Internet Medieval Sourcebook.* http://www.fordham. edu/halsall/source/rambam-oath.html (accessed on July 21, 2004).

"RaMBaM: Our Most Extraordinary Jewish Scholar." *Gates to Jewish Heritage.* http://www.jewishgates.com/file.asp?File_ID=344 (accessed on July 21, 2004).

"The Ramba'm: Rabbi Moshe ben Maimon (Maimonides) 1135–1204." *Talmud Torah: Basic Jewish Education.* http://members.aol.com/Laz erA/rambam.html (accessed on July 21, 2004).

"Teaching of Moses Maimonides." *New Advent.* http://www.new advent.org/cathen/09540b.htm (accessed on July 21, 2004).

Melisende

1105
Edessa, County of Edessa

c. 1161
Nablus, Kingdom of Jerusalem

Queen of the Kingdom of Jerusalem

Melisende was one of the most powerful women on either the Christian or Muslim side during the Crusades, several religious wars in the Holy Land spanning two centuries. The daughter of the third ruler of the Kingdom of Jerusalem—the Crusader state carved out of Palestine by the Christians after they took the city from the Muslims in 1099—Melisende ultimately became the coruler of Jerusalem, first with her husband, Fulk V of Anjou, from 1131 until his death in 1143 and then with her young son, Baldwin III, from 1143 to 1152. There were rivalries and infighting among the powerful in Jerusalem, including between Melisende and her husband and son, that made these troubled years.

During her reign, the forces of the Muslims made a comeback in the region. Under the leadership of Imad al-Din Zengi (also known simply as Zengi), a Turkish Muslim *atabeg*, or governor, the Muslims captured the fortified city of Edessa in the north and brought on the Second Crusade (1147–49). This Crusade turned out to be a major failure for the Christian forces. Melisende was perhaps a better patron, or sponsor,

> "Melisende seems to have loved power for its own sake. She knew how to make herself obeyed, but she was incapable of turning [her] authority....Her regency [rulership] was marked by military disasters and political errors caused by her inability to rise to a crisis."
>
> —*Zoé Oldenbourg,* The Crusades.

The Kingdom of Jerusalem

The Kingdom of Jerusalem was the name given to a twelfth-century Crusader state in Palestine having the city of Jerusalem as its center of power. When the Christian knights, or noble soldiers, of the First Crusade took Jerusalem from the Muslims in 1099, they knew that they would need to organize themselves in order to hold on to the land. Badly outnumbered by neighboring Muslims of Egyptian, Arabic, and Turkish origin, these Crusaders began to carve out little states and principalities (the territory of a prince) according to the same system that was being used in Europe at this time. The nobles would receive land from the king in exchange for their military service. These nobles, in turn, would have a number of vassals, or knights pledged in service to a lord, who would do the fighting, and they would also have peasants, or workers on the land, who would pay rent in return for protection from the nobles and knights. This system was called feudalism, from the Latin word for "fee."

These transplanted Europeans developed this system in the coastal lands of present-day Israel, Lebanon, Syria, and Turkey, where they set up their states. There was a big difference, however, between feudalism in Europe and in the Middle East. In Europe most of the nobles lived in the countryside, but in Outremer—another name for the Crusader kingdoms meaning "beyond the sea"—the nobles lived mostly in cities, where they built strong castles. The countryside was controlled by Muslims. Thus the economy in the Crusader states was based more on business and trade than on farming.

The Kingdom of Jerusalem was one of several such Crusader states. The first rulers built it up beyond the borders of Jerusalem to include the port cities of Jaffa, Acre, Sidon, and Beirut. Other Crusader states included the County of Edessa, the Principality of Antioch, and the County of Tripoli. Jerusalem, however, was the most powerful of these states and informally governed the others. Melisende was fourth in the line of rulers of the city and kingdom, but even during her lifetime this arrangement was falling apart. Princes in the other states competed with Jerusalem for power; some even made arrangements with the Byzantine emperor to the north in Constantinople. The nobles always had more power in the Holy Land than they had in Europe. The High Court in Jerusalem made sure the new king was elected properly, handed out money to the king, and helped raise armies.

Jerusalem fell to the Muslims in 1187, and though some of the lands nearby were recovered in the Third Crusade (1189–92), it was not until the thirteenth century that western forces once again occupied the city—and that was for just fifteen years. The title of king continued to be handed down, though this was in name only. For a time the kings ruled from other cities in the Middle East and then from the island of Cyprus, but by the end of the thirteenth century the Kingdom of Jerusalem had become a fictitious, or imaginary, realm.

of the arts than she was a ruler, for she ordered that the Church of the Holy Sepulchre, the supposed burial place of Christ in Jerusalem, be rebuilt, and she established a large abbey (institution for nuns) at Bethany, near Jerusalem.

A Child of the Middle East

Melisende was born in Edessa, a county and city located along the northern boundary of the states the Crusades had established in the Middle East at the end of the First Crusade (1095–99), a part of modern-day southern Turkey. Her father, Baldwin of Bourq, was one of the original Crusaders. From 1100 to 1118 he was the ruler of Edessa, a position given to him by his cousin, Baldwin I, who became king of Jerusalem in 1100. Baldwin of Bourq married the Armenian queen Morphia. Melisende was born in 1105, just after her father had been taken prisoner by the Muslim Turks at the Battle of Harran. She would not see her father until 1108, when he was finally ransomed, an agreed-upon amount of money being handed over for his release. When her father's cousin Baldwin I died in 1118, Baldwin of Bourq was chosen to replace him and became Baldwin II, the king of Jerusalem and unofficial leader of all the Crusader states. The family of three daughters then moved to Jerusalem, where Melisende continued her education.

The reign of Baldwin II was not an easy one. Although history records seven different Crusades, there was, in fact, fighting between Muslims and Christians on and off throughout the Middle East from the end of the eleventh to the end of the thirteenth century. In 1119 Baldwin II had to deal with invading Muslim armies by leading Crusader forces in the defense of the Principality of Antioch, another important Crusader state near the Mediterranean Sea, in the far north of Christian lands. The Crusaders were badly defeated at what became known as the Field of Blood, though Baldwin was able to drive these invading Muslim Turks out the following year. Melisende's father was again captured by the Turks in 1123 and held for ransom. He gained his freedom in 1124.

By this time it was clear to Baldwin II that he would have no sons, so he began making preparations to hand over power to his oldest daughter, Melisende, at his death. Usually, sons or male relations took over from the previous ruler, but Baldwin wanted to keep the crown in his family. Baldwin thought that his daughter would need the right husband to help her rule. He chose a European nobleman, Count Fulk V of Anjou, a powerful French region. In 1127 messengers were sent to France to make a deal with Fulk, a widower almost twice Melisende's age, who already had an older son. He was promised that he would be coruler with Melisende when Baldwin died. It took a long time to conclude the deal. When Melisende was officially declared the next queen in 1129, Fulk agreed to the marriage.

Queen of Jerusalem

Melisende and Fulk were married that same year. Soon they had two sons, the oldest being Baldwin, who would become Baldwin III, king of Jerusalem, and a younger son named Amalric, who would become king when his older brother died. As Melisende's father lay dying in 1131, he named Melisende, Fulk, and the infant Baldwin all corulers of Jerusalem. In effect, that meant that Baldwin III's parents were ruling for him until he became old enough to rule on his own. Melisende and Fulk were crowned on September 14, 1131, in the Church of the Holy Sepulchre, which was still being rebuilt by the Crusaders.

Things did not go well between the couple almost from the beginning. Melisende was accused of being the mistress, or lover, of the count of Jaffa, a rival to Fulk, whose name was derived from the port of Jerusalem. Soon the kingdom was split into two camps: those who supported Melisende and those who supported her husband. The count of Jaffa actually rebelled against Fulk, bringing in Egyptian soldiers to fight for him. Fulk put down the rebellion, and the count of Jaffa was forced to give up his property, but Fulk was not the winner. Melisende won the support of enough nobles of the Kingdom of Jerusalem so that Fulk, who wanted to rule on his own, had to share that honor with his wife, permitting her to have a real voice in governing Jerusalem. It was also said that Melisende had hired the deadly Assassins, a group of religious extremists and murderers, and that this so terrified her husband that Fulk never again made any decision without first asking Melisende for her opinion.

Within the image: *le patriarche*, *Fouques conte d'anjou*, *Melisent*

While these Franks, as the Muslims called the Christian invaders, fought amongst themselves, Zengi, a strong Islamic leader, was building up his forces in the northern Iraqi city of Mosul, hoping to unite the Islamic world to fight a *jihad,* or holy war, against these Franks. First he had to challenge other Muslims, such as the Muslim leader Unur of Damascus, Syria, to try to gain power in the Muslim world. In 1139 Fulk actually sent a Crusader force to fight with Unur at Damascus against Zengi, their common enemy. Fulk was successful in this. For the next five years things were peaceful in Jerusalem. Zengi was busy keeping his lands together in Iraq, while the Muslims in Egypt had their own internal battles and rivalries to deal with and left the Crusader states alone.

When Fulk V died in 1143, Melisende became the main ruler, since her son was still an adolescent, or under age. She also placed Manasses of Hierges, a local lord and relative of her husband's, in the powerful role of constable of Jerusalem—in effect, making him another ruler. Baldwin III,

Melisende marrying Fulk V of Anjou, France. The two would become corulers of Jerusalem along with their son, Baldwin III.
© *Bibliotheque Nationale, Paris, France/The Bridgeman Art Library.*

her son, did not like being kept in the background and was eagerly waiting for the moment when he could rule on his own. Rivalry was already growing between the powerful mother and her son. The year 1143 was an important one for the Christians in the Holy Land, for not only did the king of Jerusalem die but also John Comnenus, ruler of the Byzantine Empire, the eastern Roman Empire based in present-day Turkey and Greece.

Zengi, the Muslim leader, took advantage of these deaths and the disorganization in the Kingdom of Jerusalem to invade once again. In 1144 he and his soldiers took Edessa, an action that brought a new wave of Christian Crusaders to the Holy Land in the Second Crusade, which was led by the French king Louis VII and the German king Conrad III. In 1146 Zengi was murdered by one of his own men. His equally powerful son, Nur al-Din, took over his fight to unite Islam. When the new Crusaders arrived in 1147, they attacked Damascus instead of trying to retake Edessa and were badly defeated, further weakening the position of the so-called Latin Kingdoms, or Crusader states in Palestine and Syria.

Mother Against Son

Melisende enjoyed having power too much to want to share it with her son. When the time came for the handover of the crown to Baldwin III in 1145, she ignored the date and continued to rule on her own with the help of Manasses. In addition to her duties as queen, Melisende found the time to oversee the rebuilding of the Church of the Holy Sepulchre, which was completed in 1149. This major symbol for Christians was also the primary site that pilgrims (visitors) to the Holy Land wanted to see. Melisende and her architects gave the church a Romanesque look, a style of architecture with round arches and high ceilings. She also founded an abbey for nuns at Bethany, spent a large part of her personal fortune on a project to beautify the city of Jerusalem, and generally supported the churches of the kingdom.

By 1152 Baldwin III was twenty-two and tired of waiting for his mother to hand over power to him. He complained to the High Court of Jerusalem, a group composed of nobles and church leaders who made legal decisions. Baldwin

asked them to divide the kingdom if his mother refused to give up power. They agreed. Baldwin got the cities of Tyre and Acre, while his mother got Jerusalem and Nablus. The court also decided that Manasses had to give up his power. But Melisende would not be defeated so easily.

Tension grew between mother and son, and soon Baldwin attacked Jerusalem and forced his mother to give up both the city and her power. She moved to Nablus, where she kept a hand in government. The rivalry between mother and son was finally laid to rest, and Melisende supposedly became one of her son's closest advisers until her death in September 1161. Melisende was buried at the simple Church of Saint Mary Josaphat in Jerusalem. Baldwin III died a little over a year later. He, however, was buried in the much more important Church of the Holy Sepulchre.

Although she supported art and architecture during her rule, Melisende proved to be an ineffective leader. During

Monastery on the roof of the Church of the Holy Sepulchre, a church rebuilt by Melisende as a pilgrimage site for Christians visiting Jerusalem. © Dave G. Houser/Corbis.

her time as queen, the Muslims made large gains in recovering land from the Crusaders. The rivalries between husband and wife and between mother and son weakened the kingdom. Jerusalem would not have another female in line to become ruler again until 1186—Sybille, granddaughter of Melisende and wife of Guy of Lusignan. In that case, however, Guy had the role of king and held the real power in the kingdom. The year 1187 marked the beginning of the end of the Kingdom of Jerusalem, when the Islamic leader **Saladin** (see entry) captured Jerusalem. Although the kingdom hung on for another century along a thin strip of land next to the Mediterranean Sea, the end was in sight. Melisende's rule was only one of several reasons for this final loss, but the infighting between competing factions (groups) in Jerusalem was a sign of the loss of Crusader unity among these men and women who had come to fight the infidel (one who is not a Christian), and stayed to build a Christian kingdom in Palestine. In fact, the Christians proved that they were no better at uniting into a single state than the Muslims had been.

For More Information

Books

Jones, David. *Women Warriors: A History.* Washington, DC: Brassey's, 1997.

Mayer, Hans Eberhard. *The Crusades.* 2nd ed. Translated by John Gillingham. New York: Oxford University Press, 1988.

Millan, Betty. *Monstrous Regiment: Women Rulers in Men's Worlds.* Windsor Forest, UK: Kensal Press, 1982.

Oldenbourg, Zoé. *The Crusades.* Translated by Anne Carter. New York: Pantheon, 1966.

Web Sites

"The Great Crusades: A Woman's Role." *The Cultural Crusades.* http://www.umich.edu/~marcons/Crusades/topics/women/women-article.html (accessed on April 21, 2004).

"The Kingdom of Jerusalem." *The ORB: On-line Reference Book for Medieval Studies.* http://the-orb.net/textbooks/crusade/jerusalem.html (accessed on April 24, 2004).

"Kings of Jerusalem." *Medieval Crusades.* http://www.medievalcrusades.com/kingsofjerusalem.htm (accessed on April 16, 2004).

"Melisende Queen of Jerusalem." *Women in World History.* http://www.womeninworldhistory.com/heroine4.html (accessed on March 30, 2004).

Peter the Hermit

c. 1050
Amiens, France

1115
Liège, Belgium

Preacher

Peter the Hermit was a French preacher at the time when Pope **Urban II** (see entry) called for a Crusade, or holy war, against the forces of Islam in Palestine and Jerusalem. The pope demanded that Christians, both rich and poor, go to the Holy Land and end the centuries-long Muslim occupation there. Peter, a poor, ragged preacher living in the French region of Flanders, took the pope's words to heart. He began to preach throughout France and Germany and succeeded in raising a "people's" army of twenty thousand to forty thousand men, women, and children. Most of these people were peasants, or poor workers on the land, who listened to Peter's fine speeches about eternal salvation (forgiveness of sins) and thought it was a way out of their continual poverty and hunger. He also recruited some knights, or real soldiers, for his Crusader army, but most were common people. There were even a number of criminal types, for he attracted such people thanks to his fiery speeches and preaching.

In the spring of 1096, before the main body of Crusader forces, under the leadership of noblemen, had been assembled, Peter and his strange army set off for the Holy

"There was a priest, Peter by name.... In response to his constant admonition [scolding] and call [for a Crusade]...every class of the Christian profession, nay, also women and those influenced by the spirit of penance [seeking forgiveness of sins]—all joyfully entered upon this expedition."

—*Albert of Aix, quoted in* The First Crusade: The Accounts of Eye-witnesses and Participants.

Land. Thousands died on Peter's march across Europe and into Asia Minor due to lack of food, fights with locals on their route, and the normal illnesses and accidents that accompanied long journeys during this time period. There, not far from Constantinople, his troops were quickly cut down by the Seljuk Turks, fierce fighters who had converted to the faith of Islam. Peter later marched with the official armies of the Crusade once they had arrived, taking part in the sieges (attacks) and victories at Antioch in 1098 and Jerusalem in 1099. He returned to France not long after, founding a monastery (religious institution) where he died in 1115. His speeches in Europe from 1095 to 1096 helped spread the message and drum up enthusiasm for the First Crusade (1095– 99). Though his role was not as important in creating the Crusader movement as tradition and legend would have it, he still inspired thousands to join in and devote their lives and property to the cause.

A Man of Mystery

Peter the Hermit was born around 1050 in Amiens, France. Little is known about his early life. Some historians think he may have been the son of a Norman knight and that he was perhaps a soldier before turning to religion. There is no record of when or how he started preaching, or even if he was actually a confirmed (church-appointed) priest. It is also not known how he came by the name "hermit," for religious hermits were those who remained apart from the world, living alone and devoting their lives to religion. However, Peter most definitely went out into the world. By the early 1090s he already had thousands of followers in France. He traveled around the countryside in the area of Île-de-France, near Paris, and also in Normandy, Champagne, and Picardy, speaking to crowds of people at open-air meetings and relying on gifts from the faithful to see him through financially.

Peter was a small, thin man, who went about barefoot and always dressed in a worn-out robe. He rode a donkey and preached the benefits of charity, or giving to the poor, as well as repentance, or asking forgiveness for sins. He was one of many such grassroots preachers who roamed the countryside of Europe at the time, attracting huge crowds eager to hear him speak. He was such a good speaker that his loyal followers found him almost holy; members of the audience considered themselves lucky if they were able to snatch even a hair off Peter's poor little donkey as a keepsake, or remembrance. The German historian Hans Eberhard Mayer, writing in *The Crusades,* noted that Peter "did not look very attractive, usually being caked [covered] in mud and dirt, as he rode about the countryside on his donkey. Yet he was a man of electrifying eloquence [fine speaking ability] who radiated [gave off] an unusual power." So strong a speaker was Peter that he also attracted the rich and noble to his ranks. Many of these noblemen converted to Christianity as a result of his preaching and handed over all their worldly possessions to Peter and his charities.

Legend has it that Peter traveled to the Holy Land in 1093 as a pilgrim (religious traveler) anxious to visit the places associated with Jesus Christ. However, since about 1070 Jerusalem had been occupied by the Turks. These people from the grasslands of Asia and Persia were fresh converts to Islam and not as tolerant about letting all religions visit the holy city as the Arab Muslims had been when they held the city. A holy shrine to three faiths—Judaism, Christianity, and Islam—Jerusalem was as much a symbol of faith as a living city. Supposedly, Peter had been prevented from visiting the holy places in Jerusalem.

Returning to France, he had a vision of God, who told him that Christians could drive the infidels, or non-Christians, out of the Holy Land and Jerusalem if only they had the courage to try. According to legend, this message took the form of a letter that Peter himself delivered to Pope Urban II in Rome. Thus, Peter was the person who set the First Crusade in motion. In 1095 the pope was being guided by Peter's word when, speaking at the Council of Clermont in southern France, he called for a holy war against the Turks and Islam in the Holy Land. This legend about Peter and the origin of the Crusades was believed for hundreds of years in Europe.

In reality, it is not known if Peter visited Palestine or Jerusalem before 1095; most likely he did not. Instead, he was busy preaching in France, building up a community of faithful followers as well as enough wealth to support several charities. Certainly he never met the pope in person. After announcing the holy war at the Council of Clermont, Urban II went on to speak and preach on the same subject in other places in France. When Peter heard the call, he felt that he needed to join the cause—probably based on good intentions rather than simply to make himself more popular with the people. As the historian Zoé Oldenbourg has commented in *The Crusades:* "Adored by the people and respected by the great, Peter the Hermit was already, in 1095, a leader of crowds." She goes on to say that we do not know whether Peter used to his advantage the idea of a holy war as a way to make himself well liked among the people, but he did argue with the pope about claiming credit for the Crusade. In other words, the Crusades presented both a duty and an opportunity for Peter.

The People's Crusade

While in the company of loyal followers, Peter traveled throughout France, preaching at Berry, in Champagne, and in Lorraine. He collected money from noblemen to make the trip to the Holy Land and assembled a growing band of very unlikely soldiers to serve God. He and his crowd even received money from the Jews of Europe, a group at odds with Christian beliefs that would later be persecuted by Crusaders. Peter was also rumored to have carried with him a letter from the chief rabbi, or religious and scholarly leader, of the French city of Rouen to the Jews of Mainz, Germany, which asked for them to be charitable to him and his followers when he passed through their territory. In April 1096 Peter and his army of fifteen thousand or twenty thousand moved on to Germany to gather more faithful recruits. Even though the Germans could not understand him when he spoke, they still joined in his popular People's, or Peasants', Crusade, as it came to be called.

Most of these followers had no weapons, were poorly dressed, and had no money for a journey of the sort Peter was planning. Many of them joined not out of religious faith but in the hope of a better life. The years 1094 and 1095 had been bad ones throughout the land, with drought, or lack of rain, resulting in ruined crops. Peasants were ready, if not desperate, for a change. Peter's words, which promised salvation, or deliverance, to the faithful, fell on their ears like water on dry lips. Among the faithful was a knight who would help organize this mass of people.

Walter Sans-Avoir, or Walter the Penniless, gave some sense of military order to the mob, but there were not enough such actual knights or soldiers in Peter's ranks. Leaving Germany around May 1096, Peter and his followers were well in advance of the main Crusader armies that were still being assembled under the watchful eye of Urban II. In fact, when Urban II demanded that rich and poor alike answer his call, such an odd assortment of people as Peter had gathered was not what he had in mind. Urban had meant rich and poor knights, not Peter's rabble, or disorderly crowd. But by the time Peter and his "army" left Germany and headed for the Holy Land, they numbered between twenty thousand and forty thousand strong and had collected a considerable amount of money for food along the way.

This money soon ran out, however, for food was not always to be found along the route, and if there were not much of it, then food prices would go up. Walter's smaller group had gone first, and Peter and his large troop followed along the same route. Thus, by the time the second group passed through a region, the amount of available food was already low. This caused friction, or hostility, between the Crusaders and the local people. In Hungary

The Holy Cross

When Peter and his ragtag band of amateur soldiers set off for the Holy Land, they must have made an amazing impression on people along the route. With Peter at the front on his donkey, the knights coming behind on horseback, and the swarms of poor people following on foot, their parade stretched across the horizon. They carried banners with the Holy Cross emblazoned (stitched) on them, and on their shoulders they all wore a patch of white in the shape of a cross.

When the professional armies of nobles and knights followed later, they wore a cross of blood-red cloth on the front of their tunics, or knee-length shirts. Those that came back safely wore the same cross on the backs of their tunics. The Latin word for cross is *crux,* and soon those who went on the holy war were called "Crusaders." The Latin word for "cross" thus gave the name "Crusades" to this two-hundred-year-long battle between Christians and Muslims.

battles broke out between the two, with more than four thousand Hungarians reported as having been killed by the Crusaders. While crossing Bulgaria, further conflict broke out. When a local governor attacked the Crusaders after they set fire to his water mills, thousands of Crusaders were killed. Thousands more died of starvation and accidents along the way. It took Peter and his people four months to make the journey, but finally, in August 1096, they reached Constantinople, the capital of the Byzantine Empire, or the eastern Roman Empire, and the seat of Eastern Orthodox Christianity, as opposed to Rome, which was the center of the Roman Catholic Church.

The remains of Peter the Hermit's Crusaders after the massacre at Nicaea during the People's Crusade.

In Constantinople they were greeted by the Byzantine emperor **Alexius I** (see entry), who was less than pleased with this crowd of simple laborers and women. He had asked the pope for military aid in resisting the invasions of Seljuk Turks, who were threatening his eastern borders. Now he was stuck with thousands of poor people whom he had to feed. The crowd, eager to enter the battle and fight the infidel, was soon causing the Byzantines as much trouble as they had the

Hungarians and Bulgarians. Alexius I agreed to ferry this large force across the Bosporus Strait, the narrow body of water separating Greece from Asia Minor, where they set up camp at Civetot. Alexius I advised Peter to wait for the better-trained knights and Crusaders, who were on their way to Constantinople, before attacking the Turks, but they did not wait.

In September a band of six thousand Crusaders captured an abandoned castle, Xerigordon, and planned to use it as a base for further operations against the Turks. But soon they were surrounded by the Turks, who controlled the water supply for the castle. After a short siege, the Crusaders were killed. Before word of the disaster got back to the main camp at Civetot, Peter had returned to Constantinople to ask Alexius I for help. He made Walter the Penniless and those he had left in charge promise to remain where they were, but when they heard of the slaughter at Xerigordon, twenty thousand Crusaders set out for the Seljuk city of Nicaea to get even with the Muslims. On October 21, 1096, they walked into a trap set by the Turks, and all but a small band of Crusaders were massacred. Although this put an end to the People's Crusade, Peter nevertheless followed the other Crusader armies to the siege at Antioch, where, it seems, he deserted at one point. From there he went on to Jerusalem, where, in 1099, he preached at the Mount of Olives to inspire the men before they made their final attempt to capture that city. In 1100 he returned to Europe and founded the monastery of Neufmoustier in Liège, Belgium, where he died fifteen years later.

Peter the Hermit is the embodiment, or strong symbol, of the power of the spoken word. He, even more than Urban II, delivered the most famous propaganda (promotional information) for the Crusades. His preaching throughout France and Germany in 1095 and 1096 took the Crusader movement out of the hands of the nobles and placed it in those of the common people of Europe. The legend that formed around him sparked the imagination of the poor people of Europe for generations following the Crusades. He became a popular folk hero, the stuff of myth and legend. In reality, he was a better speaker than a leader. His poor leadership cost the lives of thousands of his followers and set the stage for bad relations between the rulers of the Byzantine Empire and future Crusader armies.

For More Information

Books

Comnena, Anna. *The Alexiad of Anna Comnena*. Translated by E. R. A. Sewter. Baltimore, MD: Penguin, 1969.

Goodsell, Daniel Ayres. *Peter the Hermit: A Story of Enthusiasm*. New York: Eaton and Mains, 1906.

Krey, August C., ed. *The First Crusade: The Accounts of Eye-witnesses and Participants*. Princeton, NJ: Princeton University Press, 1921.

Mayer, Hans Eberhard. *The Crusades*. 2nd ed. Translated by John Gillingham. New York: Oxford University Press, 1988.

Oldenbourg, Zoé. *The Crusades*. Translated by Anne Carter. New York: Pantheon, 1966.

Web Sites

"Ill-Fated Crusade of the Poor People." *About's Medieval History and the Renaissance*. http://historymedren.about.com/library/prm/bl1poorpeople.htm (accessed on July 21, 2004).

"People's Crusade." *The Crusades Bookstore*. http://www.brighton73.freeserve.co.uk/firstcrusade/Overview/Overview.htm (accessed on July 21, 2004).

"Peter the Hermit." *New Advent*. http://www.newadvent.org/cathen/11775b.htm (accessed on July 21, 2004).

"Peter the Hermit and the Popular Crusade: Collected Accounts." *Internet Medieval Sourcebook*. http://www.fordham.edu/halsall/source/peterhermit.html (accessed on July 21, 2004).

Richard I, the Lionheart

September 8, 1157
Oxford, England

April 6, 1199
Chaluz, Aquitaine, France

King of England

Richard I was king of England for a decade at the end of the twelfth century, but in that time this "absent" king spent only six months in the country he ruled. Although he was born in England, he was raised at his mother's court in the French province of Aquitaine, speaking French and practicing the noble art of poetry. But this third son of King Henry II of England (1133–1189) also practiced the manly arts of battle to such an extent that he was dubbed *Coeur de Lion,* or the "Lionheart," for his bravery and mercilessness. More famous in literature than in life, Richard I was one of those leaders who anger allies and enemy alike. Returning from the Holy Land, he was imprisoned by the Holy Roman Emperor, who headed the Christian kingdoms of Europe; the ransom paid for Richard's release nearly ruined England financially. He spent the final years of his life in France, where he battled his boyhood friend, the French king Phillip II (1165–1223). Richard's early death in 1199 ended what has been called one of the worst reigns (periods of rule) in English history in terms of the hardships suffered by his subjects.

"Since the beginning of the world we have never heard of such a knight, so brave and so experienced in arms. In every deed at arms he is without rival, first to advance, last to retreat.... His deeds are not human."

—*A Muslim leader, quoted in* Warriors of God: Richard the Lionheart and Saladin in the Third Crusade.

Richard I, the Lionheart.
© *Bettmann/Corbis.*

Born to Intrigue

Richard was the third son born to Henry II of England and **Eleanor of Aquitaine** (1122–1204; see entry). The relationship between his strong-willed parents was a stormy one. Eleanor, who was previously married to Louis VII, the king of France, preferred her cultured court at Aquitaine, in the center of France, to England. Richard was raised in Aquitaine, the favorite of his mother, as she was for him. As was the custom of the day, during his youth he wrote verses in French and in the local Provençal dialect. He also learned the arts of war from William Marshall, his tutor for jousting (combat on horseback). As Richard reached adolescence, it was clear he would be a handsome man: he was tall and powerfully built, which was exactly how a knight (noble military leader) and future king should look. Richard's older brother Henry (following the death of the first son, William) was meant to inherit his father's kingdom, but Richard had powerful ambitions in this area.

At age eleven Richard became duke of Aquitaine and left behind childish things, such as composing and reciting poetry. Soon he began plotting to gain more land and power, sometimes siding with his mother against his father or with his father against his brothers. He badly wanted to gain control of more than just the French possessions of the Plantagenet line of kings, which was also called the Angevin line after the French landholdings in Anjou. This English dynasty, or ruling family, began with Henry II in 1154 and would last until the beginning of the Stuart line of kings and queens in 1603. Besides being king of England, Henry II was also duke of the French holdings of Normandy, Brittany, Anjou, and Touraine; through Eleanor he also held title to the duchy of Aquitaine. He was thus a powerful figure both in England and in France. If the Plantagenets fought among themselves, they were also engaged in an ongoing rivalry, if not outright war, with the Capets, another French dynasty (987–1328).

At least on paper King Henry II and his holdings in France were under the control of the king of France. During Richard's lifetime the main representative of that line was Philip Augustus, son of Louis VII, the former husband of Richard's mother. Philip, who was eight years younger than Richard, spent much time at the court of Aquitaine in

Poitiers, where Henry II attempted to win through treaties what he could not win by war. Many historians believe that Richard and Philip developed a homosexual, or same gender, love for each other in adolescence and early adulthood. To complicate matters, Philip's half-sister, Alais, had been engaged to Richard from an early age. However, Richard's father, Henry II, who always had an eye for pretty women, took the girl for his own mistress, or lover. While still a youth of fourteen, Philip was declared king of France in 1179 and took the name Philip II.

Aquitaine, which was Richard's inheritance, was also a feuding (fighting) region. Its nobles were always rebelling against the rulers in Poitiers. By 1169 Henry II had managed to get these dukes and counts in line, but four years later family peace was threatened by a rebellion of sons against their father. Richard joined his older brother Henry, already proclaimed the next king, and younger brother Geoffrey, duke of Brittany, in open rebellion against Henry II. Their mother, Eleanor, angry at her husband for his continual cheating with other women, encouraged her sons. Henry II invaded Aquitaine and quickly put this rebellion down, but Richard was the last to give in. The sons were forced to pledge loyalty to their father; Richard lost the title of duke of Aquitaine and had to take orders directly from his father.

A Soldier-King in the Making

Such orders, however, were to Richard's liking. During the next five years he was constantly battling with the nobles of Aquitaine and nearby Gascony, who refused to bow to the power of King Henry II. It was during these years that Richard gained the reputation of a fierce and relentless fighter, attacking and seizing castles throughout the Plantagenet lands in France. His resourcefulness and bravery were demonstrated time and again. For example, he gained fame throughout Europe in 1179 for taking the fortress of Taillebourg, on the Charente River, which was believed to be impregnable, or too strong to conquer. Richard staged a scorched-earth campaign, burning crops and poisoning wells, which won him this prize.

Family problems broke out again when King Henry II demanded that Richard pay homage, or pledge his loyalty, to his older brother Henry, who was destined to be the future king of England. Richard stubbornly refused to do so, so in 1183 this brother invaded Aquitaine. He was joined in this campaign by Geoffrey, his other brother. Now even Henry II grew alarmed. This war between brothers threatened the Plantagenet line, for it quickly spun out of control, with Richard taking the offensive and slaughtering some of the invaders. The king rode to Aquitaine to try to stop the fighting. However, a truce was put in place only when Henry the Younger, Richard's brother, died of an illness in June 1183. Suddenly, nothing stood in Richard's way to becoming king himself—or so it seemed.

Now that Richard was the new heir, Henry II demanded that he give Aquitaine to his youngest brother, John, who had no duchies. John's nickname "Lackland" points to his landless condition. Richard would not hear of it, for Aquitaine was his homeland. A new round of hostilities broke out between father and son, in part spurred on by King Philip II, Richard's old friend and rival. With the accidental death of Geoffrey in 1186 in a jousting tournament, Richard and John became the only possible heirs to the crown. Philip II, always eager to play one Plantagenet against another, formed an alliance with Richard against Henry II, with both setting out to take the throne away from the father by force. This they accomplished by surrounding the king in his birthplace of Le Mans and burning down the town. Henry II had to flee on horseback from his own son. Deserted by most of his followers, on July 6, 1189, the aged and ill king died, with Richard at his deathbed. Then, on September 3, 1189, Richard traveled to England—one of his few brief visits to that country—to be crowned king of England. Taking the title Richard I, he set out on the new mission of saving the Christian kingdom in the Holy Land.

The Third Crusade

Word had already reached Europe of the Muslim victories under the leadership of **Saladin** (see entry), specifically his taking of the holy city of Jerusalem in 1187 from Christian Crusaders, who had held it for almost a century. The Crusaders began their struggles against the Muslims, believers in the faith of Islam, at the end of the eleventh century, in an ef-

Hic coronatus quasi tempestas ueniens federicus textus cum equitibus et potestate magna terrestri pariter eg nauali cum effusione sparsi sanguinis undicuabit.

Impio grandis aquilla nigra pennas ocius expergiscere tunde alas et rostrum im = pinge tortuosius colluber mento sufig tibi ex latere congregetur. et quasi plurimu conuentum preculdubio fortunaberis. nec obliuiscaris filios spurificos et collactes prh oleo litere. Indisluo cum alis pleteris, sed dscretis no totaliter alterabis, ceteri uiewere praesius in critico.

De angelico pastore et eius bonitate et uirtute et opter sanctis qui apparebit simus thulacoib suf dictis in sua prosperitate. et erexibus uirtuosis.

Viso et finotato p quos et qualif roana eccta plats et clerus thulari et couallesci delsri dunersimalensig ad tpra supdca federica sine tpra thulabomus duraf debeor usig ad anos dni 1974. Ouibg thady apparebit noun papa et nonus impator. Restat inde

An illumination of a Third Crusade expedition. Richard I fought in the Third Crusade, defeating the Muslim leader Saladin but never completely capturing the Holy Land. © *Archivo Iconografico, S.A./Corbis.*

fort to win back the Holy Land for Christianity. This Crusade, or holy war, would last until the end of the thirteenth century. By Richard's time there had already been two Crusades. With the First Crusade (1095–99) the Christian armies had established kingdoms in the Middle East. With the Second Crusade (1147–49) their strength was challenged by new Muslim leaders, among them Nur al-Din (1118–74). Now the pope, leader of the Roman Catholic Church in Rome, called for a

The Crusade Begins at Home

When Richard I was crowned king of England in 1189, the event seemed to inspire an outbreak of anti-Jewish feeling throughout England. Houses were burned down in the Jewish quarter of London. During one incident in 1190, five hundred Jews in the English city of York killed themselves rather than have an angry mob massacre them. Jews had long been persecuted in Europe as the enemies of Christianity. It was said that they had handed Christ over to the Romans to be crucified, or nailed to the cross, and were thus the targets of hatred for centuries. It was as if the local population in England and Europe felt that they should begin to kill the "infidels" (non-Christians) at home before they set off for the Holy Land to murder Muslims.

The Third Crusade, led by Richard I, was not the only one to inspire such terrible events. With the First Crusade (1095–99) the killings had already begun. One of many unofficial leaders of a Crusader army, Count Emich of Leiningen was especially infamous, or notorious, for his cruelty toward Jews that his army encountered along the route to the Crusades. This German set his band of mercenaries, or paid soldiers, loose on the Jewish populations in towns throughout Germany, including Spier, Worms, and Mainz, taking prisoners and demanding ransom, or payment to set them free. Even when the money was paid, Emich killed his helpless victims anyway. Another German Crusader named Volkmar did the same thing to the Jewish community in Prague while on his way to the Holy Land; however, when he tried the same deed in Hungary, he and his band were killed by the Hungarian army, one of the few countries in Europe to protect its Jewish population. Emich, too, was defeated by the Hungarians and never reached the Holy Land.

These Jewish massacres were an awful foreshadowing, or warning, of what could be done in the name of Christianity or any strong belief system. While these soldiers claimed they were only fighting the enemies of God in Europe, they were actually motivated by a shameful reason: greed. They were after the money and wealth they could steal from the Jews along the route to help pay for their travels to the Holy Land.

new Crusade to free the holy city of Jerusalem from Saladin, the latest Muslim warrior, and his armies. Even before becoming king, Richard had "taken the cross," or promised to join this new Crusade. Thus, his first act after becoming king of England was to raise enough money to outfit a Crusader army. He sold all his possessions in England, from church lands to sheriffs' positions; legend has it that Richard said he would even sell London if he could find a buyer. By the summer of 1190 he was ready to set sail for Palestine, leaving England to be ruled by his chancellor, William Longchamp. His brother John did not join the Crusade; instead, he stayed in England and immediately began to stir up factions (smaller groups) against Richard.

Richard sailed with the French king, who was also taking an army to fight the Muslims. A third army, under the German emperor Frederick Barbarossa (1123–1190), traveled by land to the Middle East. Richard, however, was not content to journey peacefully to the Crusades. He managed to fight battles and create new enemies for himself along the way. Arriving in Sicily, in the far south of Italy, he became involved in the struggle for succession to determine who would become the next king. Richard ultimately backed a man named Tancred, who had seized control after the death of the previous king. Tancred had imprisoned Richard's sister, Joan, widow of the former king, and was ruling in the place of Constance, the rightful heir to the throne and the wife of Henry VI, the man who would shortly become Holy Roman Emperor.

Although this emperor was really a ruler in name only, officially he was the head of a loose collection of kingdoms making up the Holy Roman Empire (962–1806), in present-day eastern France, Germany, Austria, and Italy. Nevertheless, it was not a good idea to anger him, as Richard would later learn. Charging ahead into this dangerous and delicate situation, Richard sacked and burned the city of Messina, won the release of his sister, and stayed on until March 1191. He then made another stopover on the island of Cyprus, where he again fought over and captured the Christian city of Limassol, looting and killing all who opposed him. In Cyprus he married Berengaria of Navarre, the woman his mother had handpicked for him. This wedding angered his Crusader partner, Philip II, because Alais, the French king's own half-sister, had long been pledged to Richard, even though she had been the mistress (lover) of Henry II.

Richard finally reached the Holy Land in June 1191, in time to aid in the siege of Acre, a Saracen stronghold. (The Saracens were a nomadic Muslim people who came from a region between Syria and Arabia and whose name was equated by the Crusaders with all Muslim or Arab forces.) Despite being sick with fever, Richard and the Crusaders finally captured the city on July 12, 1191. This victory occurred after a two-year siege, and though the Crusaders came to respect the defending Muslims, this did not prevent them from slaughtering most of the Muslims—under Richard's orders—once they had been disarmed and were defenseless. During the battle for Acre, Richard managed to anger yet another ally, Austrian duke Leopold V, who was placed in charge of the German Crusaders following the death of Frederick Barbarossa. At one point in the fighting Richard threw Leopold's standard, or flag with his battle colors, into the mud, not wanting it to stand alongside his and Philip's.

Soon Richard and Philip also had a disagreement, and the French king set sail for his homeland. Richard was now solely in charge of the Crusader army. Despite being badly outnumbered, he defeated the Muslims under Saladin at the Battle of Arsuf. These two military leaders continued to fight each other for the next few months, with talks of a truce repeatedly called off because of Richard's unreasonable demands. At one point Richard even offered to give his widowed sister to Saladin's brother in marriage if the man converted to Christianity. This offer, like his demands for total control of the Holy Land, was rejected by the Muslim leader. A final victory at Jaffa was not enough to win Richard his most desired prize—Jerusalem. Badly outnumbered, he knew that he would not be able to hold the city even if he were able to capture it. Also, word had reached him of trouble at home: His brother John and King Philip II of France were conspiring against him to rob him of his crown. In July 1192 he set sail for England, determined to hold on to his kingdom.

The Final Years

Fearful of the enemies he had made during the Third Crusade, Richard traveled secretly, in the company of pirates. When his ship was wrecked, he made his way by land, still disguised because of his earlier insult to Leopold of Austria. In the city of Vienna, Austria, Richard was recognized and thrown into a cell in Leopold's castle at Dürnstein on the Danube. From there he was handed over to Henry VI, the Holy Roman Emperor, who also had a grudge against him. Henry kept Richard as a hostage, and for the equivalent of roughly one hundred billion dollars in the currency of modern times, he agreed to set Richard free.

Meanwhile, John continued his scheming to become king. However, his mother, Eleanor of Aquitaine, now entered this battle and managed to gather supporters for Richard. The English finally raised a first installment on his ransom, and in March 1194 Richard reached England, put down the revolt, and was crowned king of England for the second time. He remained in the country for just two months, long enough to raise more funds to help him regain territory lost in France along the border of Normandy. Leaving in place Hubert Walter as governor, Richard returned to Aquitaine, where he fought for the next five years. Although the ransom paid for Richard all but ruined England economically, he demanded more funds to build a series of castles to defend his far-flung lands in England and France, the largest being the fortifications at Château Gaillard, on the river Seine, which cost almost two years' income of the British Crown. While other military leaders would end hostilities from harvest time to Christmas every year, for Richard it was always war all the time. His victories against Philip II of France kept the barons (men who had earned titles and land through service to a lord) in line and the money coming in to fuel his war machine.

In the end, however, it was not fighting his longtime rival Philip II that ended Richard's career, but rather a petty (silly) argument over discovered treasure. Philip and Richard agreed to a five-year truce in 1198, but Richard was stirred back into battle when the viscount (a rank of nobleman) of Limoges, France, refused to turn over to the king a treasure that had been discovered by a peasant while plowing his field. When Richard surrounded the castle of the viscount at Chaluz, he forgot to wear his armor and was shot in the shoulder by a crossbow. The surgery to remove the metal tip left his shoulder badly torn, and deadly gangrene (a blood infection) set in. After making his younger brother John the new king, Richard II died on April 6, 1199, and was buried in the abbey (home for nuns) church of Fontevrault, where his parents were also laid to rest.

Richard had so weakened the English treasury, or royal bank, that when John was king (1199–1216) it was impossible for him to retain the lands in France that the English had long held. Despite his reckless act of pushing the monarchy to the edge of financial disaster with his war economy, Richard was made famous by the balladeers and troubadours, or roving singers and poets, of the day. His fame became the stuff of legend in stories by the Scottish novelist Sir Walter Scott (1771–1832) and tales about the good-hearted bandit Robin Hood. Richard's claim to fame is a complex one: He was an outstanding soldier and military leader, but he was also capable of great cruelty. In many ways he was politically intelligent, but he was also ignorant of the most basic skills of diplomacy, or international relations. His overblown sense of himself made foes of friends, but his actual enemies, such as Saladin and the Muslims, respected his energy and battle skill.

Richard was one of the most famous of medieval kings because of his warlike nature, yet his accomplishments were not as great as those writing about him after his death would have us believe. As James Reston Jr. has noted, Richard I of England

> is one of the most romantic figures of all of English history. In lore that has been embellished [made larger than life] over the centuries and read to schoolboys at bedtime, Richard has become the very epitome [prime example] of chivalry [honorable behavior], the knight fighting bravely for his kingdom, his church, and his lady with axe, shield, and horse. ... Richard is remembered for his bravado [boldness] and cunning—and his extravagance [wastefulness]. He is not remembered for his compassion [kindness and caring], his tact, or his restraint.

For More Information

Books

Brundage, James A. *Richard Lion Heart.* New York: Scribner, 1974.

Gillingham, John. *Richard I.* New Haven, CT: Yale University Press, 2002.

Hallam, Elizabeth, ed. *The Plantagenet Chronicles.* London: Weidenfeld & Nicolson, 1986.

Regan, Geoffrey. *Lionhearts: Saladin, Richard I, and the Era of the Third Crusade.* New York: Walker, 1998.

Reston, James Jr. *Warriors of God: Richard the Lionheart and Saladin in the Third Crusade.* New York: Doubleday, 2001.

Turner, Ralph V., and Richard R. Heiser. *The Reign of Richard Lionheart: Ruler of the Angevin Empire, 1189–99.* London: Longman, 2000.

Web Sites

"Kings and Queens of England to 1603: The Angevins: Richard I Coeur de Lion ('The Lionheart') (r. 1189–1199)." *The Official Web Site of the British Monarchy.* http://www.royal.gov.uk/output/page63.asp (accessed on July 21, 2004).

"Richard I, King of England." *New Advent.* http://www.newadvent.org/cathen/13041b.htm (accessed on July 21, 2004).

Saladin

1137
Tikrit, Iraq

March 4, 1193
Damascus, Syria

Muslim warrior and leader

The most famous of all heroes of the Islamic faith, Saladin (pronounced sa-la-DEEN) attempted to unite the Islamic world to fight the Christian Crusaders who had taken over the Holy Land of Palestine. The two centuries of conflict between East and West, Islam and Christianity, began in 1095 with the First Crusade, when the Christians tried to recapture the holy city of Jerusalem from the Muslims. This was accomplished in 1099, leading to two centuries of intermittent (on and off) warfare between the European Christians and the mainly Arab followers of the prophet Muhammad (c. 570–632 C.E.), founder of the religion of Islam. Having been named sultan (ruler of a Muslim state) of Egypt, Yemen, Syria, and Palestine, and having established the Ayyub dynasty (1174–1258), in 1187 Saladin assembled an army of Muslim fighters to recapture Jerusalem. This victory angered the Europeans and brought on the Third Crusade (1189–92), led by the English king **Richard I, the Lionheart** (see entry), among others. Saladin was able to bring this Crusader army to a standstill, demonstrating not only great courage but also fairness and mercy to his enemies. He is one of the few warriors

Sultan Saladin.
© *Bettmann/Corbis.*

Nur al-Din

Nur al-Din (1118–1174), together with his father Zengi, proved to be a powerful model for Saladin in his bid to unite the Islamic world and retake lost lands from the Crusaders. Zengi, the *atabeg,* or Turkish Muslim governor and military leader of Syria, was one of the first Islamic rulers to fight fire with fire during the time of the Crusades. That is, the Christian knights had journeyed to Palestine and the rest of the territories of Syria to fight a holy war against Islam. Two could play at that game, Zengi thought, for the Islamic concept of jihad, or holy war, also provides for fighting against "infidels," or nonbelievers—that is, those who doubt the word of the prophet Muhammad and do not accept the Islamic faith. Interestingly, following the First Crusade (1095–99)—which resulted in the slaughter of thousands of Muslims when Jerusalem fell to the Crusaders in 1099—Muslims followed a policy of "live and let live." With Zengi this policy changed. He had a dream of uniting all of Islam in a holy war. When he and his troops attacked and captured the fortified Crusader city of Edessa in 1144, it made him one of the leaders of a renewed Islamic effort to get rid of the Franks, as the Muslims called the Christian Crusaders. This action also led to the Second Crusade (1147–49).

of the period to be equally respected by both sides, immortalized by Islamic and European writers alike.

Saladin's Kurdish Origins

Born Salah al-Din Yusuf ibn Ayyub (literally "Righteousness of the Faith, Joseph, son of Ayyub or Job"), he became known by the westernized name Saladin. His father and other ancestors were of Kurdish origin, coming from Armenia to the north and living in Tikrit, a city in Mesopotamia (present-day Iraq), at the time of his birth in 1137. Although his was an eminent, or well-respected, family, Saladin's people were not of noble blood. His father, Najm al-Din, was commander of the fortress of Tikrit when his son was born. Shortly after Saladin's birth, Najm al-Din joined the service of the powerful lord Zengi (ruled 1127–46), who governed the city of Mosul in northern Iraq. Both Saladin's father and his uncle, Shirkuh, rose to powerful positions under this ruler and his son, Nur al-Din

When Zengi was murdered in 1146, his son, Nur al-Din, took power. Born in Damascus, Syria, Nur al-Din was an unusual leader for his time. Like a modern ruler, he used public relations to spread his fame, assembling at his court poets and historians who would write of his adventures. He took the idea of a holy war further than his father, hoping one day to retake Jerusalem and also to bring Egypt under his control. During the Second Crusade he captured important cities, such as Damascus and Antioch (in present-day Turkey), from other Muslim leaders and was able to defend them against the Crusaders. He also managed to bring lands in Anatolia (the peninsula of Asia Minor in Turkey) under his control and create a new power base in Egypt.

It was there that the youth Saladin, who was then serving as lieutenant to Nur al-Din's vizier (an executive officer), came into his own. Although Saladin and Nur al-Din eventually became rivals for power in the Muslim world, they both had the same goal of uniting Islam and defeating the Crusaders. Nur al-Din did not live to see the successful completion of his plan to retake Jerusalem from the Christians. That honor was Saladin's. Nur al-Din is remembered in Islamic history as a wise and just ruler whose vision was an inspiration to Saladin and others who followed.

(1118–74), who were attempting to unite the Islamic world. Saladin grew up partly in Baalbek, in the Bekaa Valley of Syria, and later in the ancient city of Damascus, where his father commanded Zengi's militia.

This powerful ruler was partly successful in his efforts to unite Islam. In 1144 Zengi's forces captured the Crusader province of Edessa in northern Mesopotamia, an event that brought more Europeans to fight in the Second Crusade (1147–49). Although Zengi did not live to see their arrival—he died in 1146—the Crusader armies were defeated in 1148 outside the walls of Damascus. This event must have made a powerful impression on the young Saladin. It is not known whether he and his family were still living in Damascus, but the very fact that the mighty Crusaders were defeated by well-trained Muslim forces left a lasting influence on his later career. Little is known of Saladin's early years other than the fact that he was known as a bookish boy who liked to study religion and law. He also had a wild side, playing polo and drinking wine; because of his strong religious beliefs, he later gave up wine.

By the time he was fourteen, Saladin was sent to serve under his uncle, Shirkuh, in Aleppo, a city near the Mediterranean Sea. Shirkuh was by this time a military commander for Nur al-Din, who had taken over power from his father. At just sixteen years of age, Saladin was given a grant, or parcel, of land for his service. He also married the first of several wives, a practice permitted by Muslim law. (He would eventually father a total of seventeen children by his various wives.) From his father, Saladin inherited a gift for diplomacy, or managing international relations, and administration. However, as his biographer P. H. Newby has noted in *Saladin in His Time,* "Since administrators had to be soldiers, too—perhaps first and foremost—he had to be proficient [skilled] in combat: swordsmanship, the management of the horse, archery and above all how to thrust with a lance when mounted." He would need all these skills in his career, for now he knew that his mission in life was to free Palestine of the Franks.

Saladin's Meteoric Rise to Power

Saladin continued to gain more and more power. Through his uncle Shirkuh's influence and his own talents, he rose to prominence under Nur al-Din and his followers. Between 1164 and 1169 he accompanied his uncle in defending Cairo, a city in Egypt, from attacks by Crusaders. During these years he gained valuable military knowledge both from his uncle and from Nur al-Din. Shirkuh became vizier, that is, administrator of the country, in the name of the Fatimids, the political and religious dynasty that had ruled Egypt and North Africa since 909. This dynasty claimed descent from Fatima, the prophet Muhammad's daughter, and was in direct opposition to the Abbasids, the other powerful Muslim dynasty, which had its base in Baghdad. With the death of Shirkuh in 1169, Saladin himself became vizier, and he proceeded to transform the land of Egypt into a powerful economic center. He fortified Cairo, built public works and houses of worship, and encouraged the arts and sciences. Meanwhile, he was also assembling a strong army under his command. In 1171 he became supreme leader of Egypt by abolishing the old Fatimid caliphate, or successor Islamic regime.

The year 1174 marked a turning point for Saladin. His former ruler Nur al-Din had died, as had a powerful Crusader king in Jerusalem. The way seemed to be open for him to continue his program to unite the Islamic world. However, he had enemies within the Muslim world who opposed him. In 1174 he defeated two of his strongest Muslim enemies, the lords of Mosul and Aleppo, at the Battle of the Horns of Hamah. He then became governor of Egypt, Yemen, Syria, and Palestine, making him the most powerful man in the Islamic world.

Saladin Consolidates His Power

Saladin still had to overcome many obstacles to unite Islam. In 1174 and again in 1175 he survived attempts on his life by the Assassins (from the Arabic *Hashashin*), a radical sect, or branch, of Islam that murdered its enemies. He also had to put down revolts by various Arab princes. By marrying Ismat al-Din, the widow of Nur al-Din, he helped consolidate (strengthen) his position as ruler of Syria.

Beginning in 1177 Saladin determined to systematically remove the Crusaders from their fortresses along the eastern shore of the Mediterranean. He launched a series of campaigns that initially were unsuccessful, but in 1179 he had his first victory against the Franks, capturing the Crusader castle at Jacob's Ford. These efforts were slowed, however, because rival Muslim leaders rebelled against his growing power. The leaders in the cities of Mosul and Aleppo again challenged his right to rule, and in 1183 Saladin's forces laid siege to, or blockaded, Mosul. Saladin realized that to maintain control of the situation, he would have to leave his base in Egypt. He established his new power center in Damascus. Saladin was also bothered by ill health; in 1185 he nearly died of one such illness, and he never fully recovered his health.

Despite these difficulties, Saladin continued in his quest for *jihad,* or holy war, against the "infidel" (nonbelievers) Crusaders. (Ironically, the Crusaders also used the term "infidel" when referring to Muslims.) He had established truces with the Crusader states in Palestine, but in his mind there could be no peace until the Europeans were driven out and sent home.

The Breaking Point

Saladin's plans for ridding the Near East of Christian Crusaders were speeded up by the actions of a Frank named

Reynaud de Châtillon, whose fortress castle of Kerak (to the southeast of the Dead Sea) controlled the caravan and pilgrimage route between Syria and Egypt. When Châtillon attacked one of Saladin's supply trains and took his sister hostage, the Muslim leader had had enough. He gathered a force of twenty-four thousand cavalry and infantry, as well as numerous other volunteers, and moved toward Tiberias, located on the Sea of Galilee in northern Palestine. Once there, he captured the town and set a trap for the Crusader army that was being assembled by King Guy of Jerusalem, the leader of the Franks. Saladin arrayed, or spread out, his troops in a place called the Horns of Hattin, consisting of several hills near Tiberias, and waited for the Christians. Since he controlled the water supplies, he knew he had the upper hand. The Crusader knights, or professional soldiers, were dressed in armor that was both heavy and hot. Attacked by advance bands of Muslim fighters using bows and arrows, many of these knights lost their horses.

The night of July 3, 1187, the Franks were exhausted and almost out of water. The next morning, with the rising sun to his back, Saladin and his troops attacked and conquered the Crusader army, whose leaders were captured or killed. As he had sworn, Saladin beheaded Châtillon, the knight who had captured his sister. Yet he showed mercy to many others: King Guy was set free after promising that he would not fight again, and some knights were ransomed— that is, they had someone pay for their freedom.

With this victory behind him, nothing stood between Saladin and Jerusalem, the first step in his plan to recapture the Holy Land. This city was sacred (holy) to Muslims, Christians, and Jews alike, and for almost a century the Crusaders had made this the center of their foothold in the Middle East. Pushing them out of Jerusalem would send a message to all Christians that their time was up in what Saladin saw as Arab lands. He attacked the city on September 20, 1187, his troops surrounding the walls. Contemporary accounts of the siege speak of arrows falling like rain on the citizens of Jerusalem. The hospitals of the city were filled with the wounded.

After a week of direct fighting, Saladin moved his camp to the Mount of Olives to find a weaker spot in the city wall to attack. At first the citizens of Jerusalem thought he

was leaving the field. However, they were quickly disappointed when he brought in giant catapults (devices for hurling heavy objects) to shower the city with rocks and "Greek fire," a flammable mixture of pitch, naphtha (known in modern times as crude petroleum), quicklime, and charcoal that ignited whatever it struck. Worn out and running low on water, on October 2, 1187, the inhabitants of Jerusalem were finally forced to give up the fight. Saladin set a modest price for the release of the citizens of the city, and orderly evacuations began after the fall of Jerusalem. This was in marked contrast to the behavior of the Christians when they had captured the city back in 1099. Thousands were slaughtered and the streets ran ankle deep in blood. Saladin showed mercy, permitting most of the inhabitants of Jerusalem to go free and even allowing them to take their possessions with them. Such behavior won him the respect of the defeated Christians. After the fall of Jerusalem, Saladin and his forces took back much of Palestine, leaving only Antioch, Tyre, and Tripoli (the last two in modern-day Lebanon) in Crusader hands.

Saladin and his army climbing over the walls of Jerusalem on their way to overtaking the city in 1187, shortly before the Third Crusade. © *The British Library/Topham-HIP/ The Image Works.*

The Third Crusade

Saladin had partly achieved his goal of getting rid of the Franks. However, King Guy broke his word by assembling an army and attacking the Muslim fortress of Acre on the Mediterranean. At the same time, three Christian kings in Europe reacted strongly to the Muslim victory at Jerusalem. England's king Richard I, the Lionheart; France's king Philip Augustus; and Germany's emperor Frederick Barbarossa all gathered armies and headed for the Holy Land to retake Jerusalem. The army under the command of the German emperor was weakened after its leader drowned while trying to cross a mountain stream on his way to the Crusades, but it carried on under Count Leopold V of Austria. Meanwhile, King Richard I and King Philip took their men across the Mediterranean Sea to the Holy Land. Upon arrival, they joined the other Christian forces already there and laid siege to Acre. Saladin repeatedly tried to lift the blockade but was unsuccessful. In July 1191 Acre fell to the Crusaders.

For Saladin this proved to be a terrible defeat, but soon he was encouraged by conflicts within the Crusader armies. Philip and Richard—friends and rivals since childhood—quarreled, and the French king left the field, sailing for France. Richard I had other problems as well. His brother, Prince John, was conspiring with the French king to grab the English crown in Richard's absence. For fifteen months Saladin and Richard I battled up and down Palestine and Syria. At one point it seemed there would be a peaceful solution, but then Saladin decided Richard's terms were too costly to the Arab cause, and the skirmishes and battles continued.

A mutual respect grew up between the two men. It is reported that Saladin sent his personal physician to the English king after he had suffered an injury during battle; at another time the Muslim leader gave Richard a horse after his own was killed. On September 7, 1191, Richard I and his men defeated Saladin at the Battle of Arsuf, with the Islamic forces losing seven thousand men. However, Saladin was able to keep ahead of the Crusaders on their march to Jerusalem. Although Richard I came within sight of the walls of Jerusalem, Saladin prevented the English king from laying siege to the city by controlling the precious water supplies surrounding it.

Despite another minor victory for Richard I at Jaffa, the two military leaders reached a stalemate, or deadlock, in the Third Crusade, with both finally agreeing to a truce on September 2, 1192. According to the terms of this truce, called the Treaty of Ramlah, Saladin and the Muslims were left in control of Jerusalem, but the Crusaders were allowed to keep some of their holdings along the coast and also were granted the right to visit the city and its shrines as pilgrims, or religious visitors. King Richard I sailed for England the following month. Saladin, exhausted by his labors and battles, returned to Damascus and his family. He did not have much of a chance to enjoy his life away from the battlefield, for late that winter he fell ill with a fever and died on March 4, 1193.

Upon Saladin's death, civil war broke out in his kingdom between his sons and his brother, al-Adil. Al-Adil finally won, and by 1201 he had taken over all of Saladin's former lands. But Saladin was not forgotten. This first Ayyubid sultan was one of the strongest Muslim leaders since Muhammad, uniting the feuding Islamic groups to fight the Christians and returning Jerusalem to the Islamic people. Since then he has remained an inspiration to generations of Arabs who dream of uniting Arabs and Muslims. His tomb in Damascus is a major pilgrimage site for Muslims as well as a tourist attraction. It is not just Arabs who honor his memory; as Newby has written in his biography, Saladin is "Christianity's favorite Muslim." By acting in the chivalrous (honorable and courageous) manner expected of a knight, he won the respect of his enemies and found a place in western literature. In the *Divine Comedy* the Italian poet Dante Alighieri (1265–1321) honored Saladin by assigning him a place in the afterlife reserved for virtuous pagans, or non-Christians. The Scottish writer Sir Walter Scott (1771–1832) also recorded Saladin's adventures in his novel *The Talisman*. As James Reston Jr. has commented in his *Warriors of God: Richard the Lionheart and Saladin in the Third Crusade*, Saladin was "a preeminent hero of the Islamic world. ... In the seemingly endless struggle of modern-day Arabs to reassert the essentially Arab nature of Palestine, Saladin lives, vibrantly [excitingly], as a symbol of hope and as the stuff of myth."

For More Information

Books

Ehrenkreutz, Andrew S. *Saladin*. Albany: State University of New York Press, 1972.

Maalouf, Amin. *The Crusades through Arab Eyes.* Translated by Jon Roth-schild. New York: Schocken Books, 1984.

Newby, P. H. *Saladin in His Time.* London: Phoenix Press, 2001.

Reston, James Jr. *Warriors of God: Richard the Lionheart and Saladin in the Third Crusade.* New York: Doubleday, 2001.

Web Sites
"Saladin (Selahedîn)." *Uppsala Universitet.* http://stp.ling.uu.se/~kamalk/language/saladin.html (accessed on July 21, 2004).

Shajarat al-Durr

c. 1223
Armenia or Turkey

1257
Cairo, Egypt

Sultana of Egypt

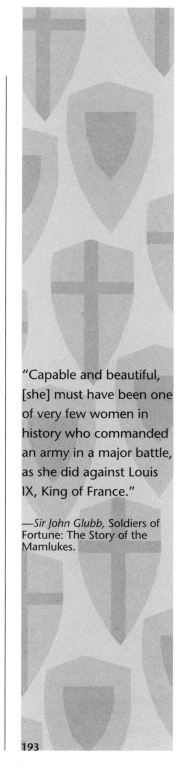

One of a handful of strong female Muslim leaders at the time of the Crusades, Shajarat al-Durr was a slave who rose from the ranks of mistress, or lover, to become the wife of the sultan (Muslim leader) of Egypt. Following the death of her husband during the Seventh Crusade (1248–54), she assumed joint control of the Muslim forces with two other counselors and helped defeat the Crusader armies of French king **Louis IX** (see entry) at the Battle of Mansurah. After a palace revolt, she was made sultana, or female leader of Egypt, a position she held for three months. She was displaced by those uncomfortable with a female leader and replaced by a Mamluk soldier, Aybeck. Yet Shajarat would not give up her power so easily. She went on to marry Aybeck and in essence continued to rule Egypt on his behalf as he fought enemies abroad until her execution for treason in 1257. Shajarat al-Durr's tale is full of plots, high adventure, and tragedy—the stuff of fiction. However, there was nothing fictional, or imaginary, about her defeat of the French forces during the Crusades. The Egyptian victory at Mansurah in effect ended enthusiasm in Europe to send more Crusaders to the Holy Land

A Trio of Strong Women

Shajarat al-Durr was not the only powerful woman involved in the events of the Seventh Crusade. While she helped rally the Egyptian troops after the fall of Damietta and contributed to the victory at the Battle of Mansurah, the French camp also had its fair share of strong women.

Louis IX's mother, Blanche of Castile, was the granddaughter of the powerful **Eleanor of Aquitaine** (see entry), who was queen of England. Blanche inherited some of her grandmother's strength of character, marrying Louis VIII, the future king of France, when she was only eleven. Once queen, she showed such leadership abilities that her husband, when lying on his deathbed, named Blanche to rule jointly with their young son, Louis IX. She became the first queen with real power in French history, putting down revolts by lesser nobles in order to secure the crown for herself and her son, finally defeating them and winning the respect of the French people. When Louis IX left for the Seventh Crusade, he put his mother in charge of affairs in France.

The king was also lucky to have a very capable and loyal wife accompany him to Egypt. Queen Margaret, who was nine months pregnant, was left in charge of Damietta when the king moved his forces to Mansurah to fight the Egyptians. Three days after her husband's capture by the Mamluks, she gave birth to a son. That same day she also learned that part of the Crusader forces were planning to abandon Damietta, thus leaving the place undefended against the Muslims. The queen realized that if they did not hold Damietta, they would have nothing to offer the Egyptians in exchange for King Louis IX. Queen Margaret managed to persuade these Crusaders to stay on, using her own money to feed them. Thus Damietta was held, and Louis IX was later released—all owing to the quick thinking of his queen.

or Egypt. Shajarat al-Durr is often called the "Joan of Arc of Islam," after that famous fifteenth-century French heroine (c. 1412–1431) who also led her armies to victory.

From Harem to Battlefield

Little is known of the early life of Shajarat al-Durr, who is also called Shajara, Shagrat, Shagar, Shaggar, and Shagarat. Her name has been translated as "Tree of Pearls," "String of Pearls," or "Spray of Pearls." It is supposed that she was born in Armenia or Turkey sometime in the early 1220s.

The first historical record of her dates from 1239. At that time she was listed as a Mamluk, or female slave living in a harem, a special area reserved for women who were the wives or mistresses of a Muslim man. According to Islamic law, men are allowed to have up to four wives. This harem belonged to al-Musta Sim, the powerful caliph, or religious leader, of Baghdad (in modern-day Iraq).

It is clear that Shajarat was not only a beautiful young woman but also a very intelligent one. In 1240 she was presented to al-Salih Najm al-Din Ayyub, the sultan of Egypt and the last member of the Ayyubid dynasty, which had begun when the powerful Muslim leader **Saladin** (see entry) conquered Egypt in 1169. Settled in Cairo, Shajarat al-Durr steadily gained in influence and won the favor of the sultan, becoming one of his wives. When the sultan was captured by a rival Muslim in 1248 and thrown into prison for a year, Shajarat al-Durr accompanied him and gave birth to their son, Khalil. After this show of loyalty, Shajarat al-Durr became al-Salih's favorite wife.

In early 1249 a Crusader army under the leadership of Louis IX arrived at the mouth of the Nile River. They, like other Crusaders before them, had made plans to capture Cairo and then move on to the Holy Land and recover Jerusalem. By this time the Crusades had been going on for more than 150 years. These Crusaders quickly captured the city of Damietta. The sultan was dying of tuberculosis (a fatal lung disease) and perhaps also some form of cancer. As his favorite wife, Shajarat al-Durr probably aided al-Salih during these difficult days, but it is not clear how much power she held while he was still alive. Al-Salih decided to direct matters from the battlefield and so left Cairo to set up defenses at the small town of Mansurah, site of a historic victory over the Crusaders during the Fifth Crusade (1218–21). This victory had been won by al-Salih's father, **Sultan al-Malik al-Kamil** (see entry), and now his son hoped to perform the same miracle.

He gathered his elite, or most highly trained, professional soldiers, called Mamluks, or foreign slaves, such as Shajarat al-Durr had been. These trained fighters had been taken as youths from outside the Muslim world—in areas of Turkey, Russia, and even northern Europe—and given a thorough and difficult education in the arts of war. Once they had undergone

An illumination of King Louis IX entering the city of Damietta after he had captured it from the Egyptians during the Seventh Crusade. *© Archivo Iconografico, S.A./Corbis.*

this training, they were considered paid soldiers; although they were no longer slaves in the literal sense, they were still referred to as Mamluks. Many of them converted to Islam.

Shajarat al-Durr accompanied the sultan to the field, and when he died on November 23, 1249, she plotted with his two advisers—Fakhr al-Din, the second in command of the troops, and Jamal al-Din, who was in charge of the palace—to keep the sultan's death a secret. They simply told the troops that he was very ill and even had a servant bring food to his tent as usual. Meanwhile, Shajarat al-Durr sent an urgent message to the sultan's son (and her stepson), Turan Shah, in Mesopotamia to return to Egypt with his men.

During this same period the French had been gathering new forces and were preparing to attack the Egyptian camp, which was on the other side of a river that separated them. In February a spy showed the French where they could cross the river. Led by Robert of Artois, the king's brother, the French attacked. They quickly took the Egyptian camp and then, contrary to their orders, followed the Egyptians to Mansurah without waiting for reinforcements. At this point the Egyptian Mamluks, led by their young general, **al-Zahir Baybars** (see entry), counterattacked and cut down the Crusaders once they had entered the narrow streets of the town. The rest of the Crusader forces were still crossing the river and were powerless to help. The French had no choice but to retreat, leaving behind the bodies of a large number of their most important knights, or professional soldiers, including the king's brother. Also killed in the battle was the Muslim commander Fakhr al-Din.

The Sultana

Not long after this victory, Turan Shah, the sultan's son, arrived in Egypt with his forces and finished off the French, capturing the king and most of his army. The rest of the Crusader force at Damietta held out, hoping to trade the city for the return of their king. During all these events Shajarat al-Durr had shown herself to be a strong and capable leader, helping run the government and the military following the death of Fakhr al-Din. With the arrival of Turan Shah, however, this role ended. Instead of showing gratitude to Shajarat al-Durr or to the Mamluks, such as Baybars, for saving his empire, he began awarding high offices, or posts, to his own men, which ultimately brought about a revolt.

The Cairo Mamluks under Baybars and Shajarat al-Durr would not let themselves be shoved aside. On May 2, 1250, the Mamluks, led by Baybars, attacked Turan Shah at a feast he was giving. Wounded, the sultan's son managed to escape to a fortified (strengthened) tower in the Nile River.

When the Mamluks set the tower on fire, Turan Shah jumped into the river. Baybars himself finished the job by killing Turan Shah with his sword. After this assassination, there were no living relatives of Sultan al-Salih to inherit the throne. Even Khalil, the son of the sultan and Shajarat al-Durr, had died by this time. Thus Shajarat al-Durr, the sultan's widow, was declared the sultana and was also proclaimed Umm Khalil, "Mother of Khalil."

Placing Shajarat al-Durr on the Egyptian throne was a way to make the new rulers seem more legitimate, or lawful and rightful heirs to the throne, for she could be considered the next in line for the Ayyubid crown. But Shajarat al-Durr had also proved herself a capable leader. It is clear that her rule was not ceremonial—that is, she did not rule in name only. In fact, she had coins made up with her name stamped on them, and her name was also mentioned during the Friday sermon at the mosques, or Islamic places of worship. Both of these honors were reserved for true leaders. In addition, she continued Turan Shah's negotiations with the French for the ransom (payment) for the king's release. The French paid a large sum, after which Louis IX was released and sailed to Acre in the Holy Land.

Shajarat al-Durr ruled as sultana for almost three months, until criticism in the rest of the Islamic world put pressure on Egypt to have her unseated (removed from the throne). It was a new thing for a woman to rule in Muslim countries. The caliph in Baghdad threatened to send troops to remove her if the Egyptians did not. A compromise was finally reached. In July 1250 Aybek, a high-ranking Mamluk, was made sultan. Although Aybek already had a wife and a son, Shajarat al-Durr realized that her power would be lost if she did not become his partner. She first won him over to her side and then married him, becoming unofficial leader of Egypt. The marriage was more than one of convenience, however, for it seems that Shajarat al-Durr really loved this military leader. For most of their marriage Aybek was far from Egypt, busily fighting Ayyubids in Syria, who claimed that the Egyptian throne rightfully belonged to them and not to the former Mamluks. In Aybek's absence Shajarat al-Durr was the real power center in Cairo. She made sure the government ran smoothly while her husband attended to military matters.

This arrangement worked well for seven years, until Aybek decided to replace her with a new wife, a woman he wanted to marry in order to secure a political alliance with the city of Mosul, in present-day Iraq. Discovering this plan, Shajarat al-Durr grew jealous and plotted the death of her husband, a man she had sacrificed so much for and who was now going to toss her aside. Despite learning of her plot to murder him, on April 29, 1257, Aybek was tricked into coming to her, where her paid assassins killed him. If Shajarat al-Durr thought that she could take over control of the empire through this action, she was wrong. Ali, Aybek's son by his first marriage, was named sultan. Aybek was so powerful that his death would not go unpunished. Shajarat al-Durr must eventually have realized this—too late. After crushing all her jewels into powder so that no one else could have them, she was arrested several days later. She was turned over to Ali's mother, the woman from whom Shajarat al-Durr had taken Aybek. The former sultana was beaten to death with the wooden shoes of this woman's

Tomb of Mamluks, constructed by Shajarat al-Durr, where she and all those who had fought for Egypt were laid to rest.
© Bettmann/Corbis.

slaves and her body thrown over the high walls of the Citadel of Cairo (the fortress of Cairo) to be eaten by dogs. Later, her remains were gathered up and taken to a mausoleum, or burial place, that Shajarat al-Durr had earlier constructed for herself. It can still be viewed in Cairo today.

Many legends and romantic stories have grown up around the life of Shajarat al-Durr. While some historians all but ignore her, treating her as just another wife of a sultan, others place her front and center during the Seventh Crusade and the Mamluk power grab in Egypt. The truth lies somewhere between these two viewpoints. Shajarat al-Durr not only ruled on her own for a brief time but also successfully (though unofficially) ran the government of Egypt for seven years. Her symbolic importance as one of the few women to gain power in the medieval Muslim world is nevertheless greater than her achievements as a leader.

For More Information

Books

Glubb, Sir John. *Soldiers of Fortune: The Story of the Mamlukes*. New York: Stein and Day, 1973.

Maalouf, Amin. *The Crusades through Arab Eyes*. Translated by Jon Rothschild. New York: Schocken Books, 1984.

Mernissi, Fatima. *The Forgotten Queens of Islam*. Translated by Mary Jo Lakeland. Karachi, Pakistan: Oxford University Press, 2003.

Waddy, Charis. *Women in Muslim History*. New York: Longman, 1980.

Ziada, Mustafa. "The Mamluk Sultans to 1293." In *A History of the Crusades*. Edited by Kenneth M. Setton. Vol. 2, *The Later Crusades, 1189–1311*. Edited by Robert L. Wolff and Harry W. Hazard. Madison: University of Wisconsin Press, 1969.

Periodicals

Duncan, David J. "Scholarly Views of Shajarat al-Durr: A Need for Consensus." *Arab Studies Quarterly* 22, no. 1 (Winter 2000): 51–69.

Web Sites

"Infamous Women: Shajar al-Durr." *Mabelyn.com*. http://www.mabelyn.com/infamous_women/shajar.htm (accessed on July 22, 2004).

"Seventh Crusade." *The ORB: On-line Reference Book for Medieval Studies*. http://the-orb.net/textbooks/crusade/seventhcru.html (accessed on July 22, 2004).

authority in the religious teachings of Islam. For Sunnis the word "imam" now sometimes has the same meaning as "caliph," but it can also refer simply to the person who leads Friday prayers. It does not have the divine meaning that Shiites give it.

Within the Shiites there were further splits. The so-called Twelvers believe that there were twelve God-inspired imams, while the Seveners believe in only seven and think that the last was Ismail, the older son of the sixth imam, Jafa al-Sadiq, who was passed over for succession. The Seveners are also called Ismailis. For the Twelvers, the last of the imams, al-Mahdi, is supposed to be hidden away from humanity until the end of the world. However, the Seveners believe that Ismail's spirit and power return through various leaders throughout time. One further schism occurred within the Ismailis over the succession of religious leaders. Breakaway Ismailis became known as "Nizaris," after the person they backed to become the new religious leader in Cairo at the end of the eleventh century.

Under the leadership of Hasan ibn al-Sabbah, around 1090 this sect established its center at the mountain stronghold of Alamut, in Iran, quickly spreading throughout Persia and Syria. Hasan's was an esoteric, or mystical, branch of Islam that rejected and went beyond human reason; it had several levels of initiation (or admission through rites and ceremonies) into secrets that supposedly gave participants special powers.

Soon the followers of this first Hasan became known as the *hashashin,* perhaps because of their use of the drug hashish in their rituals or perhaps through some corruption, or misreading, of the name Hasan. These followers included a large group of what were known as *fidai,* who, though not completely initiated into the sect's secrets, would still defend the faith with their lives. Hasan began using these *fidai* members to kill enemies of the Nizaris; their typical method was by means of a dagger in a public place. Sinan was supposedly descended from a Twelver family and converted to the Ismaili belief when he went to Alamut.

the famous fortress of Alamut in Iran, which had become the center of the Ismailis, a breakaway group of Islam. There he was accepted by the grand master Muhammad and was subsequently educated with the sons of this leader. He became friendly with one son, the future ruler Hasan II, who would later send Sinan to Syria as his emissary, or representative.

It appears that after his education at Alamut, Sinan returned to Iraq around 1160, where he was put in charge of the Ismaili sect in the district of his hometown of Basra. In 1162 Hasan

II, the new imam, or leader, sent him as his deputy to Syria. The Syrian Ismaili leader Abu Muhammad died in 1164, and thereafter Sinan was the *dai* of Syria, next in line to the imam himself. The Syrian Ismailis were not as well organized as those in Iran or Persia. They had suffered at the hands of both the Christian Crusaders, who first appeared in the Middle East in 1096 to recapture the Holy Land from the Muslims, and their fellow Muslims, many of whom were of Turkish origin and belonged to the Sunni majority. There had been massacres and acts of vengeance. A large number of Ismailis had left the cities and gathered in the mountainous region of north-central Syria. It was there, in the castle of Kahf, where Sinan began his work as chief *dai* of the Assassins, as his group of Ismailis were commonly called.

Sinan Unites the Syrian Ismailis

Abu Muhammad, Sinan's predecessor, had not been very successful in establishing a Syrian homeland for the Assassins. Under the leadership of Sinan, new fortresses were built in the mountainous region where they lived and worshiped. Besides Kahf, the most famous of these were Masyaf and Qadmus. Already famous as a teacher and healer with telepathic, or mind-reading, powers, Sinan began recruiting new members to the faith. He taught these members various languages then in use in the Middle East, including French and English, and what would come to be called spy craft: gathering information, putting all communications in a secret code, and using pigeons to send messages. He was able to keep in constant contact with various Ismaili commanders by means of this communication system; in fact, his "pigeon post" may have given rise to the stories about his telepathic powers.

It appears that Sinan, though he had been sent by Hasan II to Syria, was independent of the Persian leadership at Alamut. His followers began to believe in him as the imam and nearly worshiped him as a god. Under his leadership, the Syrian Ismaili sect became far more than just a branch of the new religion. Declaring itself independent of Alamut and Hasan II, it became a powerful new force in the Middle East, one feared by Crusaders and mainstream, or traditional, Muslims alike. Sinan's use of assassination struck fear in the hearts of all his enemies. Westerners called Sinan the Old Man of the Mountain, but actually this appears to be a mistranslation or a too-exact translation of the Persian word *pir,* which means "master" or "sheik" (chief). Sinan was not simply a fanatic (extremist); his reign in Syria proved that he was capable and talented, and he preserved Ismaili independence against the attacks of various foes.

Sinan's enemies included anyone who tried to consolidate, or organize, the region, for that would have threatened the Ismailis' independence. Thus Sinan found enemies among both the Christian Crusaders—or Franks, as the Arabs called them—and the Sunni Muslim leaders, such as Nur al-Din and Saladin, who were attempting to unite Islam. When these two men overran Egypt in 1169, they roused Sinan's anger, for that was one of the centers of Shiite and Ismaili power. In 1174, when Saladin put an end to the Fatimid caliphate, the Shiite dynasty ruling from Cairo, Sinan knew he must act. Saladin suddenly became the most powerful man in the Middle East, for Nur al-Din had died that year, as had the main Christian Crusader leader. Saladin moved into this power vacuum, and Sinan knew he must stop this military leader before he gained total control of Iraq and Syria. Twice Sinan sent his *fidai* to assassinate Saladin—and both times they failed.

In 1176 Saladin invaded Sinan's territory. After surrounding the castle of Masyaf and discovering that Sinan was not there, Saladin mysteriously withdrew. The reasons given for this retreat differ, depending on who tells the story. Abu Firas, an Ismaili historian and source of many stories about Sinan, claimed that Saladin was warned off when he discovered an Assassin's dagger on his pillow, a warning he took to heart. Others say that Saladin found that the threat from the Franks was more urgent and that fighting the Ismailis was a waste of his time. Whatever the reason, it seems that after about 1176 a truce was called between Sinan and Saladin. Some historians even report that in 1187 Assassins fought alongside Saladin and his forces in the decisive battle against the Crusaders at the Horns of Hattin, a victory that allowed Saladin to later recapture Jerusalem from the Christians.

Sinan's Relations with the Crusaders

Sinan and his followers came into direct conflict with the Crusaders because their mountainous homeland had been

A depiction of a Syrian warrior, possibly a *fidai,* on horseback, much like the ones that followed and fought for Sinan during the twelfth century. *Courtesy of the British Museum. Reproduced by permission.*

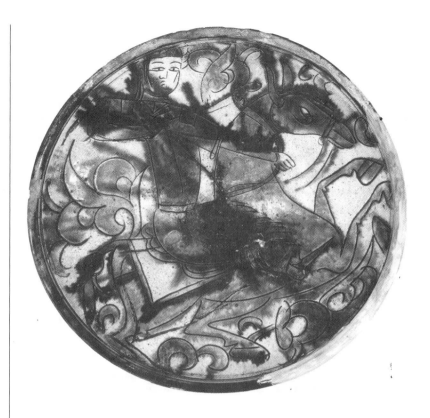

taken from these Christians. Many of the strongest Crusader fortresses, such as Krak des Chevaliers, were located very close to the Assassins' strongholds. Before Sinan's arrival, the Ismailis were forced to pay tribute (a kind of tax) to the Templar order, the group of military monks who controlled much of the region near the Ismaili lands. When Sinan came to power, he tried to achieve peace with these Crusader forces, fearful of fighting two enemies at the same time. To this end, in 1172 or 1173 he entered into negotiations with Amalric, the leader of the Crusaders and king of Jerusalem.

Some historians write that Sinan offered to convert to Christianity to further his cause. It is known that Sinan did not strictly follow the Shiite teachings; as a philosopher he was interested in the teachings of Christianity. Whether conversion was part of the bargain is unknown, but Amalric canceled the tribute Sinan was forced to pay to the Templars. This, in turn, angered the Templars, and they had Sinan's messenger killed on his return journey from Jerusalem. Thus the Crusaders lost the possibility of having Sinan and his men as their allies. With the death of Amalric in 1174, and once the disagreements with Saladin had been repaired, Sinan and the Syrian Ismailis became allies with the other Islamic forces against the Christians.

The End of Sinan

Sinan demanded absolute loyalty from his followers. Several stories tell of how many of his followers would jump to their deaths at the snap of his fingers. His telepathic powers are celebrated in tales by the Arab historian Abu Firas. Toward the end of his life Sinan was responsible for one of the most famous and hotly debated assassinations of the Crusades. Conrad of Montferrat, a Frankish leader of the Third Crusade (1189–92), arrived in the Holy Land too late to help out at the port and fortress of Acre (in modern-day Israel), which had already been taken by Saladin. He sailed on to the city of Tyre (in present-day Lebanon), which he helped defend against the Muslim forces. There, Conrad earned the hatred of most of the Islamic world for his slaughter of Muslim prisoners. Conrad was also a rival to England's **Richard I, the Lionheart** (see entry). Moreover, he had personally angered Sinan by seizing one of the Assassins' ships that had landed in Tyre. When Sinan asked for the return of this prize, Conrad refused, killing the ship's captain instead.

In 1192 Sinan had his revenge. Two Assassins who had been disguised as monks in Conrad's household attacked the man in the streets of Tyre, stabbed him repeatedly, and finished the job in a church where the injured Conrad had been taken. One Assassin was killed, and the second was captured and tortured. At first he claimed that Richard I hired him to kill Conrad. Only later did the truth come out—namely, that Sinan was again scheming from a distance.

Sinan died either that same year or in 1193. It is not clear whether he died from natural causes or if there was foul play involved, but many of his followers believed Sinan had actually gone into hiding from enemies and would reemerge to lead them once again when it was safe for him to do so. The man who became the new leader of the Assassins did not have Sinan's force of character or organizational abilities.

Never again were the Syrian Ismailis as strong as they had been under Sinan. As Enno Franzius noted in his *History of the Order of Assassins,* Sinan "was not only an outstanding personality but also an efficient administrator. He consolidated the Assassin position in Syria, organizing and training fidais (probably in the Castle of Kahf), acquiring and erecting new castles, rebuilding and fortifying old ones." For James Reston Jr. "Sinan was brilliant, clairvoyant [able to read minds], ruthless, deceitful, pious [devoutly religious] and ascetic [self-disciplined], with eyes fierce as meteors, a physician's power of healing, and a tyrant's power of awesome destruction."

For More Information

Books

Franzius, Enno. *History of the Order of Assassins.* New York: Funk & Wagnalls, 1969.

Hodgson, Marshall G. S. *The Order of the Assassins: The Struggle of the Early Nizari Isma'ilis against the Islamic World.* The Hague, Netherlands: Mouton, 1955.

Lewis, Bernard. *The Assassins: A Radical Sect in Islam.* New York: Basic Books, 1968.

Mirza, Nasseh Ahmed. *Syrian Ismailism: The Ever Living Line of the Imamite, AD 1100–1260.* Richmond, UK: Curzon, 1997.

Reston, James Jr. *Warriors of God: Richard the Lionheart and Saladin in the Third Crusade.* New York: Doubleday, 2001.

Web Sites

"Glossary." *The Institute of Ismaili Studies.* http://www.iis.ac.uk/glossary/glossary_ac.htm (accessed on July 22, 2004).

"Rashid al-Din Sinan." *Alamut: Bastion of Peace and Information.* http://www.alamut.com/subj/ideologies/alamut/mirza-Sinan.html (accessed on July 22, 2004).

Urban II

c. 1042
Chätillon-sur-Marne, Champagne, France

July 29, 1099
Rome, Italy

Pope

U rban II, a French pope (head of the Catholic Church), ruled at the end of the eleventh century. He was known as an excellent organizer and tireless worker for renewed political power for the church. Following the rule of Gregory VII, who was pope from 1075 to 1085, Urban II helped solidify gains made for the papacy, or the office of the pope, against the political power of the kings of Europe. He developed a central governing structure for the church and ultimately made the papacy a powerful player in Europe, equal to the early monarchies, or kingdoms, of the continent. Clever in the use of the spoken word, Urban's most lasting achievement was his connection with the Crusades. Speaking at a meeting of church leaders held in 1095 in the southern French town of Clermont, he urged the crowd to spread the concept of a Crusade against the Arab and Turkish Muslims—the name for believers in Islam and the word of the prophet Muhammad—who had occupied Jerusalem and the Holy Land of Palestine. His call to arms brought about the First Crusade (1095–99) and resulted in two centuries of conflict between the Christian West and Islam. Although he did not

"The Turks and Arabs have attacked....They have killed and captured many, and have destroyed the churches and devastated the empire.... On this account I, or rather the Lord, beseech you...to destroy that vile race from the lands of our friends."

—Urban II, "Speech at Council of Clermont, 1095, according to Fulcher of Chartres"; quoted in the Internet Medieval Sourcebook, *http://www.ford ham.edu/halsall/source/urban2 ,hy>fulcher.html.*

Pope Urban II. © *Archivo Iconografico, S.A./Corbis.*

live to witness the event, his speech inspired Crusader soldiers to capture Jerusalem in 1099.

Born Into the French Nobility

Born Eudes, or Odo, of Lagery, the man who would become Pope Urban II grew up in a French noble family in Rheims, located in the province of Champagne. Being the second son, it was assumed that his career would be in the church, since the firstborn son would inherit the lands. Odo studied at the Cathedral School of Rheims, where he learned the basic skills he would need to enter such a career. In the age in which Odo grew up, such skills included not just reading, writing, and a thorough knowledge of the Bible but also political skills and knowing how to accept and give orders. He was headed for greater things than being a parish, or local, priest. At Rheims he rose to the rank of archdeacon, a senior position in the church under the bishop, or head of a large religious district.

With this experience behind him, Odo left Rheims at age twenty-eight to become a monk, a member of the religious order at the famous monastery of Cluny, located in the French province of Burgundy. There he lived a strictly regulated religious life, working under the abbot Hugh, who was the head of the monastery. Ultimately he rose to the rank of prior, just below the abbot. The monastery of Cluny was known for producing monks with great ambition and a strong belief in reforming the church. These reforms included not only improving the moral lives of those inside the church but also making the church more powerful in the secular, or nonreligious, world.

Assistant to the Pope

Odo was sent by the abbot Hugh to work as an assistant to Gregory VII, one of the most important popes the church has ever produced. Gregory VII was trying to push through reforms in the church that would increase its power over the princes of Europe. His major rival in this effort was Henry IV, emperor of the Holy Roman Empire, a loose collection of German kingdoms that lasted from the tenth to the nineteenth century. This emperor claimed secular power over his subjects, which for Henry IV meant appointing bishops of the church in his lands. Gregory VII opposed this, telling the emperor that any power he had came from God and that he, Gregory VII, was God's messenger on earth. Thus, the church was more powerful than the state. Such a position was sure to bring Gregory VII into conflict not only with the emperor but with many other kings and princes in Europe as well.

In his position as assistant to Gregory VII, Odo represented the pope on missions in France and Germany, working to strengthen the role of the church in these lands. He made sure to promote bishops who displayed a sense of loyalty toward Gregory VII and who agreed with his plans for a bigger, stronger papacy, getting rid of those who did not. This work earned Odo his own promotion; he became a cardinal bishop, the step just before becoming a cardinal, an office second in power to the pope. (The cardinals elect the pope.) Odo showed that he was not afraid to act against the emperor. On one occasion he was imprisoned by Henry IV but was soon released.

At large church meetings held throughout Europe, Odo also became a tireless spokesperson for reform and directly criticized Henry IV and Clement III, the man whom Henry IV had elected as the so-called antipope, in opposition to Gregory VII. This election of a competing pope by the emperor led to fighting in and around Rome in the 1080s. The emperor's army fought the pope's hired soldiers, or Normans, who had created a kingdom in Sicily, in the south of Italy. These Norman fighters were of Viking origin and were hard to control. At one point it looked as if they would succeed in capturing Rome for Gregory VII, but they ended up destroying the city, and Gregory was forced to go into exile, eventually dying in 1085 without retaking Rome.

From Odo to Urban II

With the death of Gregory VII, the church needed to elect a new pope. Although he was nominated to become the next pope, Odo lost to Victor III, who was not terribly eager to accept the job. Rome lay in ruins, and there was still fighting going on between the church's forces and the emperor's army. Victor III held the position of pope for only three years, dying in 1088. Odo was again nominated and this time won, choosing Urban II as his official church name. His first act was to tell the world that he would continue the policies of Gregory VII. This was easier said than done. The pope's Norman armies were now fighting among themselves in Sicily, forcing him to go there to try to make peace, so that he could use the Normans for his own needs. He was successful in this endeavor, and by late 1088 he entered Rome with Norman troops at his side. Most of the city, however, was still in the hands of Clement III, the antipope. Urban II excommunicated, or excluded from the church, both the emperor and his antipope. He then went on to win a crucial battle. Urban II was now in control of Rome.

Urban II set about making friends and allies of various princes of Europe so that they would aid him in his fight against the emperor. He arranged marriages and made treaties with the Lombard League, consisting of the cities of northern Italy, to combat the power of Henry IV. While Urban II was traveling, Rome was again occupied by the antipope. He had to wander through Italy for three years before once again assembling enough forces to take the city back in time for the Easter celebrations of 1094.

By threatening excommunication for all who opposed him, Urban II managed to keep the princes and kings of Europe in line. He also spoke out against priests wishing to marry and criticized the practice of simony, or buying and selling pardons and church offices. He established a center of church government in Rome, promoting church law that increased the power of the papacy. Urban II was very modern in his approach to spreading his message. Throughout the eleven years he served as pope, Urban II traveled around Europe, organizing great councils that included the entire populace in order to advertise and popularize his reforms; the major councils were held at Piacenza (March 1095), Clermont (November 1095), Rome (1097 and 1099), and Bari (1098).

Urban II Calls for a Crusade

One of those rulers Urban II wanted to befriend was **Alexius I** (see entry), emperor of Byzantium, the eastern portion of the old Roman Empire whose capital was in Constantinople (present-day Istanbul, in Turkey). This eastern Christian empire was coming under attack by a new force in the Middle East, the Seljuk Turks, who emerged from Central Asia and subsequently converted to Islam. Under such leaders as **Alp Arslan** (see entry), the Seljuks were chipping away at the eastern portions of the Byzantine Empire and had even managed to take the holy city of Jerusalem. Alexius I sent messengers to Urban II asking him to help fight these Seljuk invaders. Urban considered this request at the meeting in Piacenza, but it was at the Council of Clermont, also held in 1095, that he made his most urgent plea for help for the eastern Christians.

This council met from November 18 to November 28, and among other business it conducted was the excommunication of France's King Philip I for having relations with a woman outside marriage. During this council Urban II also reminded the world that the pope and the papacy had ultimate power over the church. The most important speech he gave occurred on November 27, when he proclaimed the need for a holy war against the infidels (non-Christians) who held Jerusalem and Palestine. He told the Christians present that it was their duty to go to the Holy Land and fight in the name of God.

Europe during the Middle Ages was filled with knights, specially trained mounted soldiers who were bound to behave honorably. However, too often knights spent their days killing one another in battle or in tournaments. In his proclamation at Clermont, quoted in the *Internet Medieval Sourcebook,* Urban II told these knights to turn their weapons against the enemies of the Christian faith.

> Let those who for a long time have been robbers now become knights. Let those who have been fighting against their brothers and relatives now fight in a proper way against the barbarians. Let those who have been serving as mercenaries [paid soldiers] for small pay now obtain eternal reward. Let those who have been wearing themselves out in both body and soul now work for a double honor.

Urban promised that those who "took the cross" and became Crusaders would be forgiven all their sins if they died on the way to or in the Holy Land. The crowd, numbering

The Deadly Years

When Urban II called for a Crusade against the infidels, or Muslims, in the Holy Land in 1095, his timing could not have been better. The Islamic world had just lost some of its strongest leaders. In fact, between 1092 and 1094 *all* of the major political leaders in the Near and Middle East and North Africa had died. The Seljuk Turks, who threatened the Byzantine Empire and caused Emperor Alexius I to plead to the pope for help, lost their actual ruler in 1092 when Nizam al-Mulk, the vizier, or chief counsel, was killed; he had skillfully advised Seljuk sultans for three decades. Just one month after his death, Malik-Shah, the reigning Seljuk sultan, died mysteriously, ending a rule that had lasted two decades. His death was followed by those of his wife, grandson, and others close to the throne.

Two years later even worse tragedy struck during what Muslims call the "year of the death of religious and military leaders." At this time Islam was divided into two separate religious groups: the Shiites, whose Fatimid dynasty had its power base in Egypt, and the Sunnis, who were represented by the Abbasid dynasty in Baghdad. In that single year the rulers of Egypt lost their caliph (successor to the throne) when al-Mustansir died after almost sixty years in power; his vizier died shortly afterward. The Abbasid rulers likewise found themselves without experienced leaders when their caliph al-Muqtadi died. Thus, Urban II could not have picked a better time to send a Crusader army to fight Islam, for the Islamic world in 1095 was in a state of chaos as a result of these losses.

some several thousand, cheered his speech and shouted "God wills it," promising to join a Crusade.

After this rousing beginning, Urban II appointed a bishop to lead the formation of a Crusader army. This was another blow to the power of the Holy Roman Emperor, for Urban II excluded Henry IV from this great gathering and the preparations for war while he continued to travel throughout Europe preaching the need for a Crusade. A Crusader army was finally assembled by 1096 and headed for the Holy Land. Urban II was more or less in control of the papacy now, though the antipope continued to cause problems until the very end of his life. While Urban II held additional large councils in 1098 and 1099, the Crusader army reached the Holy Land and captured the cities of Nicaea and Antioch (both in modern-day Turkey). On July 15, 1099, they took the big prize of Jerusalem. Ironically, the man who inspired the

Crusades never learned of this triumph. Urban II died two weeks later, on July 29, before the news of the recapture of Jerusalem reached him.

Throughout his rule as pope, Urban II managed to continue to strengthen the reforms of his predecessor, Gregory VII. If he had simply succeeded in winning new power for the church and the papacy against the rising power of kings and princes, that would have been enough to guarantee Urban II a place in history. However, his call to arms, which started the Crusader movement, is what most people remember about this pope. In 1881 Urban II was beatified, the first step in becoming a saint, yet he is not without his critics. Most historians agree that his emotional speech at the Council of Clermont was full of half-truths about supposed atrocities (evil deeds) committed by Muslims against Christians. Many think that Urban's real motive in launching the Crusades was to extend the power of the Roman Catholic Church into the Near and Middle East. Some think that Urban II was secretly hoping to reunify the eastern and western churches. Still others believe that he was just trying to stop the fighting among landowners and princes in Europe and aim such aggression against an outside force. Whatever his motives, the fact remains that Urban II began a very costly series of wars: There were seven Crusades over the next two centuries, with numerous smaller battles in between, which took countless lives from both sides and created friction between the Christian and Islamic worlds that was still being felt in the early twenty-first century.

For More Information

Books

Bainton, Roland H. *The Medieval Church*. Princeton, NJ: Von Nostrand, 1962.

Baldwin, Marshall. *The Medieval Papacy in Action*. New York: Macmillan, 1940.

Barraclough, Geoffrey. *The Medieval Papacy*. New York: Harcourt, Brace, & World, 1968.

Cheetham, Nicolas. *Keepers of the Keys: The Pope in History*. New York: Scribner, 1982.

Cowdrey, H. E. J. *Popes, Monks and Crusaders*. London: Hambledon Press, 1984.

Morris, Colin. *The Papal Monarchy: The Western Church from 1050 to 1250.* New York: Oxford University Press, 1989.

Web Sites

"Pope Bl. Urban II." *New Advent.* http://www.newadvent.org/cathen/15210a.htm (accessed on July 22, 2004).

"Pope Urban II—1042–1099." *Templar History.* http://www.templarhistory.com/urbanii.html (accessed on July 22, 2004).

"Speech at Council of Clermont, 1095, according to Fulcher of Chartres." *Internet Medieval Sourcebook.* http://www.fordham.edu/halsall/source/urban2-fulcher.html (accessed on July 22, 2004).

Usamah ibn Munqidh

July 4, 1095
Shayzar, Syria

November 16, 1188
Damascus, Syria

Arab lord, soldier, and writer

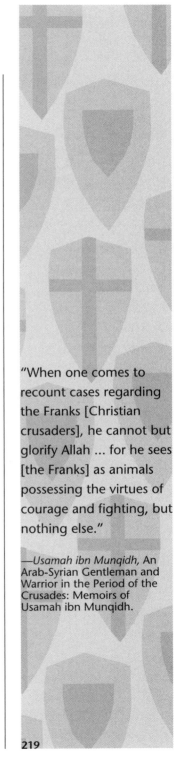

Usamah ibn Munqidh, a Syrian nobleman and soldier of the twelfth century, sat down at the end of his long and adventurous life and composed his memoirs, known in English as *An Arab-Syrian Gentleman and Warrior in the Period of the Crusades*. This autobiography presents a colorful picture of daily life in many parts of the Middle East and North Africa from roughly the time of the First Crusade (1095–99), when European Christians first came into conflict with the Islamic world over control of Jerusalem and the Holy Land, through the Second Crusade (1147–49), when Muslim fighters began to take back parts of the Middle East from the Crusaders, to just before the Third Crusade (1189–92), when the great military leader **Saladin** (1137–93; see entry) took back Jerusalem from the Christians. Usamah provides eyewitness accounts for many of the major events of the time and also presents detailed and often very critical, or negative, pictures of the Crusaders, whom the Arab world called Franks.

"When one comes to recount cases regarding the Franks [Christian crusaders], he cannot but glorify Allah ... for he sees [the Franks] as animals possessing the virtues of courage and fighting, but nothing else."

—*Usamah ibn Munqidh,* An Arab-Syrian Gentleman and Warrior in the Period of the Crusades: Memoirs of Usamah ibn Munqidh.

Ibn al-Athir

If Usamah ibn Munqidh was the most famous Arab memoirist (writer about his life) of his time, then the title of most famous historian must fall to the Muslim scholar Ibn al-Athir (1160–1233), whose full name was Abu al-Hasan 'Ali 'Izz al-Din ibn al-Athir. He was born into a powerful family in a small town on the Tigris River, located north of Mosul (in modern-day Iraq). In addition to owning land, his father was a government official in the ruling Zangid dynasty, which controlled much of Iraq and Syria at the time. Whereas his two brothers followed in their father's footsteps, Ibn al-Athir decided on a more scholarly existence, studying in Mosul and Baghdad. His long life was spent recording the events of his time, for he was an eyewitness to many of the main incidents of the Third Crusade (1189–92) as well as some of the later Crusades. Thanks to his well-placed family members, he had inside information about political affairs.

Ibn al-Athir's most famous historical work is his *al-Kamil fi at-Tarikh* (translat-ed as "The Perfect History" or "The Complete History"), though he also wrote a history of the Zangid dynasty as well as reference works. Ibn al-Athir's *Kamil* is a chronicle of the Islamic world. It begins with Creation, covers the Persian and Roman Empires as well as the world of the Hebrews, and then focuses on the Muslim world from the time of the Prophet Muhammad (founder of the religion of Islam) in the seventh century until Ibn al-Athir's own period. Although he did not list his sources, his "Perfect History" remains an invaluable source for events during the Crusades. Like Usamah, he mixes firsthand experience—and occasionally even second-hand gossip—with other written texts to paint a picture of the Islamic world during the Crusades. His work has been praised for its detailed survey of Islamic history and its many rulers and leaders as well as for the global, or wider, view he takes of events not just in the Middle East but also in Spain and southern Italy.

A Syrian Gentleman

Born on July 4, 1095, into the noble family of Munqidh, in northern Syria, Usamah grew up in the ancestral castle of Shayzar, not far from the city of Hama. Usamah came into the world months before Pope **Urban II** (see entry) delivered his famous speech demanding a holy war against the Muslim world to recapture Jerusalem for Christianity. It was one of the most powerful speeches in all of history, for it started what became almost a two-hundred-year conflict between East and West, Christianity and Islam. The castle where Usamah was born sat atop a rocky hill called the Cock's

Comb and was protected by the Orontes River on three sides. Since anyone who occupied this castle controlled the major inland route going north and south in Syria, it was often attacked by enemy armies. It was so perfectly located and designed that the invading Crusaders were never able to capture it, although they eventually established their own military outposts nearby.

Usamah was greatly influenced by his father, Murshid, who was of noble Arab blood and was both a man of action and of intellect (brains). Although Usamah's father loved to hunt and fight, he also spent several hours each day copying parts of the Koran, the Islamic holy book. During his lifetime Murshid copied the Koran forty-three times in black, red, and blue ink. In an article titled "Memories of a Muslim Prince," Viola H. Winder noted that Murshid's life, "as would that of his son later, exemplified Arab culture and the code of chivalry [honorable behavior]." Like many educated Muslims, the father was deeply religious, yet he also had a curious mind and studied astronomy (the science of space) and philosophy (the study of systems of beliefs and principles). When it was Murshid's turn to rule the small kingdom of Shayzar, he refused to accept the position. He did so because he hated politics and feared the damaging effects of power. As a result, in 1098 Murshid's younger brother, Izz al-Din, became the local leader at Shayzar and also accepted responsibility for educating young Usamah.

As Usamah noted in his memoirs, since his family "never felt secure on account of the Franks, whose territory was adjacent," this education focused on military skills as well as more academic subjects. For ten years Usamah studied science, languages, religion, and philosophy in addition to mastering the bow and arrow and sword. Above all, Usamah loved studying literature and reciting poetry. In his memoirs he tells how he and his teacher would often ride along the nearby Orontes River, find a quiet spot under the trees, and recite poetry to each other. His father did not remain totally in the background in Usamah's youth. He encouraged his favorite son to engage in physical activities and taught him courage by his own example.

In his memoirs Usamah recalled one boyhood incident that occurred at Shayzar following the capture of some

Franks. When an agreement had been reached with other Franks, these prisoners were released. However, soon after they left the castle several Muslim thieves attacked them. Encouraged by his father, Usamah rode out to save these former enemies and took some of the Muslim thieves prisoner. It was this sort of honorable behavior that Usamah's father had taught his son.

From an early age Usamah saw the horrible effects of war. As a young boy he accompanied his father to battlefields where Muslims fought the invading Crusaders. He saw men slaughtered in battle and also witnessed what happened to prisoners. One of his father's best soldiers was captured by the Franks during the First Crusade. After he had had one of his eyes painfully gouged (forced) out by his captors, the Muslim soldier was sold back to Usamah's father in exchange for the best horse in Shayzar and a chest of money.

Usamah was no stranger to violent behavior himself. As he wrote in his memoirs, when he was only ten years old he killed an older servant at Shayzar who was beating a servant boy. However, as Winder commented, "the days of Usamah's youth were made up of more than the forays [raids] and skirmishes [incidents] of battle." In an age when there were still lions and panthers roaming about in Syria, hunting was a daily pastime for the young man. Usamah was as comfortable on a horse as he was at a desk reading his poetry. He became a master hunter by the age of thirteen, using falcons both as aids in hunting and as messenger birds. While he was still a teenager, he was tested in life-and-death situations involving lions, hyenas, and Crusader knights. As Winder noted, "In such an environment Usamah grew to manhood. The years of his long lifetime never tarnished his high standards of honor, honesty, courage, and kindness."

Into the World

As long as his uncle, the sultan (leader of the kingdom) had no male children, life at Shayzar was agreeable for Usamah. In fact, as Philip K. Hitti commented in the introduction to his translation of *An Arab-Syrian Gentleman,* this uncle's "period of rule furnishes the background for most of the interesting events" in Usamah's memoirs. Unfortunately,

this situation changed when his uncle had a male child. Suddenly Usamah was no longer in favor. In 1129 he left Shayzar for a time and then returned, but when his father died in 1137 Usamah left the fortress of Shayzar for good. The line of the Munqidh family came to a tragic end at Shayzar when a huge earthquake struck the region in 1157, destroying all the buildings and killing everyone in the castle except the new sultan's wife.

Meanwhile, Usamah had made his way in the world, traveling first to Damascus, where he stayed until 1144, and then moving on to Cairo, where he served as a high-ranking government official from 1144 to 1154. He later recorded the jealousies and inside fighting that went on at the court of the Fatimids, who ruled Cairo. During these years he also fought the Franks in the Second Crusade. From 1154 to 1164 he served the powerful sultan Nur al-Din (1118–1174) in Damascus, once again fighting the Franks as well as other Muslims who opposed the sultan's attempts to unify the entire Islamic

A fresco of one of the many battles in Syria during the Crusades that Usamah witnessed as adviser to the Muslim leader Saladin.
© Archivo Iconografico, S.A./Corbis.

world. Usamah later joined the service of the powerful Muslim leader Saladin, who made him a trusted adviser. Saladin also appointed Usamah, by then an old man, governor of Beirut. Throughout his long and distinguished career Usamah came into close contact not only with powerful Islamic leaders of the day but also with the Franks, whom he regarded as enemies but occasionally as friends.

The Memoirs

Usamah's love of poetry led him to write twelve volumes of verse. During his lifetime he was known to his fellow Arabs primarily as a poet. However, when he reached the age of ninety, Usamah decided to turn to autobiography and wrote the often rambling story of his life, *Kitab al-I'tibar* ("The Book of Instructive Example"), which has been translated into English as *An Arab-Syrian Gentleman and Warrior in the Period of the Crusades*. These memoirs do not follow any chronological order; instead, Usamah jumps from topic to topic. A description of the hunting life might be followed by an account of fighting Franks and other Arabs or a detailed report of his life and works involving various leaders. As Hitti observed, "The author intends his book to be didactic [a tool for teaching]. ... The favorite theme is that the duration of the life of a man is predetermined [arranged in advance], that its end can neither be retarded [delayed] or advanced by anything man might or might not do." For Usamah, a faithful Muslim, a person's life was determined by Allah, the Muslim God.

The tone of the book, however, is not preachy. His observations on the behavior of the Franks are especially interesting and often humorous. "They are first hand and frank," according to Hitti, "and reflect the prevalent [common] Moslem public opinion" that the Crusaders were mighty warriors but were lacking in most other skills. Usamah is amazed at their medical and legal practices. He watches a Frankish doctor kill two patients that he, Usamah, was trying to save. On another occasion he witnesses the Franks' trial by ordeal, in which a suspected criminal is forcibly kept under water; if the person survives, he or she is pronounced innocent. Usamah found these practices inferior to Islamic medicine and law. He was also shocked by the loose morals of the Crusaders and their women. At the same time, however, he found a common sense of honor among the monk-soldiers of the Teutonic Knights, a fighting religious order, who protected him on various occasions. He found them to be closer to the Arab ideal: courageous but also true to the teachings of their God.

Usamah also wrote in his memoirs of the sadness he felt at having reached old age. As a young man he was "more terrible in warfare than nighttime, more impetuous [hotheaded and hasty] in assault/Than a torrent [flood], and more adventurous on the battlefield than destiny!" But with the approach of old age all this changed:

> But now I have become an idle maid who lies/ On stuffed cushions behind screens and curtains./ I have almost become rotten from lying still so long, just as/ The sword of Indian steel becomes rusty when kept long in its sheath.

Usamah did not have long to complain about his old age, for he died in 1188, shortly after finishing his memoirs. His son later had the book copied, and it spread from the Islamic world to the West. According to Hitti, Usamah's book is "a unique piece of Arabic literature." His stories "open before our eyes a wide and new vista [view] into medieval times and constitute [represent] an invaluable contribution to our knowledge of Arabic culture." Writing in the foreword to this same translation of *An Arab-Syrian Gentleman,* Richard W. Bulliet noted that "nothing in all of medieval Islamic history quite matches [the book's] vivid and detailed descriptions, and there are few instances of such lucid [clear] first-person writing in the history of Christian Europe."

For More Information

Books

Irwin, Robert. "Usama ibn Munqidh: *An Arab-Syrian Gentleman and Warrior in the Period of the Crusades* Reconsidered." In *The Crusades and Their Sources.* Edited by Bernard Hamilton and William G. Zajac. Aldershot, UK: Ashgate, 1998.

Maalouf, Amin. *The Crusades through Arab Eyes.* New York: Schocken Books, 1984.

Usamah ibn Munqidh. *An Arab-Syrian Gentleman and Warrior in the Period of the Crusades: Memoirs of Usamah ibn Munqidh.* Translated by Philip K. Hitti. New York: Columbia University Press, 2000.

Web Sites

"Autobiography, Excerpts on the Franks." *Internet Medieval Sourcebook.* http://www.fordham.edu/halsall/source/Usamah2.html (accessed on July 22, 2004).

Winder, Viola H. "Memories of a Muslim Prince." *Saudi Aramco World,* 21, no. 3 (May/June 1970). Available online at http://www.saudi aramcoworld.com/issue/197003/memories.of.a.muslim.prince.htm (accessed on July 22, 2004).

Index

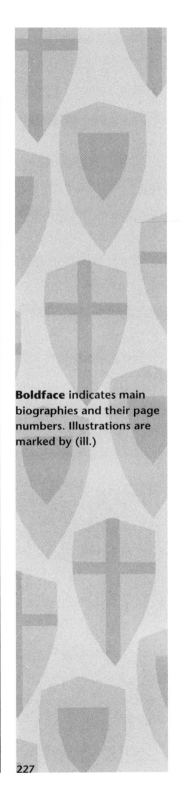